Finite Element Essentials in 3DEXPERIENCE 2021x

Nader G. Zamani
University of Windsor

SDC
PUBLICATIONS

SDC Publications
P.O. Box 1334
Mission, KS 66222
913-262-2664
www.SDCpublications.com
Publisher: Stephen Schroff

ISBN-13: 978-1-63057-453-6
ISBN-10: 1-63057-453-8

Printed and bound in the United States of America.

Dedicated to my parents,

Mostafa and Shamsi Zamani

and my grandchildren,

Zidan, Jahan, Veda, and Maeve

Preface

This book introduces the reader to the powerful FEA simulation tool in the 3DEXPERIENCE business platform. It specifically deals with the "Native" finite element solver embedded and integrated within 3DEXPERIENCE.

The format of the book is of the tutorial style which leads the reader in a step-by-step fashion from the start to the end. The chapters utilize the standard topics in a Mechanical/Civil engineering curriculum worldwide.

The chapters deal with both the structural and thermal problems involving the static and dynamic cases. Furthermore, nonlinearities at the material and geometric levels are also applied in some problems. All three-standard element types, solids, beams, and shells, and their combination are represented in the document.

There are two other tutorial style textbooks on 3DEXPERIENCE by the same author and publisher that the reader may find very useful as a supplement to the material in the current textbook. All chapters in the 2021x edition of this book also have companion videos which are posted on YouTube for public access on the "Nader Zamani" channel.

I sincerely hope that you enjoy this book and find it useful in your future academic endeavors.

Nader Zamani
Windsor, Ontario

TABLE OF CONTENTS

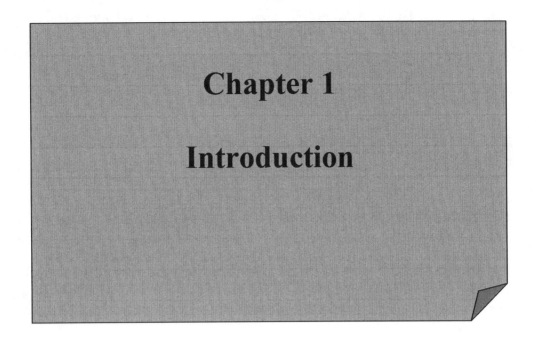

Chapter 1

Introduction

The first edition of this book was published in 2017 which was only three years past the inception of the 3DEXPERIENCE platform by Dassault Systèmes (DS). At that time, there were very few resources in the public domain available to the general engineering community. This prompted DS to aggressively push academia and training outfits to develop educational materials for the CAD/CAE public. Since then, the software itself has dramatically transformed and improved. An important vehicle to achieve some of the goals of DS has been YouTube. To name a specific channel, I can refer to 3DEXPERIENCE.edu.

To have a better understanding of the rationale behind the original writing of this book, a brief historical description of the development of FEA in Dassault Systèmes (DS) is in order. The Dassault organization was created in 1981 in support of the aviation industry in France. After substantial investment in software development, they marketed their CAD software known as the "Computer Aided Three-Dimensional Interactive Application" or Catia for short. At the time, this software was the state-of-the-art technology for CAD applications, and after almost four decades they still enjoy that reputation. The domain of applications of the software was quickly expanded to cover other areas such as aerospace, automotive, naval architecture, and consumer products.

During the mid-nineties, Dassault expanded its market share by including robotics and virtual manufacturing in their software products. They also formed an alliance with the IBM corporation in marketing their Catia software but made the wise decision of not limiting themselves to the mainframe computers. They tailored and optimised their software for adaptation on the windows-based operating system. This move enabled the smaller size companies to rely on and benefit from the services and products offered by Dassault Systems.

To give the software users the ability to perform some analysis capability, a homebrewed finite element software known as "Elfini" was bundled in the Catia program. Although this program met its original purpose, namely, to offer limited FEA capabilities, it was considered as Catia's nemesis. One could only perform linear material properties and small deflections and strains. Despite these limitations, the industrial designers with a limited FEA knowledge could use this CAE functionality to improve their designs dramatically.

Realizing this issue, in 2005, Dassault Systèmes acquired the software company known as HKS (Hibbit, Karlsson & Sorensen) in Providence, Rhode Island. The HKS company was the developer and marketer of the commercial FEA software known as Abaqus. At the time, Abaqus was well known as the state-of-the-art technology in finite elements and dominated that market. The HKS company was immediately renamed as Simulia with its headquarters remaining in the greater Providence area. The first attempt to offer Catia users a respectable FEA capability was to market the AFC software (Abaqus For Catia) which was the stripped-down version of Abaqus, integrated within the Catia program. The license, however, had to be obtained separately and the interface was rather clumsy. This software can still be acquired from Simulia and loaded on top of Catia. In all likelihood, AFC will not be supported in the near future. Dassault Systèmes also acquired the program known as SOLIDWORKS in 1997 as a less expensive and more affordable CAD package. The FEA engine within the SOLIDWORKS program was known as "Cosmos". In principle, the geometric models can be created with Catia or SOLIDWORKS and the resulting model passed on to the FEA solver directly. This can also be arranged through a "dumb" solid generated by any other CAD package.

For the past fifteen years, Dassault Systèmes has made many acquisitions in diverse areas of modern software technology. This has led to a major shift in the company's strategy to attract new sectors of the industry. This strategic shift has been accompanied by introducing the "3DEXPERIENCE" business platform. In a nutshell, 3DEXPERIENCE is a business platform providing software solutions to all divisions within a company ranging from engineering to sales and marketing. One can safely refer to this platform as an integration of many, many, other software which can be offered to industry and tailor made to their needs. Clearly, the reader's interest in this book are the finite element aspects which are elaborated below.

As far as the Simulia applications are concerned, there are several finite element packages which can be found within 3DEXPERIENCE. The most well known of these is the Abaqus program. Currently, the implicit version of the software is available with the explicit and fluid flow analysis to be implemented soon. Other recently acquired software related to FEA and integrated within 3DEXPERIENCE are Tosca (structural optimization), Simpoe-Mold (injection molding), and FE-Safe (durability analysis). There are numerous other engineering/computer science software that have been added and bundled in the business platform since 2016.

The book consists of many standalone chapters which make an attempt to present several important aspects of the general FEA code. In order to maintain the independence between the chapters, we were forced to introduce duplications and repetitions of some common topics. We are fully aware of this issue but unfortunately were unable to avoid it. This format gives a reader the opportunity to select topics of interest, and without having completed the previous chapters to proceed through the tutorial. Although a previous knowledge of Abaqus is not required, it is assumed that the reader has basic skills in 3DEXPERIENCE CAD modeling. These skills are quite basic and are limited to creating simple parts and assemblies.

There are two other important comments that can be helpful to the reader and provide a better perspective of 3DEXPERIENCE data management. When it comes to saving the results and intermediate work, under normal circumstances, it is saved on the "cloud" server. This arrangement can be altered and negotiated between Dassault and the licensee. Even the data that is labeled to be stored "locally" is encrypted and not useful to the user. In the event that the software is used in an academic institution by students, they should check with the instructor on this issue.

The developers at Dassault are making a major push for users to employ the "Shape Abstraction" concept. This basically allows you to insert a copy of the original geometry (Abstraction Shape) allowing you to modify it without effecting the original part. Modifications can include hole and fillet removals and operations of this type. In this book, the concept of "Shape Abstraction" is only discussed and used in chapter 2 for modeling the elastic response of a block with a circular hole.

The examples in the current book are run with very coarse meshes. This is intentional because accuracy is not the main focus of the presentation. Our focus is the "How to Do" process.

The reader may find the following supplementary materials published by SDC Publications extremely useful.

CAD Modeling Essentials in 3DEXPERIENCE 2016x Using CATIA Applications, by Nader Zamani, SDC Publications, ISBN 978-1-63057-095-8.

Mechanism Design Essentials in 3DEXPERIENCE 2016x Using CATIA Applications, by Nader Zamani, SDC Publications, ISBN 978-1-63057-095-8.

The videos for different chapters of this book have been posted on the YouTube channel of the author. To reach the channel please search under "Nader Zamani" in YouTube.

https://www.youtube.com/channel/UCiY-yqqmRC4pQWV_yb4PN0A

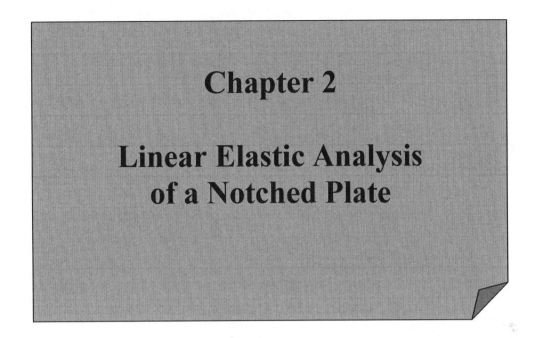

Chapter 2

Linear Elastic Analysis
of a Notched Plate

Introduction:

In this tutorial, a solid finite element model of a plate with central hole is created. The loading is in the plane of the plate and the deformation is small enough to warrant a linear elastic analysis.

NOTE: It is assumed that you have basic familiarity with CAD modeling in 3DEXPERIENCE allowing you to create a block with a central hole. If that is not the case, please consult the following tutorial book.

CAD Modeling Essentials in 3DEXPERIENCE, by Nader Zamani, SDC Publications, ISBN 978-1-63057-095-8.

Problem Statement:

The steel plate shown below is subjected to a pressure load P at the two ends. Although the problem has three planes of symmetry, you will be modeling the full geometry. The loading is assumed to be small enough to cause a linear elastic behavior.

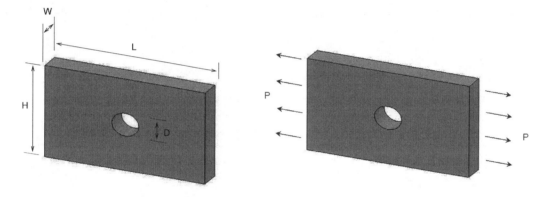

The dimensions of the part to be analyzed are such that the parameter $r = \dfrac{D}{H}$ is 0.25. The chart below gives a stress concentration factor of $K_t = 2.4$. This chart is based on $L \gg H$ which is not true in the modeled block. However, the value of K_t will be used for comparative purposes.

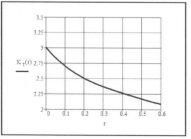

There are many types of solid elements available in the software; however, in this chapter, tetrahedron elements are used. They come in linear and parabolic forms. Both are referred to as tetrahedron elements and shown below.

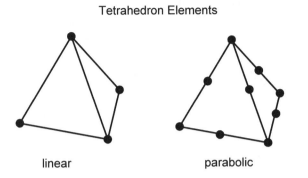

Tetrahedron Elements

linear   parabolic

The linear tetrahedron elements are faster computationally but less accurate. On the other hand, the parabolic elements require more computational resources but lead to more accurate results. Another important feature of parabolic elements is that they can fit curved surfaces better. In general, the analysis of bulky objects requires the use of solid elements.

In a solid continuum, the state of deformation is described by the six components of the Cauchy stress $\{\sigma_x, \sigma_y, \sigma_z, \tau_{xy}, \tau_{xz}, \tau_{yz}\}$ which vary from point to point. The von Mises stress is a combination of these according to the following expression:

$$\sigma_{VM} = \sqrt{\frac{1}{2}\left[(\sigma_x - \sigma_y)^2 + (\sigma_x - \sigma_z)^2 + (\sigma_y - \sigma_z)^2 + 6(\tau_{xy}^2 + \tau_{xz}^2 + \tau_{yz}^2)\right]}$$

For an obvious reason, this is also known as the effective stress. Note that by definition, the von Mises stress is always a positive number. In terms of principal stresses, σ_{VM} can also be written as

$$\sigma_{VM} = \sqrt{\frac{1}{2}\left[(\sigma_1 - \sigma_2)^2 + (\sigma_1 - \sigma_3)^2 + (\sigma_2 - \sigma_3)^2\right]}$$

For many ductile materials, the onset of yielding (permanent plastic deformation) takes place when $\sigma_{VM} = \sigma_Y$ where σ_Y is the yield strength of the material. For design purposes, a factor of safety "N" is introduced leading to the condition $\sigma_{VM} = \dfrac{\sigma_Y}{N}$.

Therefore, a safe design is one where $\sigma_{VM} < \dfrac{\sigma_Y}{N}$. The von Mises stress contour plot allows you to check the above condition.

The Model and Material Properties:

First, using the Part Design App 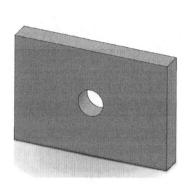, create a block with a central hole with the dimensions L = 0.15m, H= 0.1m, W = 0.02m, and D = 0.025m as shown below.

The first task is to apply a material property to this part. From the bottom row of icons (i.e. the action bar), select the "Tools" tab.

Select the "Tools" tab

From the Tools menu, select the dropdown to the right of the "Material Browser" icon . This opens up the section menu as shown. Follow the steps outlined below to select the "Create Material" .

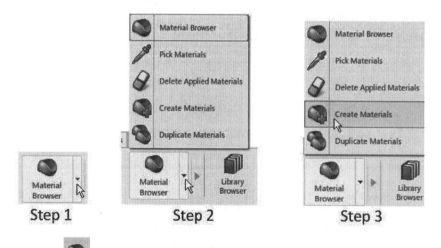

The selection of opens up a dialogue box shown on the next page. This box allows you to supply a proper name for the material should you decide to do so. Our assumption is that you do not have a material of interest in the "cloud" database and would like to follow the steps to create it. It is a rather tedious process but will be clearly spelled out.

Select the "Create Material" ⬤ icon. Make sure that you check "Add domain" section of the dialogue box, and that the "Simulation Domain" is picked. Note that this creates a shell (a placeholder) and the material information needs to be supplied later.

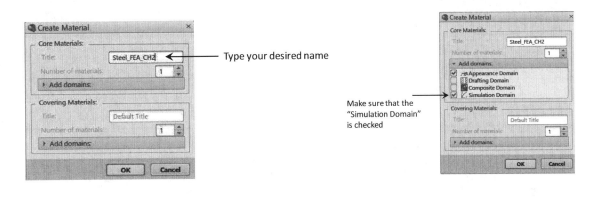

Type your desired name

Make sure that the "Simulation Domain" is checked

Here is the material property that you created. This is just a "shell", information needs to be inputted later.

Once you close the dialogue box by clicking on "OK", you will find yourself in the material database and can identify the material that you just created, namely "Steel_FEA_CH2". The database screen is shown on the right.

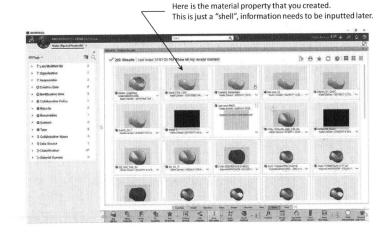

Place the cursor on your created material in the database, right click and select "Apply". You still have to return to the screen where the geometry exists and continue. This necessitates the closure of the current screen (the database screen).

Position the cursor here on the screen, right click, select "Apply"

Select the "X "on the top right margin of the database screen to close the window.

Close this window by clicking on "X".
Be careful not to close the App. instead.

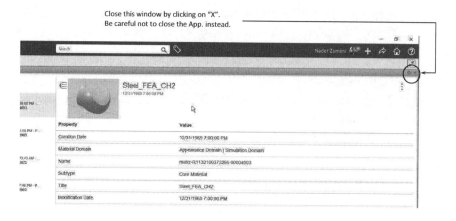

You will return to the geometry window; however, the shape of the cursor is modified as shown below.

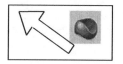

Place the cursor on the part on the screen or on the top branch of the tree and double click.

You will notice that the "Materials" branch is created at the very bottom of the tree as shown below. You can then use the cursor to select the "Green" check mark to proceed.

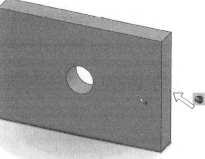

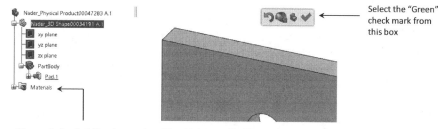

Select the "Green" check mark from this box

The created material has been assigned but this is just a "shell" , information needs to be inputted later.

Please note that the actual material properties are yet to be inputted. Expanding the "Materials" branch reveals two other branches. The location where the properties are inputted is the last branch "Material Simulation Domain00004139" as shown on the right.

Input material properties by double clicking on this branch

Double click on the last branch and follow the steps below.

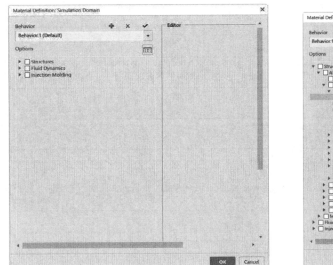

Step 1

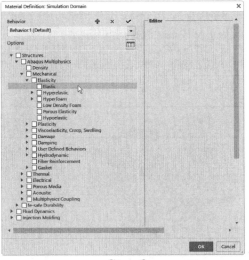

Step 2

Step 3

Steps:
1. Expand the Structures Option
2. Continue Expanding until the Elastic Option is visible
3. Click on the Elastic Option & input the Young's modulus and Poisson Ratio.

In Step 3, the Young's modulus and Poisson ratio can be inputted. For the present problem, $E = 2 * 10^{11}\ Pa$ and $\nu = 0.3$, which are the standard values for carbon steel. Properties can be changed by simply double clicking on the last branch shown.

Creating an Abstraction Shape:

When performing a structural analysis, one often simplifies the model. These simplifications may include modeling a symmetric portion of a component, removing small non-critical features, or even modeling a solid component as a shell. Modifying the 3D Shape used for designing and manufacturing the component could cause costly errors. Fortunately, **3DEXPERIENCE** provides a feature called an "Abstraction Shape". The Abstraction Shape provides a container with a dependent copy of the design 3D Shape.

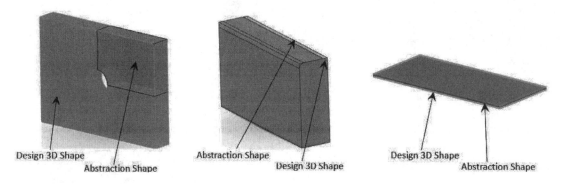

Inserting an Abstraction Shape is a straightforward process. As shown below, right click on the part, select Insert, and then select Abstraction Shape.

Step 1   **Step 2**   **Step 3**

Creating a dependent copy of the 3D Shape, used for the design and manufacturing, and placing it in the Abstraction Shape requires a bit more effort. To accomplish this task:

1. Double click on the 3D Shape to activate it
2. Right click on the PartBody associated with the 3D Shape
3. Select Copy
4. Double click on the Abstraction Shape to activate it
5. Right click on the PartBody associated with the Abstraction Shape
6. Select Paste Special
7. Select "As Result With Link" and then click on OK.

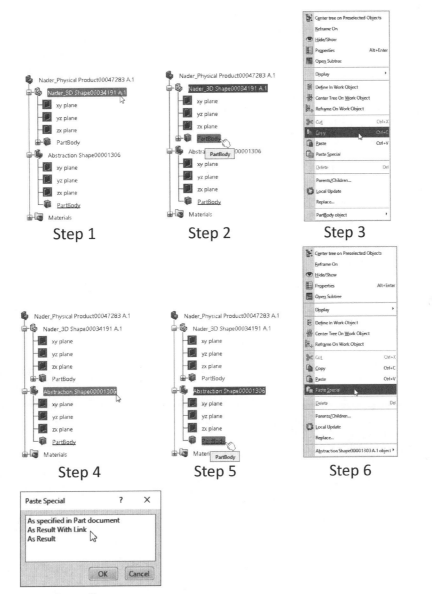

Step 1   Step 2   Step 3

Step 4   Step 5   Step 6

Step 7

For most simulations, we could leave the model as it is. But some of the functionality used by the simulation apps requires the solid to be located under the PartBody. Therefore, we perform the following three steps to clean up the model.

1. Drag and drop the solid to the PartBody
2. Right click on the now empty body container
3. Select delete

The steps to clean up the model and the final model tree are depicted below.

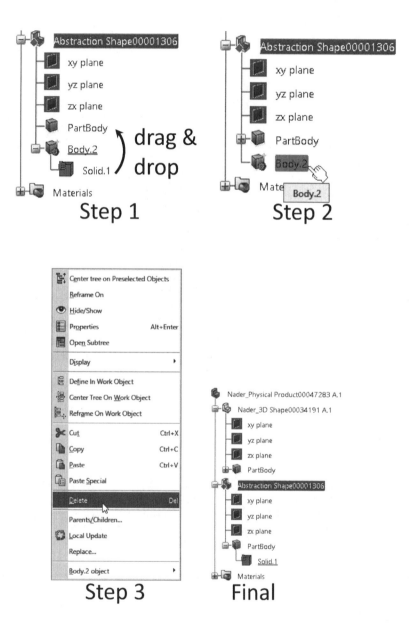

Creating the Finite Element Model:

Click on the compass at the top left corner of the screen. Be sure that the "ME" and "As a System of Operations" choices are active as depicted in the figure to the right. If you have difficulty locating any app, you can activate the search capability by clicking on the magnifying glass. You can also drag any app into your "My Favorite Apps" for easy access in the future. Scroll through the applications and select the

Structural Model Creation

"Structural Model Creation" App   .

The "Create Finite Element Model" dialogue box appears. For now, select the "Automatic" option for the Initialization Method. The other initialization methods provide a user with additional control over the meshing process. The selection of "Automatic" creates parabolic tetrahedral elements. Next, activate the geometry selection and click on the PartBody under the Abstraction Shape. Then click on OK.

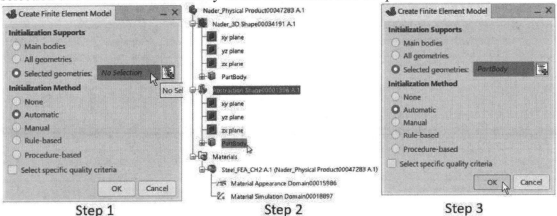

The row of icons at the bottom of your screen (action bar) changes and will appear similar to the one displayed below.

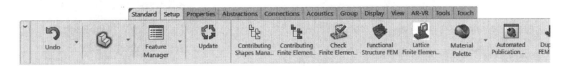

Mesh and Properties are created

The tree indicates that a mesh and the corresponding solid section has been created.

Expanding the branch "Finite Element Model0003095" further indicates that the elements are of "Tetrahedron" type and the property is "Solid Section" as expected.

Upon double clicking on the "Tetrahedron Mesh.1" branch, the corresponding dialogue box shown on the right pops up. Here, one can change the type (linear or quadratic), the size and sag, and certain other parameters. For example, local mesh refinement can be accomplished through the "Local Specifications". Click on "Initialize from geometry" and then click on OK.

There are different methods for displaying the mesh. The instructions given below are one method of achieving that objective.

From the bottom row of icons, select the "Mesh" icon  .

The bottom row's appearance now looks similar to below.

Select the "Update" icon

.

Upon updating, the mesh appears on the screen as shown on the right.

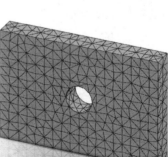

There are also different ways of
hiding the mesh. For example, first
select the "Display" tab from the
bottom row of icons.

you can select the "Visualization Management" icon 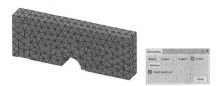 from the
choices. The resulting dialogue box shown on the right appears.
You can then use the dropdowns to show or hide the various
features.

There are a few other icons that are worth mentioning here.

Selecting the "Sectioning" icon cuts the
mesh with the standard xy, xz, and yz planes as
shown.

The "Clipping Box" icon enables you to select a region of your mesh.

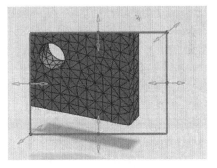

There are several other mesh visualization tools available including changing element
color and shrinking the elements. We do not discuss those further but will highlight the
mesh "Mesh Visualization Quality" plot. This allows one to quickly identify poor quality
elements that could produce erroneous results.

Creating a Scenario:

The nature of the analysis, namely Static, Dynamic, Buckling, etc., is set in the "Structural Scenario Creation" App. Furthermore, the loads, restraints, and interaction are also defined in this application.

It is also important to point out that that one could have created the Scenario before the "Finite Element Model Creation" step. In fact, the latter can be created from within the "Structural Scenario Creation" App.

Click on the compass in the top left corner of the screen as shown here. Scroll through the applications and select the "Structural Scenario

Structural
Scenario Creation

Creation" App.

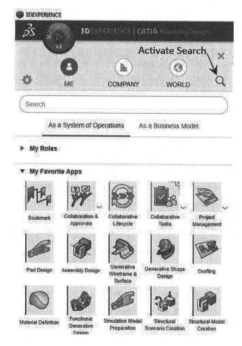

The pop-up window "Simulation Initialization" shown below appears on the screen. Since this is strictly a structural problem, the radio button "Structural" should be selected. A quick glance of the tree confirms that a "Scenario" has been created.

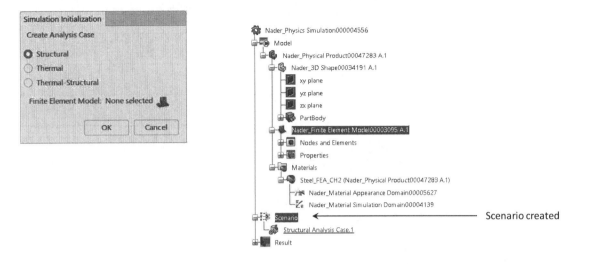

Scenario created

The row of icons at the bottom of your screen changes and will resemble the one displayed below.

Checking the middle bottom section of the screen reveals that there are two red exclamation signs.
These pertain to "Structural Analysis Case.1" and "No Procedures Exist".

Red exclamation signs

From the "Setup" tab, click the "Finite Element Model" icon 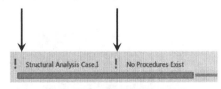. The following pop-up window displayed on the next page appears.

Since there is already a finite element model created, it appears in the list. Be sure that you select that row. Notice that there is also an option to create a finite element model. As mentioned earlier, the FE model can also be created within the Scenario, and this is where you would complete that task. In this case, it does not apply because an FE model was already created and selected.

Select the "Procedures" tab from the action bar (bottom row).

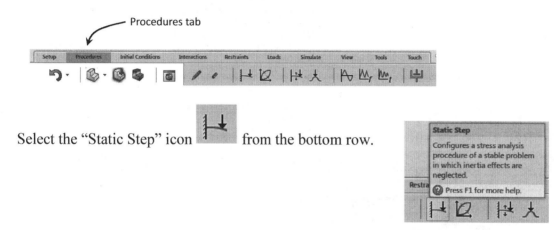

Select the "Static Step" icon from the bottom row.

The "Static Step" dialogue box pops up. Accept all the defaults. Note that if the "Advanced" pulldown list is selected, it becomes clear that this is the point in the software where "Geometric Nonlinearities" are included, or excluded.

A quick glance at the bottom middle section of the screen reveals "Green" checkmarks instead of "Red" exclamation marks.

Note the "Green" checkmarks instead of "Red" exclamations

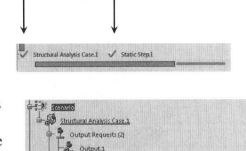

The tree indicates that "Static Step.1" has been created. There are default basic output entities that are requested upon the creation of a Step.

Accessing the Model, Scenario and Results Quickly:

Clearly this can be done by double clicking on the corresponding branches of the tree. However, it can also be done efficiently by selecting the appropriate icon among these three:  . The first one on the left is "Model and Mesh", the middle one is "Scenario" and the one on the far right is "Results"; that is the postprocessor.

Applying the Pressure Load:

A pressure load of -100000 Pa is to be applied on the end faces. Note that positive pressure by convention is a compressive load. Since the notched block is under tension, pressure value is inputted as a negative number.

Select the "Loads" tab

Select the two end faces of the block; keep in mind the multiple selection is done with holding the Ctrl key down.

Select the "Pressure" icon 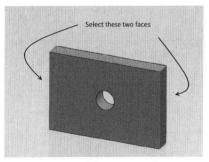 from the bottom row of icons and input the pressure value.

Select these two faces

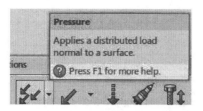

Applying the Restraints:

The problem under consideration is in static equilibrium without imposing any restraints. However, due to the geometrical and loading symmetries, it possesses three planes of symmetry. Therefore, in principle, one needs to model 1/8th of the geometry only.

In the present model, no symmetry considerations will be made. Since the structure can move as a rigid body and still remain under equilibrium, the so called {1,2,3} rule will be imposed. This is illustrated in the figure on the right. The arrows represent a zero displacement in the shown direction.

The (1,2,3) restraint representing (x,y,z) prevents the block from flying away. The (1,2) restraint representing (x,y) prevents rotation about the x and y axis. Finally, the (3) restraint representing (z) eliminates the rotation about the z axis.

Select the "Restraints" tab from the bottom toolbar (the action bar).

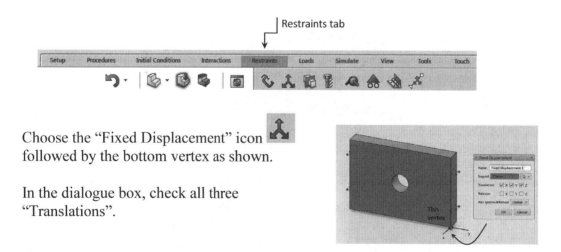

Choose the "Fixed Displacement" icon followed by the bottom vertex as shown.

In the dialogue box, check all three "Translations".

Repeat the same process for the other two vertices and choose the appropriate translations as shown.

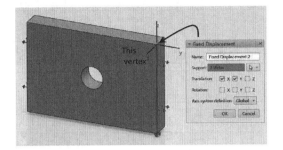
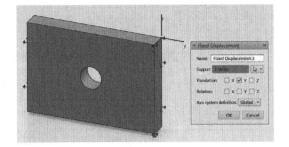

As a side comment, instead of using the "Fixed Displacement" icon and checking all three x,y,z translations, one could have used the "Clamp" icon .

Note that the imposed restraints are now reflected in the tree.

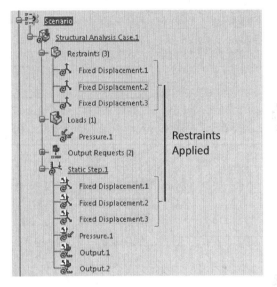

Consistency, Model Check, and Simulation:

Select the "Simulation" tab from the bottom row of icons on your screen

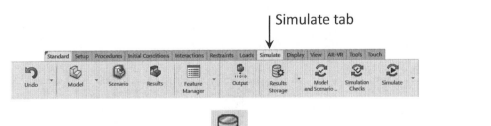

Select the "Results Storage" icon from the bottom row to define where the simulation results will be stored. While model and scenario data is always stored on the server, simulation results may either be stored on the server or on the local machine. If the "Local" option is selected, the results will be stored in C:\Users*WinUsername*\AppData\Local\DassaultSystemes\PLM_LocalResult.

However, the data is masked, encrypted, and only accessible by the owner of the data. <u>Students should check with their instructor to determine the proper location for storing their simulation results.</u> For this case, we select the "Server" radio button.

It is a good practice to perform the consistency and consistency check before submitting the work for the final run.
Select the "Model and Scenario Check" icon from the

bottom row .

The software goes through a check phase and if there are no issues, a message with a "Green" check mark is returned.

Next select the "Simulation Checks" icon from the bottom row of icons. Accept the number of "Cores" in the pop up box below.

Upon the completion of the "Simulation Check", any errors or warning messages will be available in the pop up box below.

Simulation Checks Status

✓ Simulation checks completed.

▸ **Errors (0)**

▾ **Warnings (1)**

   Output request cf has been removed as there are no applicable loads in this step

▸ **Information (0)**

Assuming that there are no serious issues (i.e. no error messages), you are ready to submit the job for "Simulation".

Select the "Simulation" icon ⟳ from the bottom row.
Accept the number of "cores" in the pop up box, and wait for the simulation to complete.

During this phase "Simulation Status", important messages such as "Licenses", "Plots", and "Iterations" are recorded in the main pop-up window. These can be viewed by selecting the appropriate tab.

Successfully completed

In the present run, if you select the "Iterations" tab you will see a single iteration as the problem in linear.

The "Plots" tab reveals nothing interesting. The problem being linear, there is only one iteration to get the solution.

From the "Feature Manager" dropdown, select the "Diagnostic Viewer" [icon] from the menu. This can also be launched by typing Alt+v.

Once the window pops up, click on the arrows to expand the records.

Click to Expand

Under the "Advanced" section, use the pulldown menu to expand the choices. Here, you can select an item of interest to get information about.

For example, if you are seeking information about "Iterations", make that selection and click on "Status". A text file (Notepad) is generated which pertains to the requested item.

Select the type of report you are seeking

Select the Item that you want a report on

```
1b28e5b6_1bb8_58d5e2d2_db6d_0_STA - Notepad                    —    □    X
File  Edit  Format  View  Help
Abaqus/Standard 3DEXPERIENCE R2017x HotFix 1              DATE 24-Mar-2017 TIME 23:24:22
SUMMARY OF JOB INFORMATION:
STEP   INC ATT SEVERE EQUIL TOTAL  TOTAL     STEP      INC OF      DOF   IF
                DISCON ITERS ITERS TIME/     TIME/LPF  TIME/LPF    MONITOR RIKS
                ITERS              FREQ
   1    1   1    0      1     1    1.00      1.00      1.000

THE ANALYSIS HAS COMPLETED SUCCESSFULLY
```

Results (Post processing):

Once you close (or move) the obstructing dialogue boxes, you must be in the "Results" section and the bottom row should appear as shown on the right.

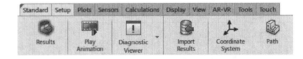

If not, click on the "Results" icon .

In the background, you should see the "Plots" dialogue box which shows the results of Frame1, and the initial results and the results after the first iteration. If the first of the "Plots" dialogue box is highlighted, the value of the von Mises stress is zero as shown on the right.

This is not surprising as the first row is before any incremental load is applied. If the load is zero, the displacement and stress are both zero. Use the cursor to select the second row of the "Plots" dialogue box. One can then see the von Mises stress distribution in the part.

The stress concentration graph given on page 2-1 indicates a factor of 2.4 for the given dimensions. Since the magnitude of the applied pressure was 1.00E+5 Pa, a maximum von Mises stress of 3.19E+5 Pa is in reasonable agreement with theory. Keep in mind that this is a coarse grid.

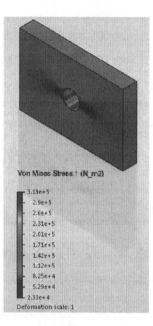

In order to display the "Displacement.1", use the "Plot" pulldown menu in this window and select "Displacement.1" as shown below.

The "Plots" dialogue box can be closed to make room on the screen if needed. Use the cursor and select the arrow on the top left corner of the window; this will collapse the box as seen next.

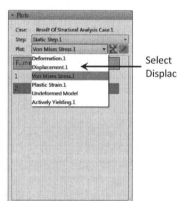

Select Displacement.1

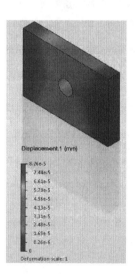

Every time a new plot is to be generated, the previous one is deactivated. Checking the status of the tree on the right indicates that the "Displacement" is "Active", whereas the other 5 (including von Mises) are "Not Active".

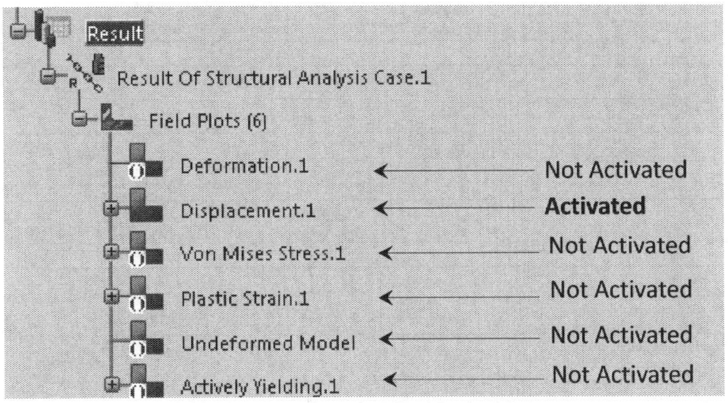

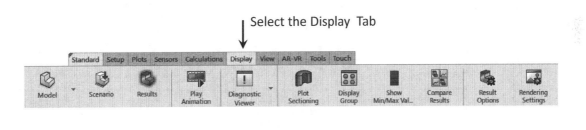

Plots which are "Not Active" have a marker  ⬤ next to them. There may be good reasons that you want several plots on the screen side by side. Suppose that you want the contour plots of the displacement and the von Mises stress side by side.

Select the "Display" tab from the bottom row of icons.

Select the Display Tab

Select the "Compare Results" icon 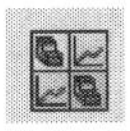  from the bottom row.

The "Compare Results" dialog will appear as shown below. Click on the X's to remove the two right panes.

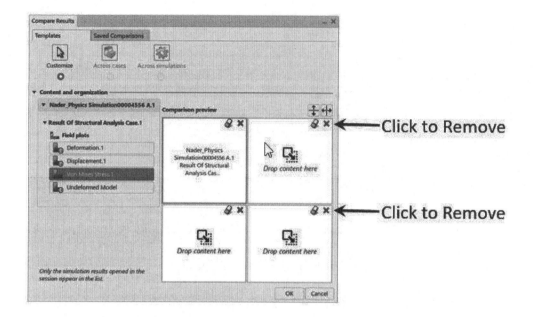

Then, drag and drop the displacement field plot into the remaining lower pane.

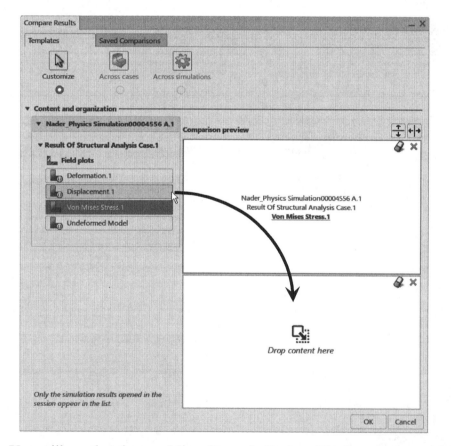

You will see that the von Mises Stress is displayed in the top sector of the screen and the displacement is displayed in the bottom sector of the screen as shown below.

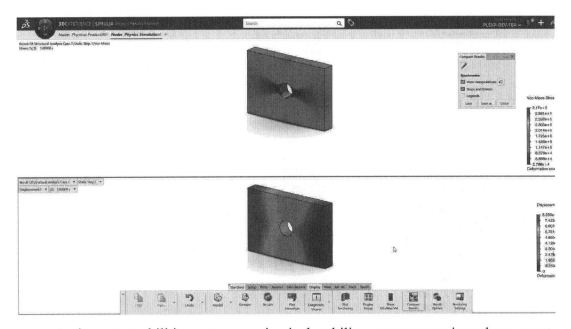

An important skill in post processing is the ability to pan, zoom in and zoom out of the contour legend. In order to explain the process, plot the contour of "Displacement.1". Point the cursor to the contour legend and select it (left click). You will see that the contour plot (on the block) becomes dim. This is an indication that the contour plot is "Not Active", whereas the contour legend is. Now, selecting the legend with the middle mouse button down, the legend can be panned. Selecting the contour legend, a single click of the middle mouse button, and forward/backward motion of the mouse enables you to zoom in and zoom out of the legend. Once you are done, select the contour legend again which will activate the contour plot.

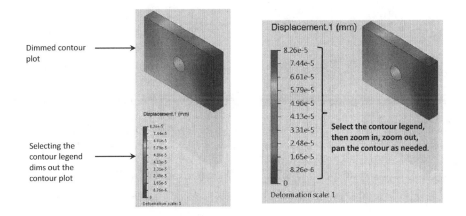

The group of icons 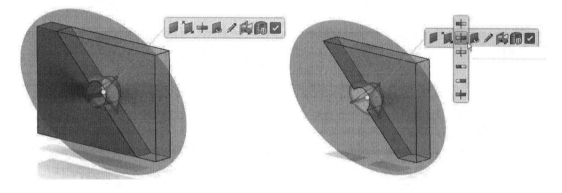 on the bottom of screen are very useful in post processing. The compare results icon has already been discussed. We will now review the plot sectioning icon. Once this icon is selected, the part can be cut at an arbitrary orientation by rotating/translating the "Robot"; two random cuts are shown below.

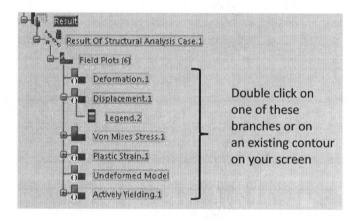

Manipulating the contour plots as far as formatting and setting the parameters is very important. To explore such features, double click on an existing contour on the screen (or simply double click on a branch of the tree which corresponds to a contour in the "Results" section).

Double click on one of these branches or on an existing contour on your screen

Once the contour appears on the screen, double click on it again. This action leads to the "Contour Plot" pop up window shown on the right. This window has three tabs and many pulldown menus which enables you to customize the plot.

The three tabs are immediately below the "Name".

In the first tab, one can select the different variables to be plotted.

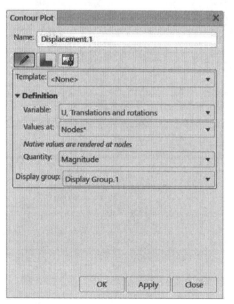

Selecting the middle tab 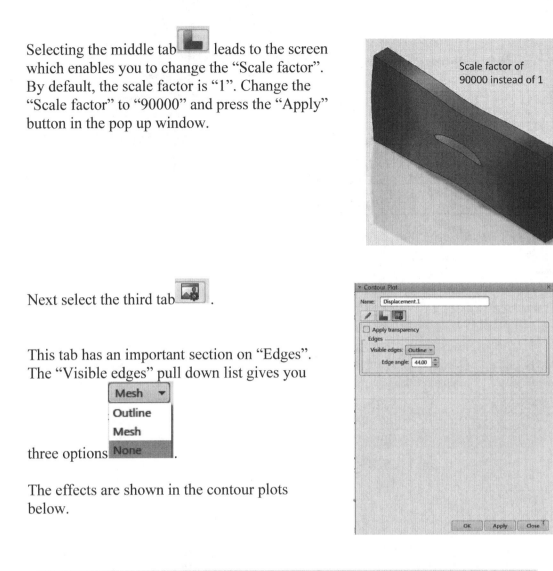 leads to the screen which enables you to change the "Scale factor". By default, the scale factor is "1". Change the "Scale factor" to "90000" and press the "Apply" button in the pop up window.

Next select the third tab .

This tab has an important section on "Edges". The "Visible edges" pull down list gives you three options .

The effects are shown in the contour plots below.

Looking at the above contour plots one notices that there are no distinct color separation borders. It could be that for certain reasons, having a smooth transition between colors is not desirable. This can easily be changed by double clicking on the contour legends which will open the "Legend Options" dialogue box. The box is shown on the next page and gives you many other options regarding the contour.

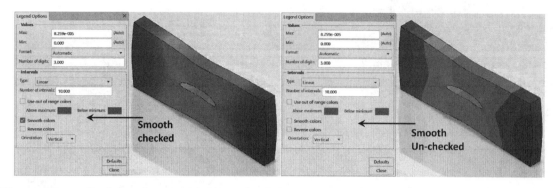

The number of colors, the maximum and minimum range for the variable can also be set in this window. Note that the setting which allows you to orient the legend "Horizontal" or "Vertical" is at the bottom of the window.

Select the "Create Report" icon from the bottom of the screen. This will lead to the dialogue box shown below.

A professional looking report in "Word" or "PowerPoint" formats can be generated. Personalized information such as company/university logo can be automatically inserted.

The results animation tool is located on the "Standard" tab. It is good practice to pin the "Standard" tab to the Action Bar. To do this, right click on the tab and select "Pin Section" as shown on the right.

Select the "Play Animation" icon from the bottom row.

This loads the animation player as shown below.

You can change the animation properties and save the animation by clicking on the "Animation Options" icon .

This loads the "Animation Options" dialog as shown on the right. Finally, looping control is achieved by clicking on the  icon. You can click through the options: loop, bounce, and one shot.

A very useful post-processing feature is the "Show Min/Max Values" icon ■ from the bottom row of icons.

Up until this point, the post processing dealt with contour plot fully rendered. The next activity deals with generating plots which are "symbol" based; for example, the y-component of the displacement vector (or symbol) but plotted as a vector. In this example, y is the direction where the part is loaded.

Select the "Symbol Plot" icon  from the "Plots" tab at the bottom of the screen. Note that the icon "Isocontour Plot" is essentially the same as "Create Contour Plot" ■, except that there is no rendering.

Follow the instructions below to select "UT, Translation" with "Vector Component 2".

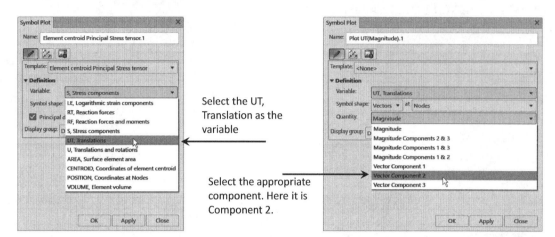

Select the UT, Translation as the variable

Select the appropriate component. Here it is Component 2.

For Symbol shape, select "Vectors"

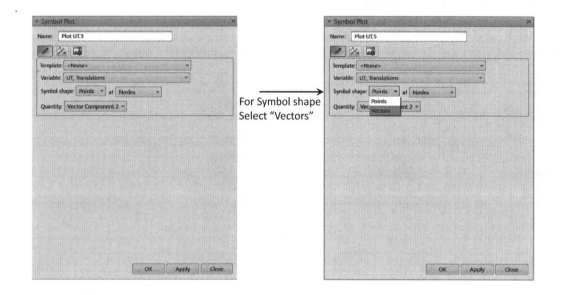

For Symbol shape Select "Vectors"

Finally press "Apply". The symbol plot (vector plot) shown below appears. The issue with this plot is that there are too many symbols (arrows).

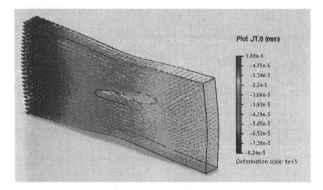

Follow the instructions given below in the middle tab of this window  to reduce the arrow density.

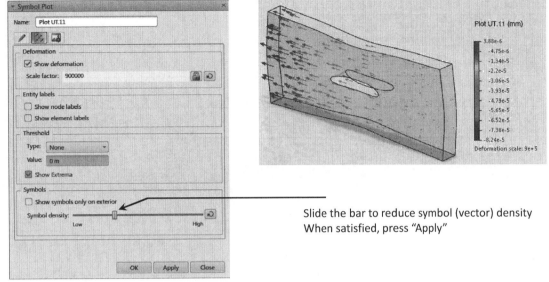

Slide the bar to reduce symbol (vector) density
When satisfied, press "Apply"

The final activity is to explore the "Feature Manager" ▦ in the context of the simulation results. This selection leads to the "Feature Manager" dialogue box below which contains valuable information.

	Name	Min	Max	Fields	Units
	Deformation.1	N.A	N.A	U	mm
	Displacement.1	0 mm	8.26e-5 mm	U, U	mm, mm
	Von Mises Stress.1	2.796e+4 ...	3.17e+5 ...	S, U	N_m2, mm
	Undeformed Model	N.A	N.A		
	Plot UT(Magnitude).1	0 mm	8.259e-5 ...	UT, U	mm, mm

Plots / Sensors / Display Groups

It is worth mentioning that dialogue boxes such as "Feature Manager" and the "Diagnostic Viewer" ![ ] can be accessed any time by right clicking on the screen as shown below.

There are many, many other important features that were not touched upon in this chapter but will be explored in later ones.

Exercise 1: Analysis of a Foot Pedal

The foot pedal shown below is made of steel with Young's modulus 30E+6 psi and Poisson ratio 0.3. The pedal is loaded with a normal force of 100 lb along the edge shown. The other end of the pedal is clamped. The geometrical dimensions are provided at the bottom of the page where all the dimensions are in inches.

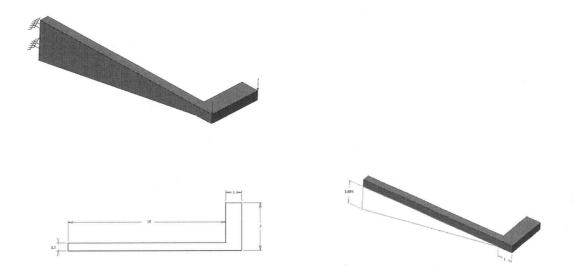

Try running the model with the two different element "size" and "sag" with both the linear and parabolic type of elements. Record the results in terms of the maximum displacement and the maximum von Mises stress in a table and comment on the results. The run time of the parabolic elements with element size of 0.1 could be substantial depending on the type of processor used.

Partial Answer:

Size = .3, sag = .05		
Element Type	Linear	Parabolic
Maximum Displacement	.0158 in.	.0227 in.
Maximum von Mises Stress	5.32E+3 psi	1.1E+4 psi

Size = .1, sag = .05		
Element Type	Linear	Parabolic
Maximum Displacement	.021 in.	.0229 in.
Maximum von Mises Stress	9.43E+4 psi	1.6E+4 psi

The above tables reveal an extremely important fact about finite element analysis. Making a single run and accepting the results at face value is a serious mistake. Note that for linear elements as the mesh is refined, there is a significant change in both displacement and von Mises stress. The user should not accept either value as being correct and must refine the mesh further. The refinement should reach a point at which the difference with the previous mesh is not deemed to be significant to the user. This process is referred to as a mesh convergence study.

Keep in mind that the refinement need not be uniform throughout the part. One should perform the refinement in the critical areas only. It is clear that parabolic elements are superior in accuracy to linear elements. Furthermore, note that although the displacement seems to have stabilized, the von Mises is still unreliable. It is well known that the displacements in FEA are more accurate than stresses. The reason is that the stresses are obtained by differentiating the displacement, a process which magnifies the error.

Exercise 2: Analysis of a Cylindrical Bar under Torsion

The cylindrical bar shown below has a clamped end. The other end is subjected to a couple caused by opposite forces on magnitude 1000 lbf separated by 1.5 in. This is equivalent to a torque of 1500 lbf.in applied to the cylinder. The material is steel with Young's modulus 30E+6 and Poisson ratio of 0.3.

The diameter of the cylinder is 1 in. and the dimensions of the loaded end are shown below. Although not showing, the length of the padded cylinder is 5 in. and the length of the padded rectangle is 0.5 in. All sharp corners at the loaded end have surface fillet of radius 0.1 in.

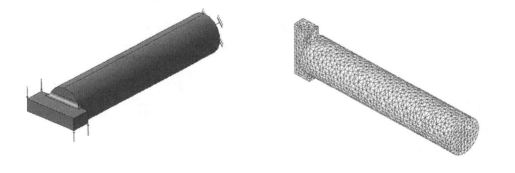

draw the rectangle on the circular face, then pad it away .5 in

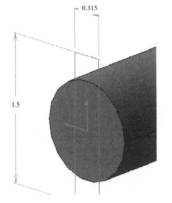

Model the part with linear solid elements with size = 0.1 and sag = 0.025 which results in the mesh shown in the previous page. Compare the hoop stress (The hoop stress is the largest principal stress "C11") with the theoretical solution from strength of materials.

Partial Answer:

The strength of materials solution is based on $\tau = \dfrac{Tr}{J}$ where T is the applied torque, r is the radius of the cylinder and J is the polar moment of inertia. In terms of the diameter, $r = \dfrac{D}{2}$, and $J = \dfrac{\pi D^4}{32}$. The hoop stress "C1" which numerically equals τ is calculated from $\dfrac{16T}{\pi D^3}$. For the present problem, $T = 1500$ lb.in and $D = 1$ in. Based on these parameters, a value of 7643 psi for the hoop stress is predicted.

Notes:

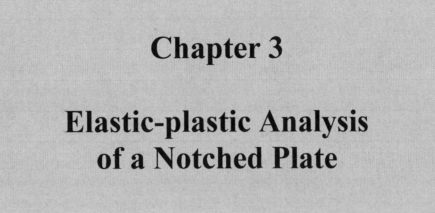

Chapter 3

Elastic-plastic Analysis
of a Notched Plate

Introduction:

This tutorial is an extension of the problem described in chapter 2. The plate with a central hole is pulled with a high load (50 MPa instead of 0.1 MPa of chapter 2) which drives the part into the plastic range. The true stress/true strain curve is provided in tabular form for the plasticity model.

NOTE: It is assumed that you have basic familiarity with CAD modeling in 3DEXPERIENCE allowing you to create a block with a central hole. If that is not the case, please consult the following tutorial book.

CAD Modeling Essentials in 3DEXPERIENCE, by Nader Zamani, SDC Publications, ISBN 978-1-63057-095-8.

Problem Statement:

The steel plate shown below is subjected to a pressure load P at the two ends. Contrary to the earlier model in chapter 2, the three planes of symmetry are used to reduce the finite element model as shown.

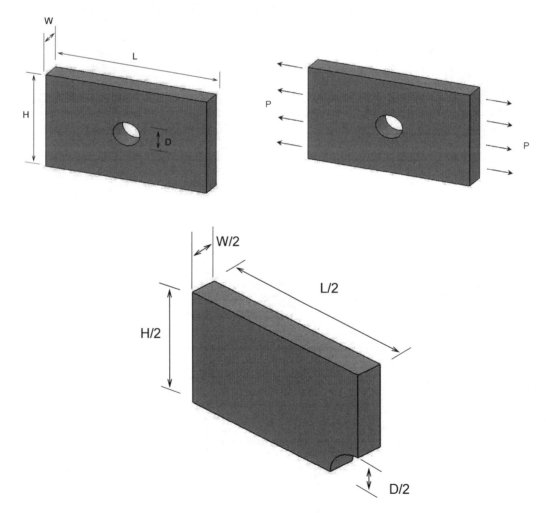

The Model and Material Properties:

Using the Part Design App 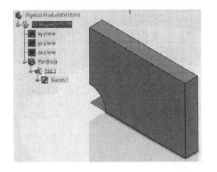 , create a 1/8 model of a block with a central hole with the dimensions L = 0.15m, H= 0.1m, W = 0.02m, and D = 0.025m as shown below.

The first task is to apply a material property to this part. From the bottom row of icons (i.e. the action bar), select the "Tools" tab.

From the menu, select "Material Browser" icon 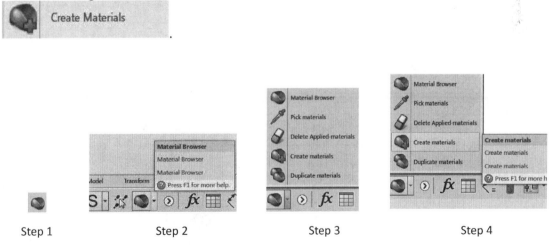. This opens up the menu as shown. Follow the steps outlined below to select the "Create Material"

The selection of opens a dialogue box shown on the next page. This box allows you to supply a proper name for the material should you decide to do so. Our assumption is that you do not have a material of interest in the "cloud" database and would like to follow the steps to create it. It is a rather tedious process but will be clearly spelled out.

Select the "Create Material" ![icon] icon. Make sure that you check the "Add domain" section of the dialogue box, and make sure that "Simulation Domain" is picked. Note that this creates a shell (a placeholder) and the material information needs to be supplied later.

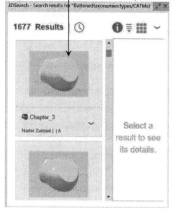

Type your desired name

Make sure that the "Simulation Domain" is checked.

Once you close the dialogue box by clicking on "OK", you will find yourself in the material database and can identify the material that you just created, namely "FEA_CH3". The database screen is shown below.

Here is the material property that you created This is just a "Template". Information will be inputted later.

Place the cursor on your created material in the database, right click and select "Apply". You still must return to the screen where the geometry exists and continue. This necessitates the closure of the current screen (the database screen).

Place the cursor here, right click, select "Apply"

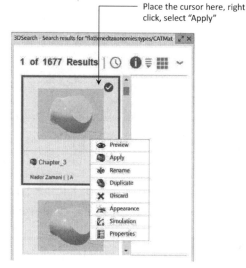

Select the "X "on the top right margin of the database screen to close the window.

Close this window by clicking on " X ".
Be careful not close the App. instead.

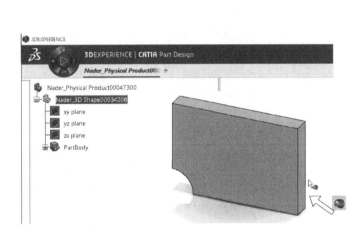

You will return to the geometry window. However, the shape of the cursor is modified as shown below.

Place the cursor on the part on the screen or on the top branch of the tree and double click.

You will notice that the "Materials" branch is created at the very bottom of the tree as shown below. You can then use the cursor to select the "Green" check mark to proceed.

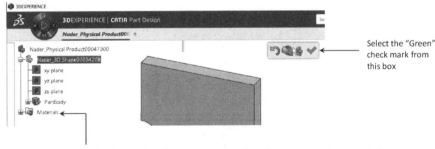

Select the "Green" check mark from this box

The created material has been assigned but this is just a "shell" , information needs to be inputted later.

Please note that the actual material properties are yet to be inputted. Expanding the "Materials" branch reveals two other branches. The location where the properties are inputted is the last branch as shown on the right.

PartBody
Materials
Steel_FEA_Ch3 (Nader_Physical Product00047300 A.1)
Nader_Material Appearance Domain00005647
Nader_Material Simulation Domain00004159

Input material properties by double clicking on this branch

Double click on the last branch and follow the steps below.

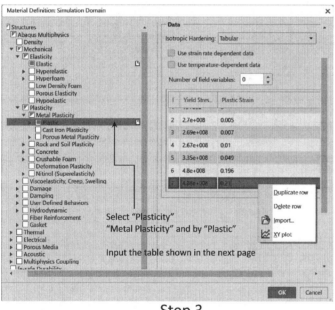

Step 1

Step 2

Step 3

In the steps 1 through 3, the linear elastic properties are inputted. In the next task (Step 3), the nonlinear stress strain curve (true stress vs true strain) must be inputted by filling the table or uploading an Excel spreadsheet. If experimental data is used, it is generally in the form of engineering stress vs engineering strain. The following expressions are used for conversion purposes.

$$\varepsilon_{true} = \ln(1 + \varepsilon_{eng})$$
$$\sigma_{true} = \sigma_{eng}(1 + \varepsilon_{eng})$$

In the present problem, the conversion has led to the data on the right, representing σ_{true} vs ε_{true} . Note that the first line represents the yield strength of the material (at zero plastic strain).

Stress(Pa)	Strain
1.0 e+008	0
2.7e+008	0.005
2.69e+008	0.007
2.67e+008	0.01
3.35e+008	0.049
4.8e+008	0.196
4.88e+008	0.21

An Excel file can also be imported as shown on the right.

E7			×	✓	f_x	
	A		B		C	
1	yield stress (N_m2)		plastic strain			
2	1.00E+08		0			
3	2.70E+08		0.005			
4	2.69E+08		0.007			
5	2.67E+08		0.01			
6	3.35E+08		0.049			
7	4.80E+08		0.196			
8	4.88E+08		0.21			
9						

In the event that the "Material Definition Simulation Domain" dialogue box is not open, double click on the appropriate row of the tree to access it.

PartBody
Materials
Steel_FEA_Ch3 (Nader_Physical Product00047300 A.1)
Nader_Material Appearance Domain00005647
Nader_Material Simulation Domain00004159

Input material properties by double clicking on this branch

You can have a plot of this data generated. Position the cursor in the middle column, right click, and select "XY plot". This will generate the requested plot.

Finally, close the "Material Definition Simulation Domain" by clicking "OK"

Elastic-plastic Analysis of a Notched Plate

Creating the Finite Element Model:

Locate the compass on the top left corner of the screen, and left click. Scroll through the applications and select the "Structural Model Creation" App

The row of icons in the bottom of your screen changes and will appear as displayed below.

The dialogue box shown below, "Create Finite Element Model" appears. For now, use the "Automatic" radio button. Other options are for user control of the meshing process. In the case of "Automatic", tetrahedral parabolic elements are created. There are additional steps required if "Abstraction" is to be used. This is explained in chapter 2.

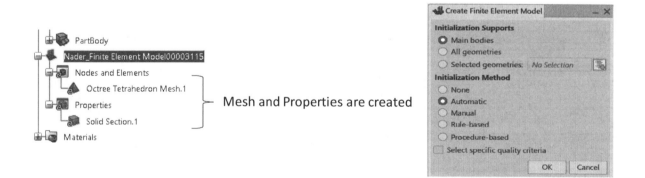

The tree indicates that a mesh and the corresponding solid section has been created. The elements are of "Tetrahedron" type and the property is "Solid Section" as expected. However, the "Updating" icon is displayed in the tree.

Although it is not necessary, in order to "Update" and get rid of the ⟳ symbol, follow the instructions below.

Select the "Setup" tab from the bottom row of icons.

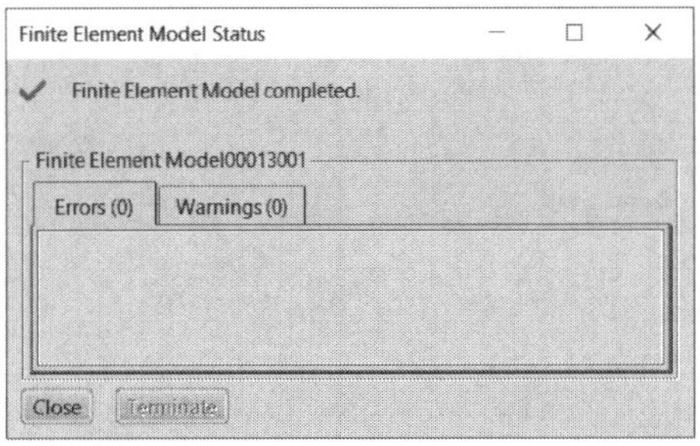

Select the "Setup" tab

Click on the "Check the Finite Element Model" icon  ☑ from your choices.

The finite Element check will take place while a window pops up and assuming there were no issues, the window looks as shown to the right.

Finite Element Model Status — □ ×

✓   Finite Element Model completed.

Finite Element Model00013001

Errors (0)   Warnings (0)

Close   Terminate

At this point the branches of the tree containing the "Nodes/Elements" and "Properties" are fully updated.

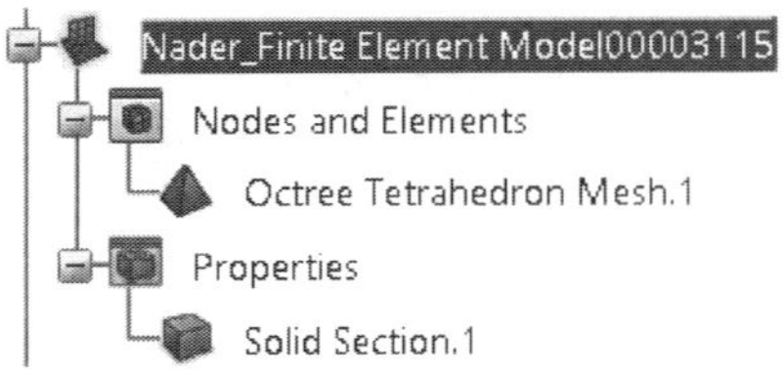

Nader_Finite Element Model00003115
- Nodes and Elements
  - Octree Tetrahedron Mesh.1
- Properties
  - Solid Section.1

Upon double clicking on the Tetrahedron Mesh branch, the corresponding dialogue box shown on the right pops up. Here, one can change the type (linear or quadratic), the size and sag, and certain other parameters. For example, local mesh refinement can be accomplished through the "Local Specifications". Use the default settings.

There are different methods for displaying the mesh. The instructions given below are one method of achieving that objective.

From the bottom row of icons, select the "Mesh" icon 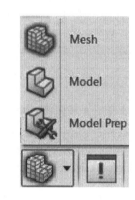 .

The bottom row's appearance resembles what is shown below.

Select the "Update" icon  .
Upon updating, the mesh appears on the screen as shown on the right.

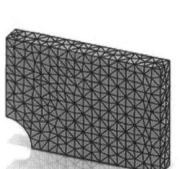

There are also different ways of hiding the mesh. For example, first select the "Display" tab from the bottom row of icons.

You can select the "Visualization Management" icon 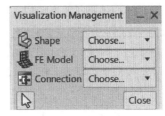 from the choices. The resulting dialogue box shown on the right appears.

Choose the "pull-down" next to 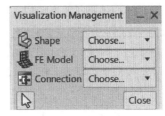 and make the indicated selection. This hides the mesh.

There are a few other icons that are worth mentioning here.

The "Clipping Box" icon enables you to select a region of your mesh.

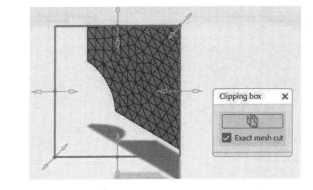

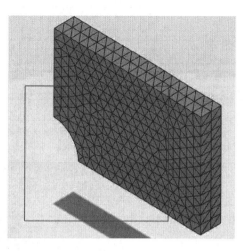

One can also shrink the elements, particularly useful for 2D elements such as shells. Select the "Element Shrink" icon

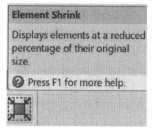

The resulting dialogue box has three sliding bars which allow you to shrink the elements as desired. As indicated earlier, this is not very useful for three dimensional solid elements; however, they are presented here for the sake of completeness.

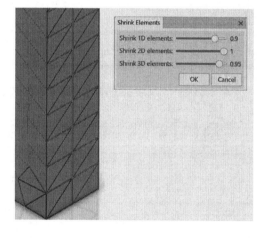

Creating a Scenario:

The nature of the analysis, namely, Static, Dynamic, Buckling, etc. is set in the "Structural Scenario Creation" App. Furthermore, the loads, restraints, and interaction are also defined in this application.

It is also important to point out that that one could have created the Scenario before the "Finite Element Model Creation" step. In fact, the latter can be created from within the "Structural Scenario Creation" App.

Locate the compass on the top left corner of the screen, and click.

Scroll through the applications and select the "Structural Scenario Creation" App.

Structural Model Creation

The row of icons in the bottom of your screen changes and will appear as displayed below.

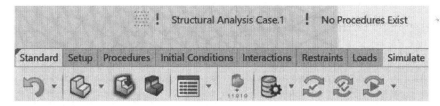

The pop-up window "Simulation Initialization" shown below appears on the screen. Since this is strictly a structural problem, the radio button "Structural" should be selected.

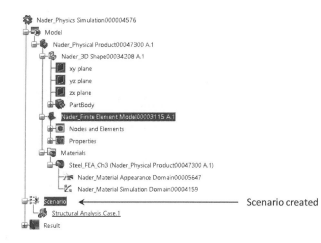

A quick glance at the tree confirms that a "Scenario" has been created.

Checking the bottom middle section of the screen reveals that there are two red exclamation signs.

These pertain to "Structural Analysis Case.1" and "No Procedures Exist".

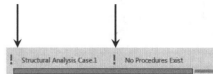

Click the "Select the Finite Element Model" icon from the bottom row. This is referring to the FemRep which is already created. The following pop-up window opens up.

Since there is already a finite element model created, it appears in the list and make sure that you select that row.
Click on "OK".

Select ⟶

Note that there is another icon 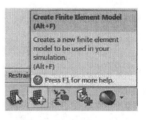 , namely, the "Create Finite Element Model" in the bottom row. As it was mentioned earlier, the FE model could have also been created in Scenario, and this is the icon to achieve that task. It does not apply to you as it was already created and selected above.

Pick the "Procedures" tab from the bottom row.

Select the "Procedure" tab

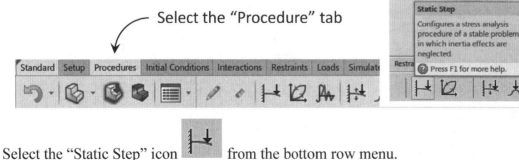

Select the "Static Step" icon from the bottom row menu.

The "Static Step" dialogue box pops up. Accept all the defaults except the "Initial Time Increment" that should be "0.1s". Note that if the "Advanced" pulldown list is selected, it becomes clear that this is the point in the software where "Geometric Nonlinearities" are included, or excluded.

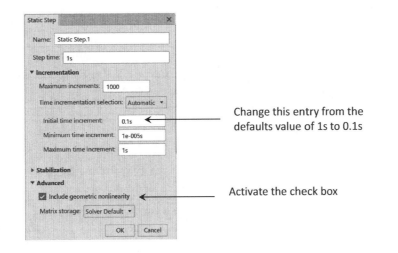

Change this entry from the defaults value of 1s to 0.1s

Activate the check box

A quick glance at the bottom middle section of the screen reveals "Green" checkmarks instead of "Red" exclamation marks.

Note the "Green" checkmarks instead of "Red" exclamations

The tree indicates that "Static Step.1" has been created. There are default basic output entities that are requested upon the creation of a Step.

Accessing the Model, Scenario and Results Quickly:

Clearly this can be done by double clicking on the corresponding branches of the tree. However, it can also be done efficiently by selecting the appropriate icon among these three  . The first one on the left is "Model and Mesh", the middle one is "Scenario" and the one on the far right is "Results" that is the postprocessor.

Applying the Pressure Load:

A pressure load of -50000000 Pa (-50 MPa) is to be applied on the end faces. Note that positive pressure by convention is a compressive load. Since the notched block is under tension a pressure value is inputted as a negative number.

Select the "Loads" tab

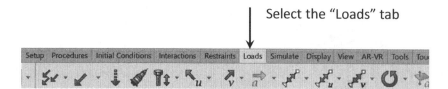

Choose the end face of the block as shown, select

the "Pressure" icon 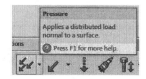 from the bottom row of
icons and apply –0.5E+8 Pa.

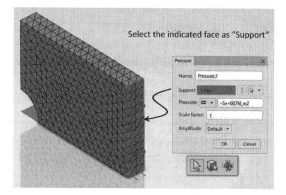

Applying the Restraints:

Pick the "Restraints" tab from the bottom row of icons as shown (i.e. from the action bar).

Select the "Restraints" tab

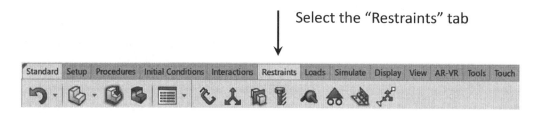

Make three, separate and consecutive selections of each of the planes of symmetry. Each time one of these selections is made, click

on the "Slider" icon from the bottom row of icons.

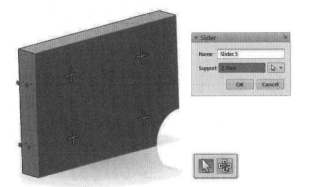

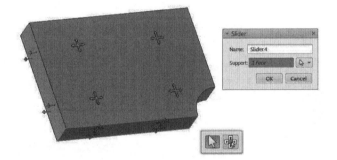

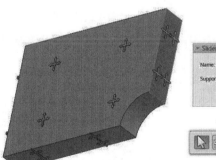

The "Slider" restraints are now recorded in the tree. Your numbering may be different though.

Nader_Physics Simulation000004576
Model
    Nader_Physical Product00047300 A.1
Scenario
    Structural Analysis Case.1
        Restraints (3)
            Slider.1
            Slider.2
            Slider.3
        Loads (1)
        Output Requests (2)
        Static Step.1
    Result

Slider restraints just applied.
Your numbering labels may be different.

Requesting the desires "Outputs" beyond the default outputs:

First select the "Simulate" tab and then pick the "Outputs" icon [icon] from the menu.

"Simulate" tab

| Standard | Setup | Procedures | Initial Conditions | Interactions | Restraints | Loads | Simulate | Display | View | AR-VR | Tools | Touch |

Note that if the problem is nonlinear, regardless of its type, a large amount of data at different iterations may be generated. One should consider the storage requirements on the hard drive.

In case the results are stored on the "cloud" it can affect the data communication overhead.

Select the type of field output needed and the frequency of recording the data for future post-processing

Output

Name: Output.3
Support: Whole Model
Frequency: Every n increments
n: 1
Output group: Field
    Apply preselected defaults
    Stresses
        S, Stress components
        TSHR, Transverse shear stress (for thick shells)
        ☑ MISESMAX, Maximum Mises equivalent stress
    Strains
        E, Total strain components
        ☑ PE, Plastic strain components
        ☑ PEEQ, Equivalent plastic strain
        PEEQMAX, Maximum equivalent plastic strain
        ☑ EE, Elastic strain components
Section points: Default
Element output at: Integration points
                            OK   Cancel

It is a good practice to perform the model and consistency check before submitting the work for the final run.
Select the "Model and Scenario Check" icon from the bottom row

The software goes through a check phase and if there are no issues, a message with a "Green" check mark is returned.

Simulation Checks Status

✓ Simulation checks completed.

▶ Errors (0)

▶ Warnings (1)

▶ Information (0)

Close   Terminate

Next select the "Simulation Checks" icon from the bottom row of icons. Accept the number of "cores" in the pop up box below.

Simulation Checks

Location: Local interactive ▾

Performance: ●————————○ 4 / 4 cores

                Baseline   Fast

▼ Analysis case

Experience content Generate ▾

Results   Overwrite previous ▾

Description for previous results

▶ Units: m, kg, s, Kdeg, mol.

OK   Cancel

Upon the completion of the "Simulation Check", any warning messages will be available in the pop-up box below.

Simulation Checks Status

✓ Simulation checks completed.

▼ Warnings (7)

C3D10HS AND HYBRID TETRAHEDRAL ELEMENTS WILL ENFORCE PRESSURE CONTINUITY ACROSS MATERIAL BOUNDARIES. IN ORDER TO ALLOW DISCONTINUITIES IN THE VOLUMETRIC FIELD USE *TIE.

DEGREE OF FREEDOM 4 IS NOT ACTIVE IN THIS MODEL AND CANNOT BE RESTRAINED.

DEGREE OF FREEDOM 5 IS NOT ACTIVE IN THIS MODEL AND CANNOT BE RESTRAINED.

DEGREE OF FREEDOM 4 IS NOT ACTIVE IN THIS MODEL AND CANNOT BE RESTRAINED.

DEGREE OF FREEDOM 5 IS NOT ACTIVE IN THIS MODEL AND CANNOT BE RESTRAINED.

Assuming that there are no serious issues (i.e. no error messages), you are ready to submit the job for "Simulation".

Select the "Simulation" icon 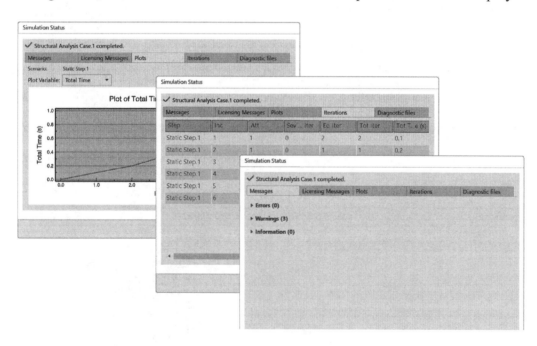 from the bottom row.

Accept the number of "cores" in the pop up box, and wait for the simulation to complete.

The present simulation will satisfactorily complete but in other cases, it may terminate at an earlier stage. This can be due to lack of convergence or excessive iterations in a particular sub-step. In that situation, one can still do the post-processing for the previously converged sub-steps. Furthermore, using the different tabs in the final dialogue box, valuable information on how simulation proceeded can be displayed.

For the readers who are not familiar with performing nonlinear analysis, they need to be reminded that the reference to the total time of t = 1second is fictitious. The present

problem was solved with the "Static Step" and therefore there is no time dependence. The time here refers to the proportion of the "pressure" value that was imposed on the side face.

Results (Post processing):

Once you close (or move) the obstructing dialogue boxes, you must be in the "Results" section and the bottom row should appear as shown on the right.

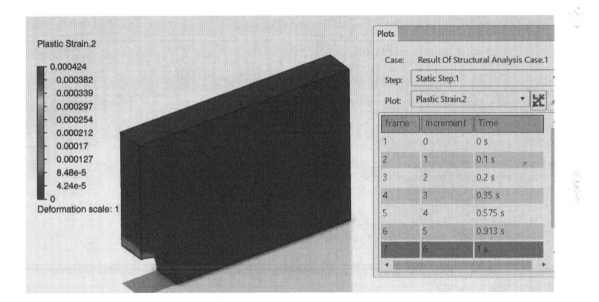

If the postprocessing (results) dialogue box does not appear automatically, click on the "Results" icon.

Although it does not apply to the present run, a warning box may appear informing the user that these are intermediate results. In that situation simply close the "Warning" pop up box.

From the pulldown menu, you can select the nature of the contour plot desired and below the dialogue box choose the time specified. Here the plastic strain at the end of the run (t = 1s) plotted. If the run involves several steps, that can also be set using the pulldown menu.

Under normal circumstances, once a contour plot is generated, the previous one is automatically removed from the screen. However, multiplot simultaneously appearing on the screen can easily be created.

The plots of the von Mises stress at four different times are given below. Note that the time equal to zero means no load is applied yet.

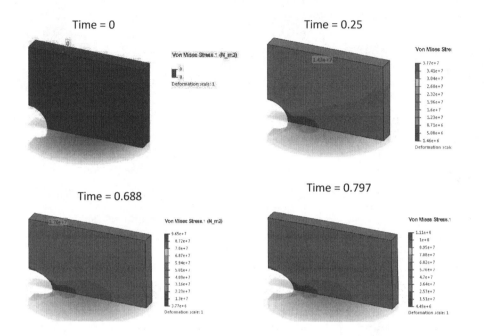

The plots of PEEQ (equivalent plastic strains) are also shown below. There is no plasticity in action in the initial stages of loading.

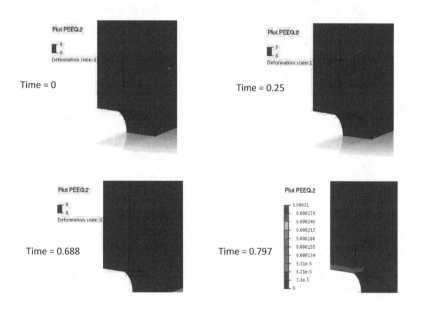

Changing the Element Type:

There are several ways to change the type of elements used.
Here is one procedure for changing the element type. Double click on the branch of the tree called "Tetrahedron Mesh.1" which opens the dialogue box shown below.

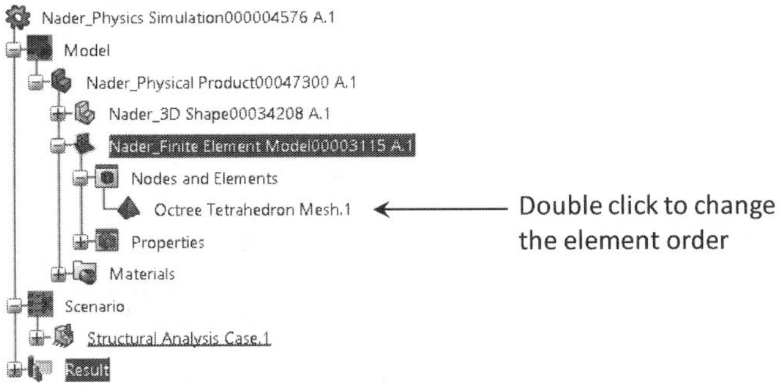

Nader_Physics Simulation000004576 A.1
Model
  Nader_Physical Product00047300 A.1
    Nader_3D Shape00034208 A.1
    Nader_Finite Element Model00003115 A.1
      Nodes and Elements
        Octree Tetrahedron Mesh.1 ← Double click to change
                                         the element order
      Properties
    Materials
  Scenario
    Structural Analysis Case.1
  Result

Note that the parabolic element is highlighted. Use the cursor to select the linear elements as shown.

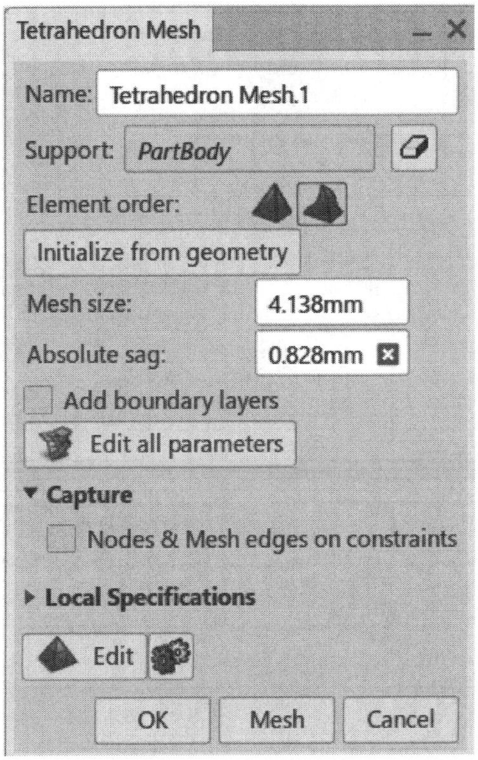

Tetrahedron Mesh — ✕

Name: Tetrahedron Mesh.1

Support: *PartBody*

Element order:

Initialize from geometry

Mesh size: 4.138mm

Absolute sag: 0.828mm ✖

☐ Add boundary layers

    Edit all parameters

▼ **Capture**

    ☐ Nodes & Mesh edges on constraints

▶ **Local Specifications**

    ◆ Edit

    OK   Mesh   Cancel

There are alternative and more systematic approaches to achieve the above objective.

Select the "Mesh" icon 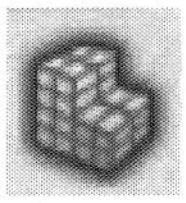   from the main menu at the bottom of the screen.

Select the "Setup" tab

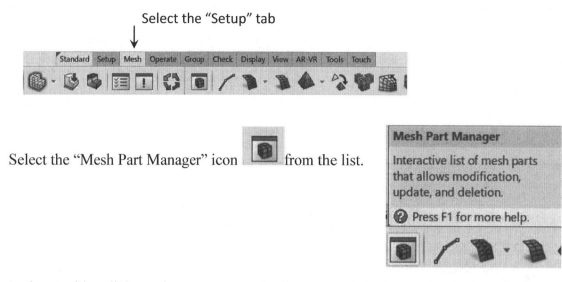

Select the "Mesh Part Manager" icon 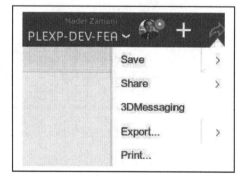 from the list.

In the resulting dialogue box, one can make the appropriate changes and create the new mesh.

Before concluding this chapter, the reader is reminded that regular saves on the "Cloud" need to be made. This is placed at the top right corner of your screen as shown on the right. However, depending on the institution you are stydying at (or working at) you may have other options. Please check with your instructor/system administrator to learn the details.

Exercise 1

In this exercise, you will explore the finite element modeling of an elasto-plastic material. The background material needed for you to achieve this goal is provided below.

Polystyrene Crazing is the phenomenon that produces a network of fine cracks on the surface of the polystyrene material. One of the early attempts to model this process is due to Howard and Owen. They idealized their model as shown below.

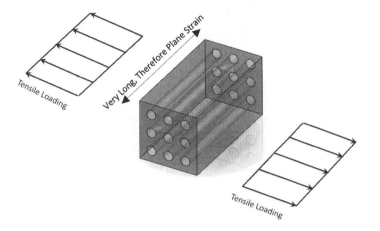

The polystyrene is assumed to be infinitely long in all directions and it is under uniaxial tension. The load is perpendicular to the direction of the crack/void network. Due to the infinite length along the crack direction, the problem can be approximated as a plane strain problem. Furthermore, the infinite dimensions perpendicular to the crack directions, implies symmetry conditions that can be applied. The details of such assumptions are shown below.

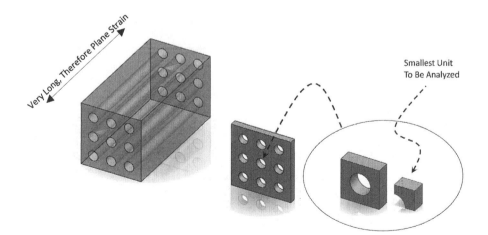

The boundary conditions for the plane strain problem are described below.
Note that due to the plane strain condition, the surfaces ABCDE and A' B' C' D' E' are roller supported.

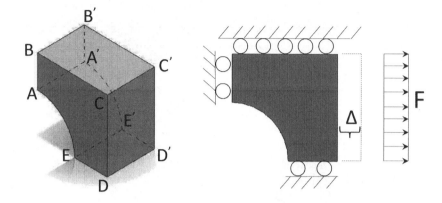

The material is assumed to be an **elastic perfectly-plastic** type with the following numerical data.

Young's Modulus = 42000 MN/m^2
Yield Strength = 105 MN/m^2
Poisson's Ratio = 0.33

The spacing and the void dimensions are governed by the ratio $\frac{d}{a} = 0.5$ where "a" and "d" are described on the right.

The mesh that was originally used by Howard and Owen is also shown below. They employed eight noded, isoparametric, plane strain elements.

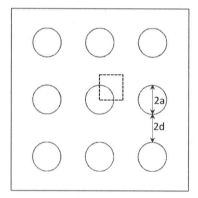

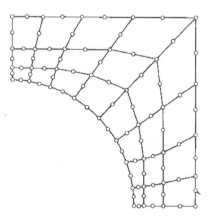

The findings of Howard and Owen are summarized in the non-dimensional force deflection curve presented below.

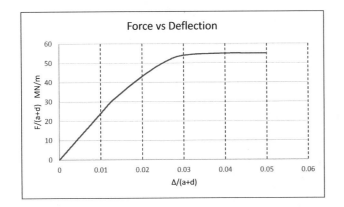

Since you are limited to three dimensional elements in 3DEXPERIENCE, your model will be fully composed of such entities.

NOTES:

Chapter 4

The Need for the Mesh Convergence Study

Objective:

This tutorial is a further look at the problem described in chapter 2 with some modifications made. The main focus of the chapter is to conduct a mesh convergence study by taking a sequence of meshes which become progressively finer and finding the maximum von Mises stress whose location is at the notch.

For the geometry, the plate with a central hole is pulled on both sides to cause a total elongation of 1mm. In chapter 2, the pressure at the two ends was specified, whereas here, the displacement is given. Due to symmetry, only a sector of the geometry needs to be modeled, for example, in the case of solid elements, 1/8th of the part is modeled (as in chapter 3), whereas if shell elements are employed, 1/4th of the part is discretized. In this chapter, shell elements are in fact used.

One of the nice features in 3DEXPERIENCE is that many different meshes (Finite Element Models) can be generated beforehand and included in the model. These meshes can be used when needed and this simplifies the mesh convergence study drastically.

NOTE: It is assumed that you have basic familiarity with CAD modeling in 3DEXPERIENCE allowing you to create a block (a surface) with a central hole. If that is not the case, please consult the following tutorial book.

CAD Modeling Essentials in 3DEXPERIENCE, by Nader Zamani, SDC Publications, ISBN 978-1-63057-095-8.

Problem Statement:

The steel plate shown below is subjected to a fixed displacement at the two ends. The deformation is assumed to be linear and elastic and the plate is modeled with a surface, and therefore, shell elements need to be used.

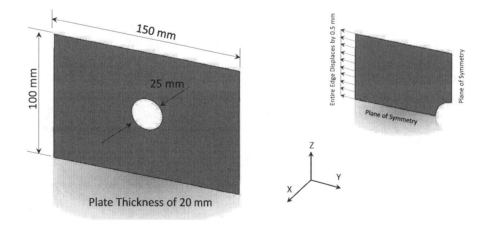

Shell Elements, their Advantages and Limitations:

If the topology of the part is such that one dimension is significantly smaller than the other two dimensions, the part can be reasonably modeled with a surface of a given thickness. Examples of such parts are all sheet metals, thin-walled pressure vessels, car bodies, and aircraft fuselage. The appropriate elements to analyze such structures are shell elements.

Linear triangular shell elements in space have three nodes with each node having six degrees of freedom. Those are three translations and three rotations. The thickness of the shell must be provided as an input to the software. A typical shell element is displayed below. As in the case of solid elements, 3DEXPERIENCE has linear and parabolic shell elements with the latter one being more accurate. Other more sophisticated shell elements are also available but not being considered in this chapter.

The degrees of freedom are given by the following vector.

$$(u_x \quad u_y \quad u_z \quad \theta_x \quad \theta_y \quad \theta_z)$$

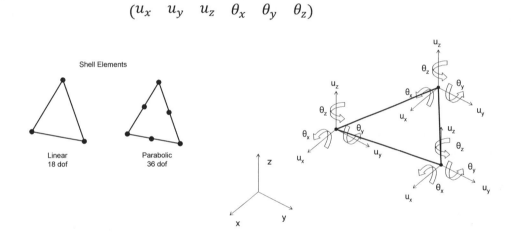

The symmetry plane restraints are imposed according to the following table.

PLANE	u_x	u_y	u_z	Θ_x	Θ_y	Θ_z
yz	zero	free	free	free	zero	zero
xz	free	zero	free	zero	free	zero
xy	free	free	zero	zero	zero	free

For example, if yz is a plane of symmetry, $u_x = 0 \quad \theta_y = 0 \quad \theta_z = 0$
if xz is a plane of symmetry, $u_y = 0 \quad \theta_x = 0 \quad \theta_z = 0$
if xy is a plane of symmetry, $u_z = 0 \quad \theta_x = 0 \quad \theta_y = 0$

The paragraphs below are quoted from the following paper by the author:
"14th LACCEI International Multi-Conference for Engineering, Education, and Technology: "Engineering Innovations for Global Sustainability", July 2016.

The reader may be familiar with the SAE Mini-Baja competition in which engineering schools from across the world have the opportunity to participate (see Fig below). One of the aspects of this competition is to design a frame which has the structural integrity based on the SAE specifications. Ordinarily, because of the complexity of the geometry, the participating teams use a commercial FEA software to investigate their design. It is very common that they use solid elements to model components (such as tubes) to predict the stresses. This will frequently lead to poor results as it cannot be discretized with sufficiently small solid elements. The student's reasoning for this decision is based on convenience and the lack of familiarity with the beam and shell elements.

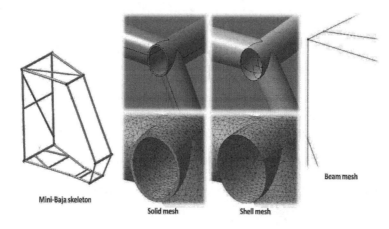

Mini-Baja skeleton   Solid mesh   Shell mesh   Beam mesh

In order to make the current FEA packages "look" user friendly, the number of warning messages is kept at a minimum. This is partly the reason that some users look for the "deflection" plot without paying much attention to the actual numbers. Clearly, changing the element size can dramatically affect the stress values and to a lesser extent, the deflection values. To convince the students of the significance of the mesh size, a simple cantilever beam problem can be used. To be more specific, a 1x1x10 inch steel beam whose end face is clamped, and the top face is subjected to a pressure of 50 psi is considered. This simple geometry is used to avoid confounding the issue.

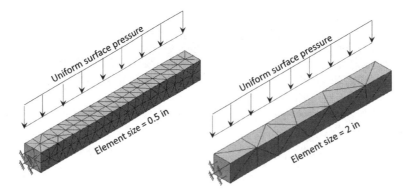

The two different discretizations of the cantilever problem (with solid elements) are shown in the previous page, where the coarse mesh is 2 in., whereas the fine mesh is 0.5 in. The results of using linear tetrahedral elements with the coarse and fine mesh are described in the table below. The quantities compared are the maximum deflection and the maximum von Mises stress.

Element size (inches)	Maximum Deflection (inches)	Maximum von Mises Stress (psi)
2.0	0.0056	3410
0.5	0.0155	8200

A beginner, having seen such a comparison, may arrive at the conclusion that a smaller element size results in a more reliable solution. Therefore, they select an extremely small size which can cause the computer to stall trying to complete the job.

The reader should be convinced through a good example that although small elements are preferred, their effectiveness depends on where they are deployed. These elements are to be used in locations where the stress contours are tightly packed together. A good demonstration problem is precisely the problem that will be discussed in this chapter, namely a plate with central hole under tensile loading.

Shell elements, although very efficient, do not consider the variation of stress through the thickness of the part and therefore, in certain situations erroneous results can be produced.

The Model and Material Properties:

In the "Objectives" section of this chapter it was mentioned that the reader should be sufficiently familiar with the CAD modeling in 3DEXPERIENCE to be able to create a plate with a central hole. However, the steps to create the geometry are outlined for completeness.

Select the "Generative Shape Design" icon  to enter the App.

After landing in that App., select the "Wireframe" tab.

"Wireframe" tab

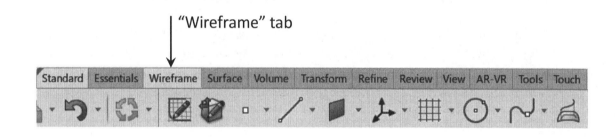

Using the "Positioned Sketch" icon  draw a profile as shown and dimension it accordingly.

Exit the sketcher

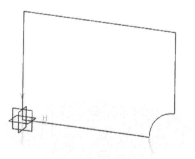

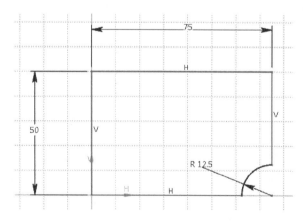

Select the "Surface" tab from the bottom row (the action bar).

"Surface" tab

Click on the "Fill" icon and in the resulting dialogue box, select "Sketch.1" just drawn.

This operation will create a surface bounded by "Sketch.1".

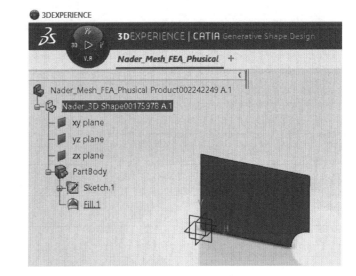

The next step is to apply material properties to this surface. Since linear elastic analysis is to be performed, there are two pieces of information that are needed. The Young's modulus is assumed to be E = 2e+11 Pa and the Poisson's ratio is ν = 0.3.

The steps needed to apply material properties to the part were explained in its entirety in chapter 2 and can be carried out without any changes. We leave it to the reader to complete this task. Upon completion, the "Material Definition Simulation Domain" dialogue box should look as follows.

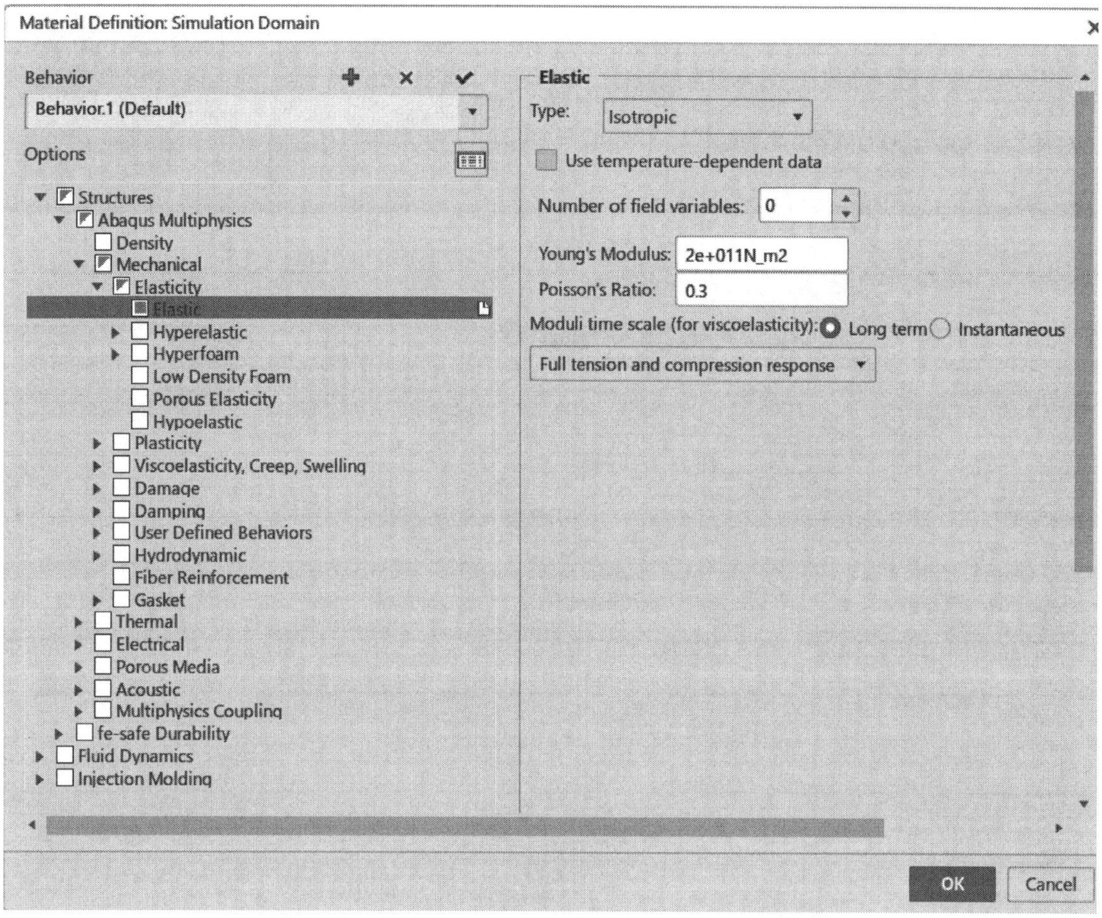

Creation of Four Finite Element Models:

In 3DEXPERIENCE, a "Finite Element Model" refers to mesh and the appropriate section properties of the mesh.

Locate the compass on the top left corner of the screen, and select it as shown on the right. Scroll through the applications and select the "Structural Model Creation" App

Structural Model Creation

The row of icons on the bottom of your screen changes and will appear as displayed below.

"Setup" tab

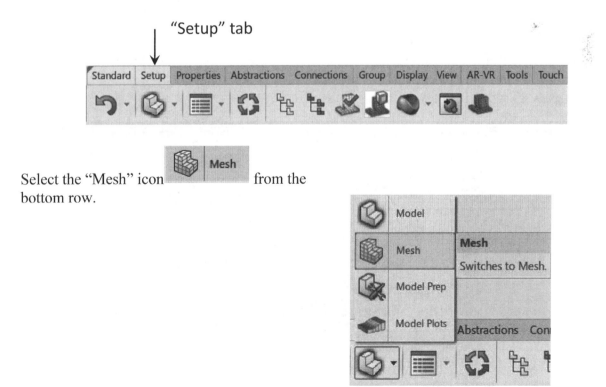

Select the "Mesh" icon ⬚ Mesh from the bottom row.

The bottom row of icons (the action bar) changes contents as shown below.

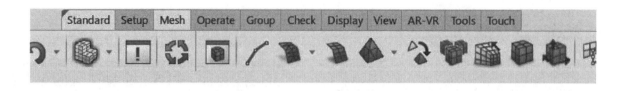

From the menu, select the "Surface Triangle Mesh"

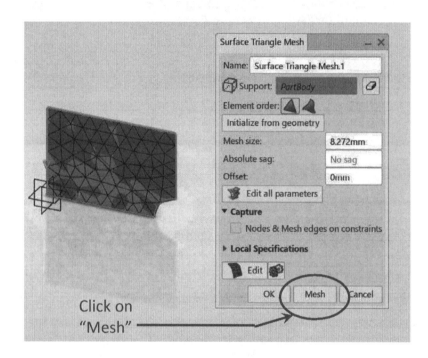

and for the "Support", choose the created surface, i.e. "Fill.1". This can be done from the screen, or from the tree.

Please make sure that the "Linear" element is checked. Click on the "Mesh" button at the bottom of the window and the mesh with corresponding parameters (size and sag) will be displayed.

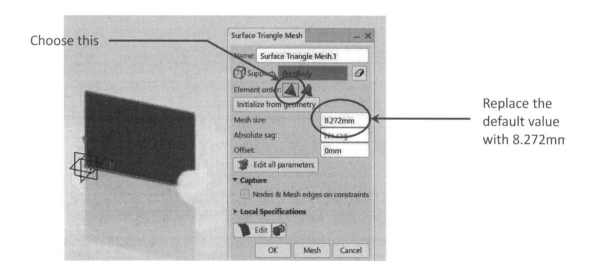

Upon selecting "OK", the window closes, and the mesh appears on the screen.

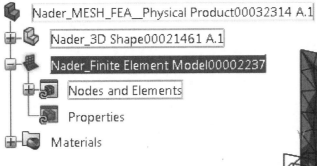

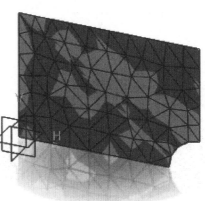

Once filtering out the part, the mesh by itself is plotted.

For filtering, right click on the screen and select "Visualization Management".

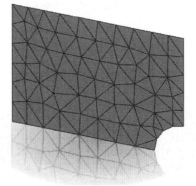

This mesh corresponds to an element size $d = 8.272mm$ and a default *sag*.
In the subsequent "FE Models", the size is progressively reduced. The tree indicates that the "Properties" branch is yet to be assigned.

Select the "Setup" tab from the bottom row.

Setup tab

Click on the "Model" icon followed by the "Properties" tab. The menu transforms and appears as shown below.

"Properties" tab

Pick the "Shell Section" icon from the menu and enter 20mm for the "Thickness". For the "Support" select the mesh from the screen. Note that the tree indicates that the mesh needs updating.

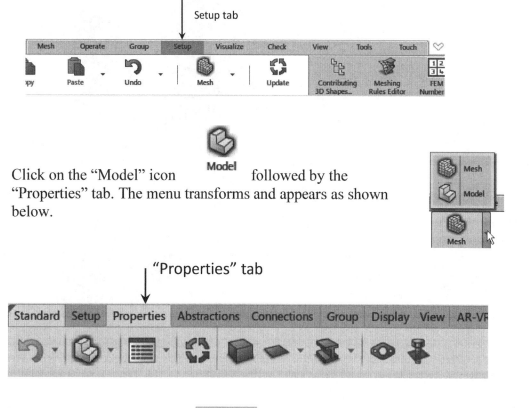

Select the "Setup" tab followed by the "Mesh" tab and update .

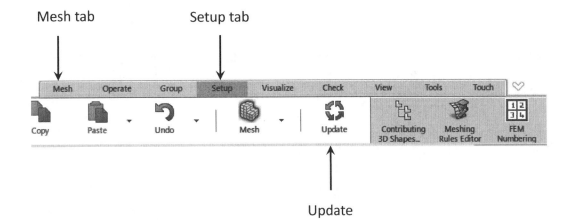

Mesh tab   Setup tab

Update

The steps followed in the creation of this "Finite Element Model" must be repeated four times; all are identical to the first model except for the element size. The subsequent sizes are $\frac{d}{2} = 4.136mm, \frac{d}{4} = 2.068mm, 2d = 16.544mm$ and the corresponding meshes are shown below.

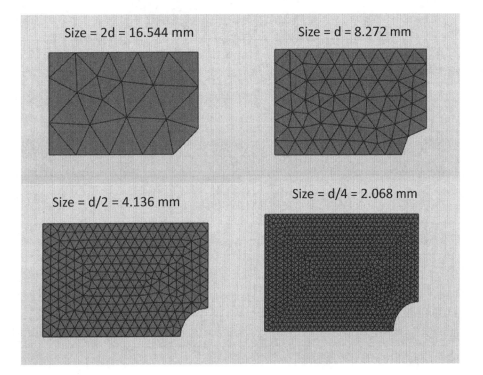

For helping the reader and avoiding confusion, I will repeat the steps needed to create the "second" finite element model.

Select the "Setup" tab from the action bar.

From the choices, pick the "Duplicate FEM within" icon

.

Once the icon is selected the dialogue box appearing below will appear on the screen.

Duplicate FEM within

Duplicates the FEM assembly within the same model, with the option to duplicate connections.

❓ Press F1 for more help.

Duplicate FEM within		— ✕
FEM to duplicate: *Finite Element Model00013221*		

Product structure	FEM	Duplicate
🧊 Nader_Mesh_fea_Physical P...	🔩 Finite Element ...	

Duplication prefix: [   ]

Connections: ◉ Include   ○ Duplicate and include

[OK] [Cancel]

In the older releases of 3DEXPERIENCE, the procedure for adding other "Finite Element Models" was more straightforward. All that one needed to do was to use the icon "Create Finite Element Model" which is no longer avaliable. With the present release of the software, this needs to be done through the above dialogue box. Select the radio button "Duplicate and Include" 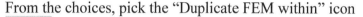 radio button and add a "Duplication prefix". This will create a second finite element model. Upon pressing "OK", a second "Finite Element Model" in the tree is created. However, the element size for the second model has to be changed.

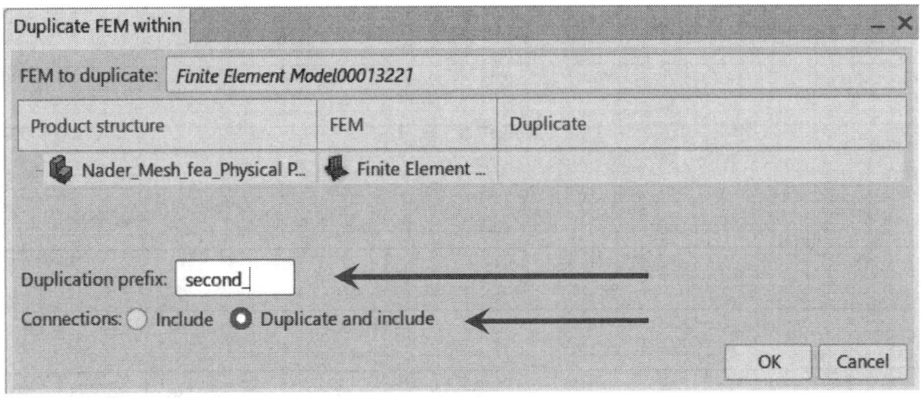

The tree displays the presence of the second "Finite Element Model" just constructed.

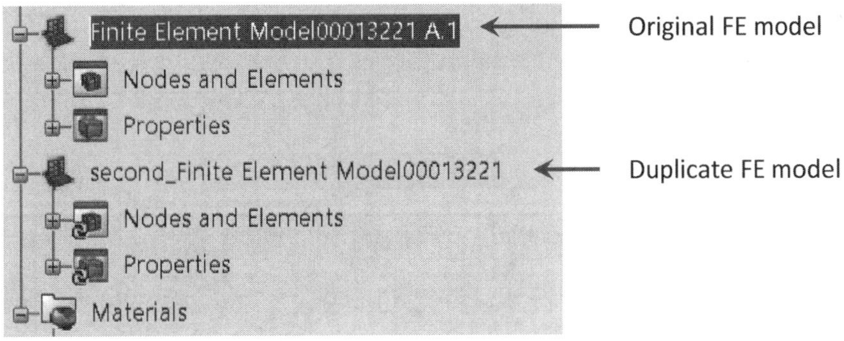

Double click on the "Nodes and Elements" in the new branch of the tree and change the "Mesh size" to 4.136mm as shown below.

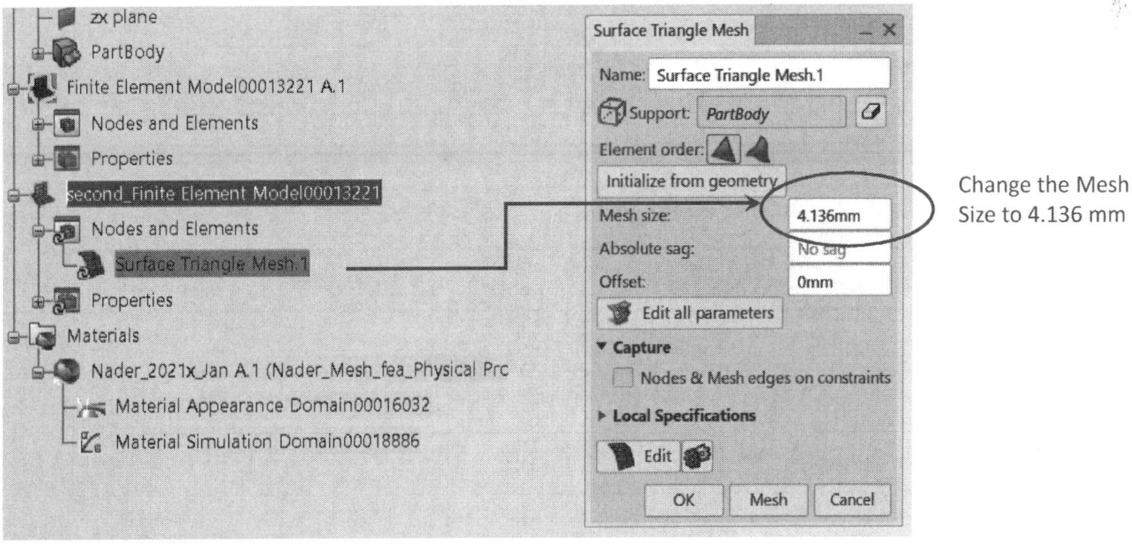

Upon pressing the "Mesh" button at the bottom of the dialogue box, the new mesh will appear.

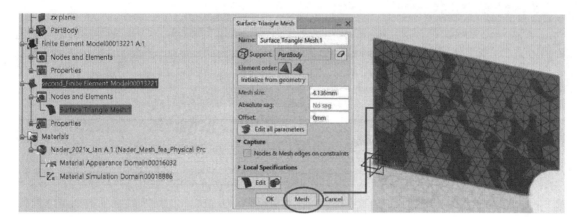

Once again select the "Setup" tab from the action bar.

"Setup" tab

Repeat the above process two more times with "Mesh size" 2.068mm and 16.544mm. The tree will now have 4 branches of the "Finite Element Model" as displayed below.

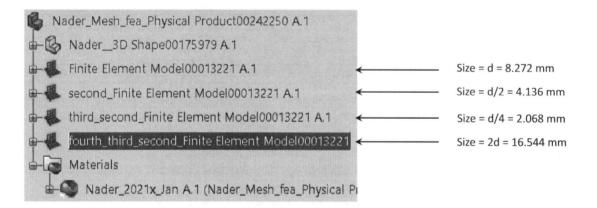

Note that although it is not the case for this problem, the thickness of the model can also be changed by modifying the section property.

Creating a Scenario, Running the Finite Element Models One at a Time:

Locate the compass on the top left corner of the screen, and select it as shown on the right. Scroll through the applications and select the "Structural Scenario Creation" App

Structural Scenario
Creation

The row of icons in the bottom of your screen once you select the "Setup" tab changes and will appear as displayed below.

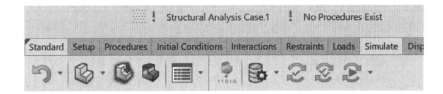

The pop-up window "Simulation Initialization" shown on the right appears. Since this is strictly a structural problem, the radio button "Structural" should be selected.

A quick glance at the tree confirms that a "Scenario" has been created.

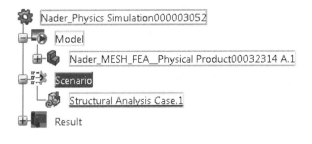

You will notice two red "exclamation" marks in the bottom middle section of the screen as shown below. This stems from the fact that at this point, no "Finite Element Model" has been selected and no "Step" has been defined.

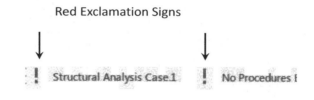

Red Exclamation Signs

Click the "Select the Finite Element Model" icon from the bottom row. This is referring to the "FE Model" which is already created. The following pop-up window appears.

Since there are four "Finite Element Models" present, you must select the one that is to be used.

As soon as you select an "FE Model" and close the window, the first red exclamation sign turns into a green check sign.

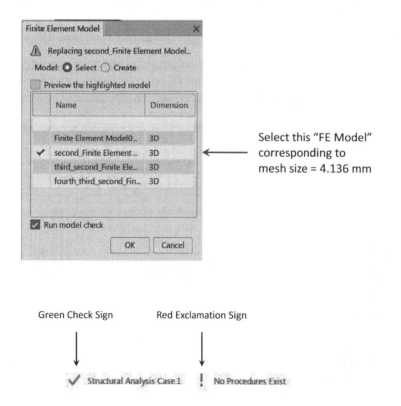

Select this "FE Model" corresponding to mesh size = 4.136 mm

Green Check Sign   Red Exclamation Sign

Note that there is a "Create Finite Element Model" option in the previous dialogue box. Therefore the "FE Model" can also be created within a "Scenario".

Select the "Procedures" tab from the bottom row.

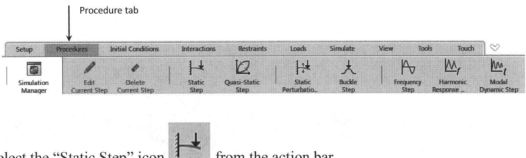

Select the "Static Step" icon  from the action bar.

The "Static Step" dialogue box pops up. Accept all the defaults. Note that if the "Advanced" pulldown list is selected, it becomes clear that this is the point in the software where "Geometric Nonlinearities" are included, or excluded. **The present problem is solved as a linear problem and therefore the NLGEOM box should be unchecked**.

Note that upon closing "Static Step" window, both check marks in the bottom left margin are green. Good sign!

Applying Restraints:

Select the "Restraints" tab from the bottom row.

"Restraints" tab

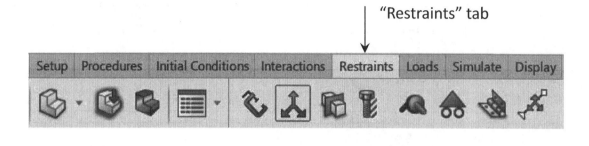

Use the "Fixed Displacement" icon and when the dialogue box opens, for the "Support" select the vertical edge of the geometry generated, and check the boxes shown.

If you are having difficulties with picking the edge, make sure that in your model, "Sketch.1" is hidden and "Fill.1" is showing (not hidden). Also see the tree on the next page.

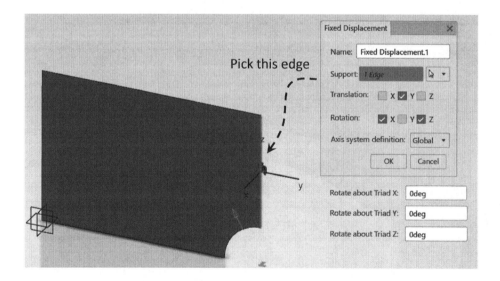

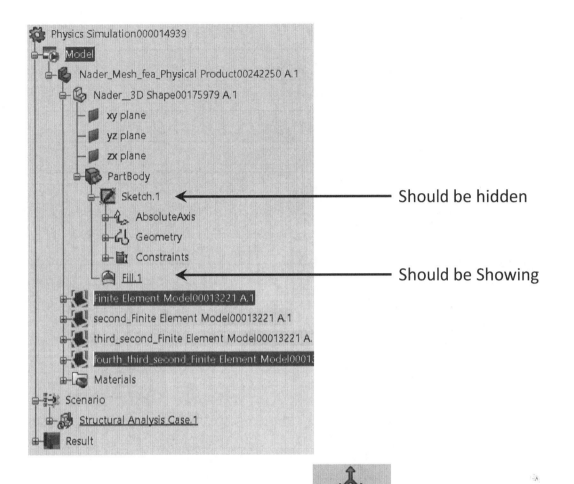

Once again, use the "Fixed Displacement" icon ![Fixed Displacement] and when the dialogue box opens, for the "Support" select the horizontal edge of the geometry generated and check the boxes shown.

Note that despite these restraints, the structure can move as a rigid body in the x-direction. To prevent the rigid body motion, we can take one of the corner points and give it a zero displacement in the x-direction.

Pick the "Fixed Displacement" icon and when the dialogue box opens, for the "Support" select the vertex of the geometry and check the box shown.

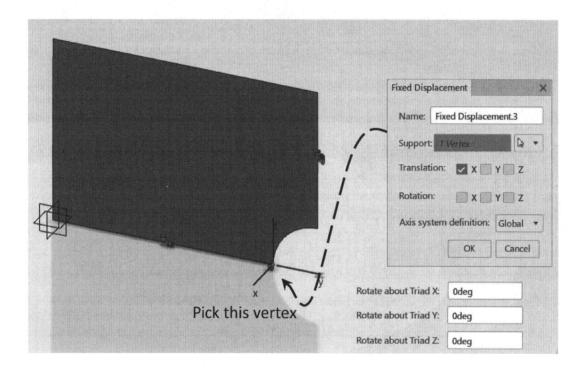

Applying Loads:

Select the "Loads" tab from the bottom row (action bar).

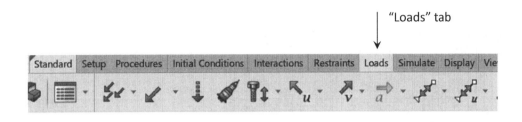

"Loads" tab

Use the "Applied Translation" icon and for the "Support" the left vertical edge of the plate. For "Translation" input -0.5mm. The pulldown menu allows you to specify the direction (-Y in the present problem).

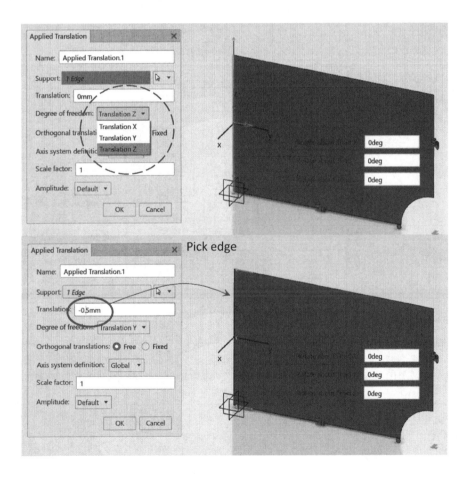

Consistency, Model Check, and Simulation:

Select the "Simulation" tab from the bottom row of icons on your screen.

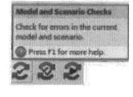

It is a good practice to perform the model and consistency check before submitting the work for the final run.
Select the "Model and Scenario Check" icon from the bottom row.

The software goes through a check phase and if there are no issues, a message with a "Green" check mark is returned.

Next, select the "Simulation Checks" icon from the bottom row of icons. Accept the number of "Cores" in the pop up box below.

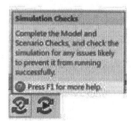

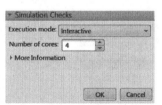

Upon the completion of the "Simulation Check", any warning messages will be available in the pop-up box below.

Assuming that there are no serious issues (i.e., no error messages), you are ready to submit the job for "Simulation".

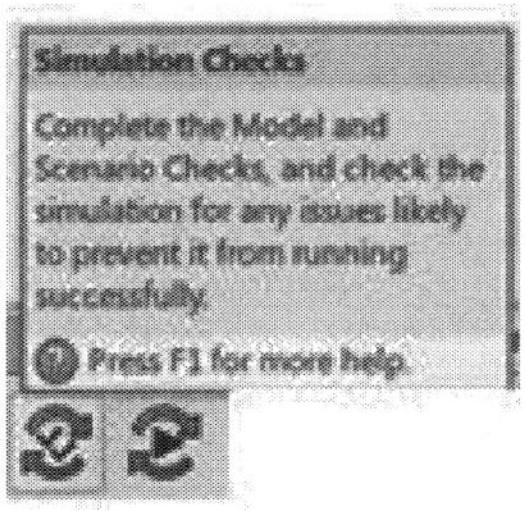

Select the "Simulation" icon from the bottom row.

Accept the number of "cores" in the pop up box, and wait for the simulation to complete.

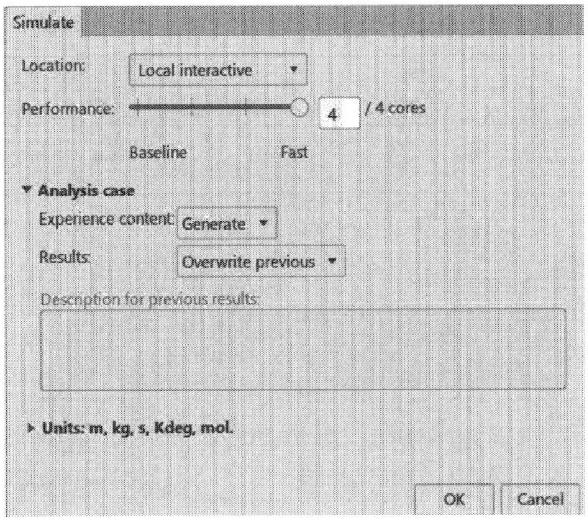

During the "Simulation Status" phase, important messages such as "Licenses", "Plots", and "Iterations" are recorded in the main pop-up window. These can be viewed by selecting the appropriate tab.

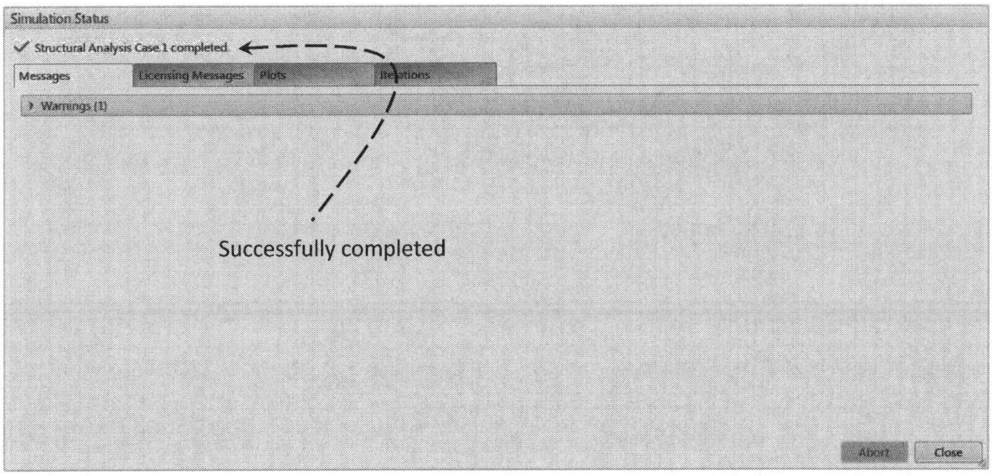

Results (Post processing):

Once you close (or move) the obstructing dialogue boxes, you must be in the "Results" section and the bottom row should appear as shown on the right.

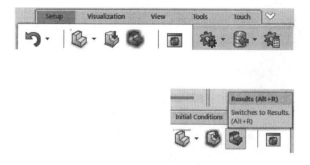

If not, click on the "Results" icon .

In the background, you should see the "Plots" dialogue box which shows the results of Step1, and the initial results and the results after the first row. If the first row of the "Plots" dialogue box is highlighted, the value of the von Mises stress is zero.

This is not surprising as the first row is before any incremental load is applied. If the load is zero, the displacement and stress are both zero. Use the cursor to select the second row of the "Plots" dialogue box.

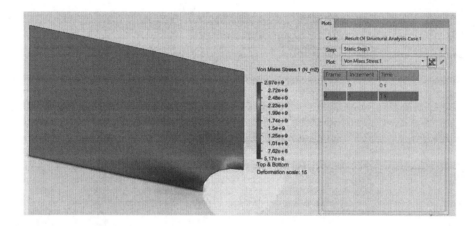

The contour of the displacement vector is shown below and agrees with the intuition. The maximum displacement is the imposed displacement of 0.5mm on left vertical edge.

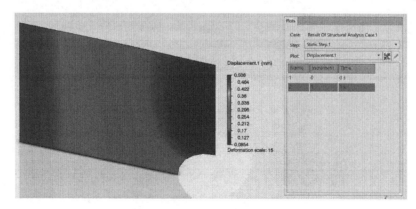

If you double click on the contour legend, it will open the dialogue box below allowing you to change certain features in the generated plot.

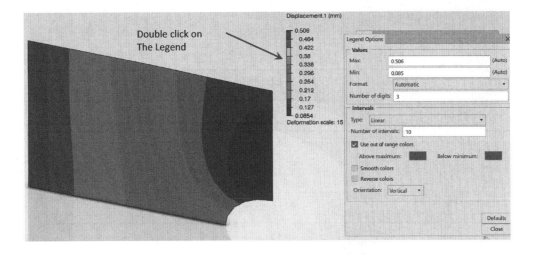

This process must be repeated three more times for the different "Finite Element Models". Only the first few steps of this repetition will be reproduced here.

Here is How the Repetition Goes:

Select the "Scenario" icon.

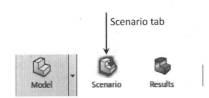

Pick the "Setup" tab.

Use the "Finite Element Model" icon to choose a different model (remember, there are four of them that were created earlier).

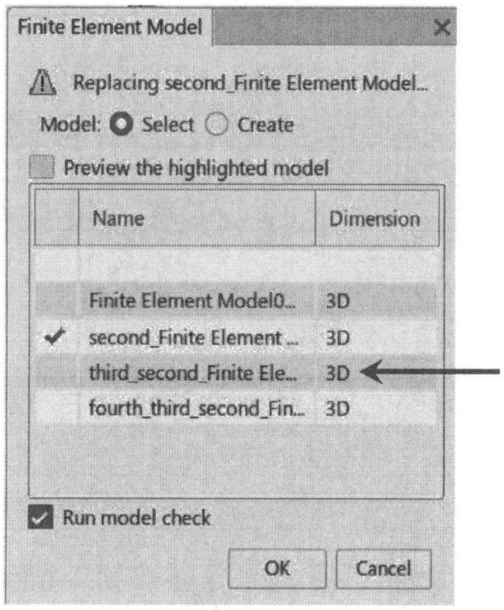

Finite Element Model   ✕

⚠ Replacing second_Finite Element Model...

Model: ● Select ○ Create

☐ Preview the highlighted model

Name	Dimension
Finite Element Model0...	3D
✓ second_Finite Element ...	3D
third_second_Finite Ele...	3D ←
fourth_third_second_Fin...	3D

☑ Run model check

OK   Cancel

Select this "FE Model" corresponding to mesh size = 2.068 mm

Finally, use the "Simulate" icon ⟳ to run, postprocess and record the maximum von Mises stress. These were done four times and the data recorded. In fact, it was also done for a total of 8 runs (including d/8, d/16, d/32, and d/64).

The table below summarizes the value of the maximum von Mises stress for different values of the mesh size. Recall that $d = 8.722 \ mm$ corresponds to the default mesh size suggested by the software.

Symbolic size	Element size (mm)	Max von Mises (GPa)	# Elements	# Nodes
2d	16.544	2.502	59	42
d	8.272	2.385	119	77
d/2	4.136	2.881	423	242
d/4	2.068	3.096	1713	916
d/8	1.034	3.584	6789	3515
d/16	0.5027	3.865	29035	14766
d/32	0.25135	3.835	115685	58338
d/64	0.125625	3.851	460461	231215

The plot of the above data is also shown below. The two graphs are identical information except that for the one on the left, the horizontal axis is the number of nodes, whereas the one on the right is the logarithm of the number of nodes. This data indicates that there is substantial change in the prediction when refinement is made.

Checking the data in the graph also indicates that making all elements small is a poor strategy, and perhaps it would have been sufficient to reduce the element size only in the critical area where the stress concentration exits.

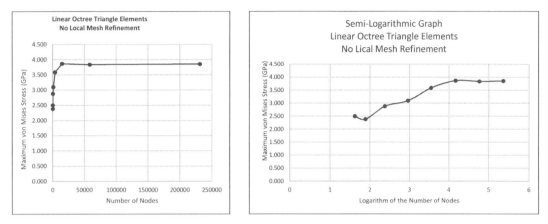

Performing Local Mesh Refinement:

In order to perform local mesh refinement, double click on the branch of the tree which has the "active" finite element model to open the "Surface Triangle Mesh" dialogue box.

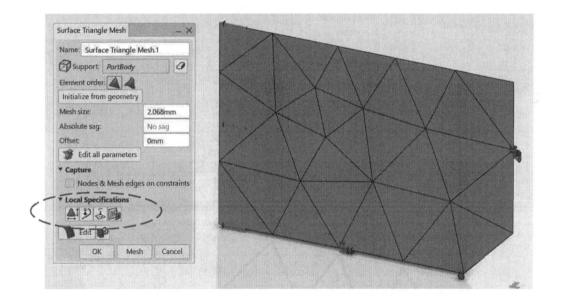

Use the "Local Specifications" arrow to get your selection choices. From the available choices choose the "Local Mesh" size.

For the sake of illustration, select the edge and for the "Size" indicate 1mm.

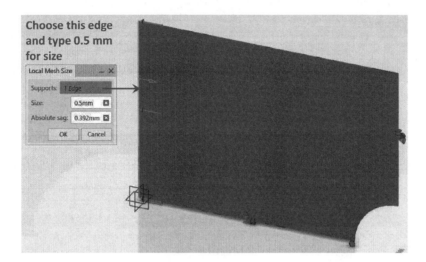

Close the dialogue box and click on "Mesh" The mesh will be locally refined about that edge as shown below.

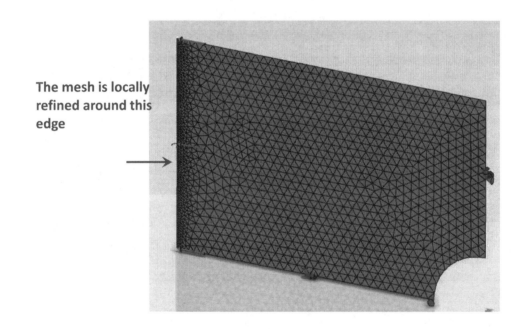

Before concluding the chapter, it is obvious that the location where the mesh is to be refined is in fact around the hole and not the vertical edge as done.

Exercise 1

Consider the L-shaped region shown below. This geometry is said to have a reentrant corner. The top face of the part is clamped whereas the side face is subject to load in the direction shown and assume that the response of the material is elastic. Can you guess where the part is stressed most? What do you think the theoretical stress value at that location is?

Perform an FEA analysis of the part with mesh refinement (both global and local mesh refinement) and plot the information as a function of element size. Finally modify the part with a generous fillet radius and repeat the above calculations.

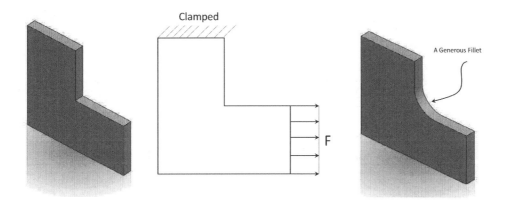

Exercise 2

Consider the three dimensional object below. Can you guess the location where the part is most stressed? Assume a steel part (and linear elasticity), use dimensions of your choice and a torque value to predict the stresses in the part. Upon completing this task, apply a generous fillet at the root and repeat the calculations above. Do not forget the need for mesh refinement.

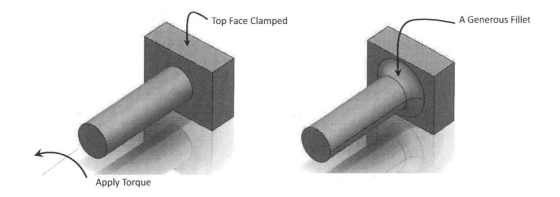

Notes:

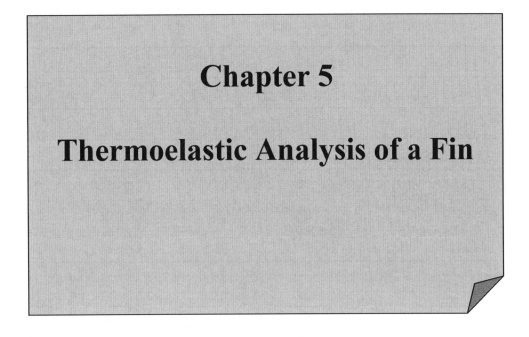

Chapter 5

Thermoelastic Analysis of a Fin

Objective:

In this chapter a relatively simple fin is subjected to steady state heat transfer and the resulting temperature distribution is used to perform elastic analysis of the fin due to the restraints which are preventing the axial movement of the structure. The major assumption is that the deformation of the fin does not affect the heat transfer aspects of it. This is precisely what is commonly referred to as a "Sequential" thermomechanical analysis.

NOTE: It is assumed that you have basic familiarity with CAD modeling in 3DEXPERIENCE allowing you to create the simple part. If that is not the case, please consult the following tutorial book.

CAD Modeling Essentials in 3DEXPERIENCE, by Nader Zamani, SDC Publications, ISBN 978-1-63057-095-8.

Problem Statement:

Consider the long fin shown below. The cavity is filled with a fluid with a constant temperature of 232 °C while the exterior of the fin is subjected to an ambient temperature of 21°C. The top and the bottom rings of the fin are prevented from motion in the axial direction. This fact and the thermal expansion of the fin leads to deformation and the thermal stresses in the part.

It is assumed that the deformation is elastic and therefore only Young's modulus and Poisson's ratio are needed. The chosen values are $E = 200\ GPa$, $v = 0.3$. Furthermore, since steady state heat transfer analysis is conducted, only thermal conductivity of the material is needed. This value is assumed to be $k = 26$ W/m.K. The coefficient of thermal expansion is assumed to be $\alpha = 13E - 6$ mm/mm.K.

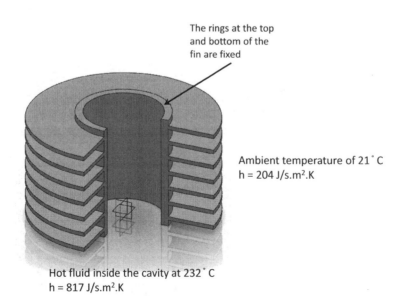

The rings at the top and bottom of the fin are fixed

Ambient temperature of 21˚ C
h = 204 J/s.m².K

Hot fluid inside the cavity at 232˚ C
h = 817 J/s.m².K

If the fin is assumed to be long, the restrained ends make it a prime candidate for the plane strain condition. This statement together with the symmetric nature of the fin indicates that a sector (say 45 degrees) of the geometry can be selected for analysis purposes. The arbitrary sector needed is shown below and the nature of the boundary conditions are also shown.

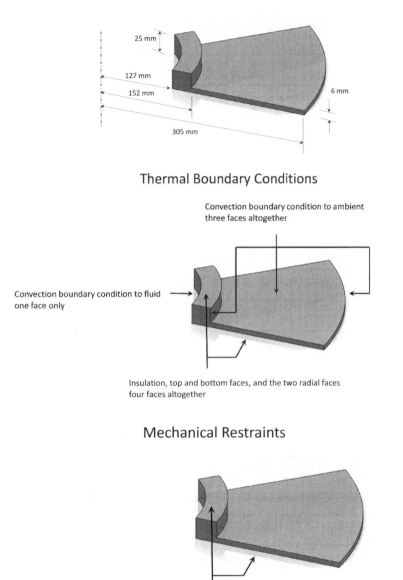

The reader should keep in mind that the analysis of the reduced sector is valid only for the fins that are reasonably far away from the two ends. This is mainly due to the fact that the boundary conditions in the vicinity of the two ends are perhaps very complicated and sometimes even unknown. Many years ago, reductions of this type were necessary because of the computing hardware resources but that is no longer the case.

The Model and Material Properties:

Using the Part Design App 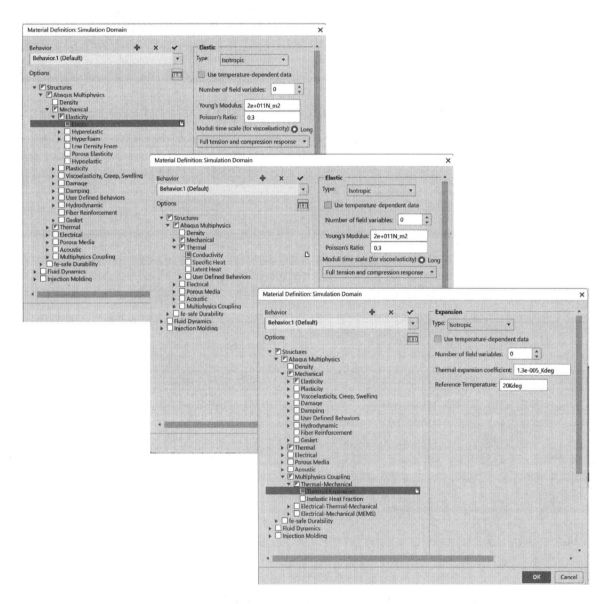, create the reduced section of the fin with the given dimensions. Once the part is available, apply the material properties using the "Create Material" icon . This icon can be found in the "Tools" tab of the action bar. The details of this process were explained in chapters 2 and 3 and will not be repeated here. However, once the material is created the appropriate dialogue boxes should look like the ones below.

Creating the Finite Element Model:

Locate the compass on the top left corner of the screen and click on it. Scroll through the applications and select the "Structural Model

 Structural Model Creation

Creation" App   .

The row of icons in the bottom of your screen (the action bar) changes and will appear as displayed below.

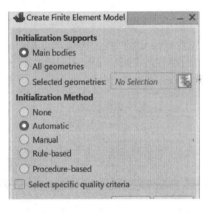

The dialogue box shown on the right "Create Finite Element Model" appears. For now, use the "Automatic" radio button. Other options are for user control of the meshing process. In the case of "Automatic", tetrahedral elements are created.

There are additional steps required if "Abstraction" is to be used. This is explained in chapter 2.

The tree indicates that a mesh and the corresponding solid section have been created.

There are different methods for displaying the mesh. The instructions given below is one method of achieving that objective.

From the bottom row of icons, select the "Mesh" icon 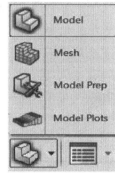 .

Choose the "Update" icon 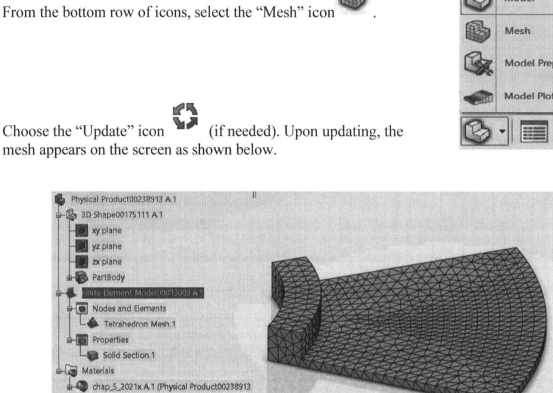 (if needed). Upon updating, the mesh appears on the screen as shown below.

There are also different ways of hiding the mesh. For example, first select the "Display" tab from the bottom row of icons.

"Display" tab

You can select the "Visualization Management" icon from the choices. The resulting dialogue box shown on the right appears.

Then use the pulldown menu in . This hides the mesh.

Creating a Scenario:

The nature of the analysis, namely, Static, Dynamic, Buckling, etc. is set in the "Structural Scenario Creation" App. Furthermore, the loads, restraints, and interaction are also defined in this application.

It is also important to point out that that one could have created the Scenario before the FemRep. In fact, FemRep can be created from within the Structural Scenario App.

Locate the compass on the top left corner of the screen, and click on it. Scroll through the applications and select the "Structural Scenario

 Structural Scenario Creation

Creation" App   .

The row of icons on the bottom of your screen changes and will appear as displayed below.

The pop-up window "Simulation Initialization" shown below appears on the screen. The radio button "Thermal-Structural" should be selected.

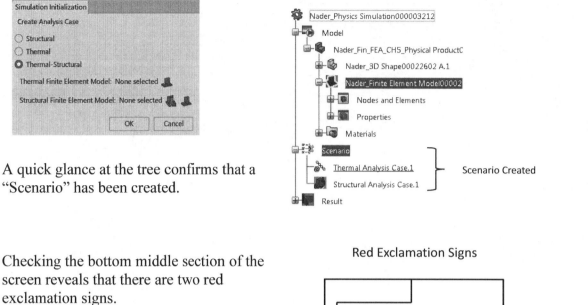

A quick glance at the tree confirms that a "Scenario" has been created.

Checking the bottom middle section of the screen reveals that there are two red exclamation signs.

These pertain to "Thermal Analysis Case.1", "Structural Analysis Case.1" and "No Procedures Exist".

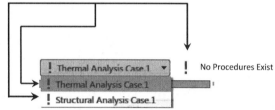

Make sure that in the bottom left margin, the "Thermal Analysis Case.1" is selected.

Choose the "Finite Element Model" icon from the action bar.

The resulting dialogue box is displayed below. In this box, select the row shown.

Select this row

Upon pressing "OK" and closing this dialogue box, a "Green" check mark appears in front of "Thermal Analysis Case.1".

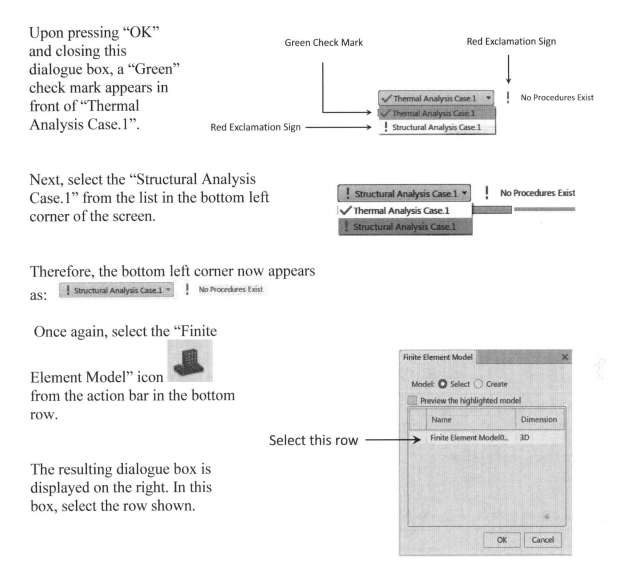

Next, select the "Structural Analysis Case.1" from the list in the bottom left corner of the screen.

Therefore, the bottom left corner now appears as: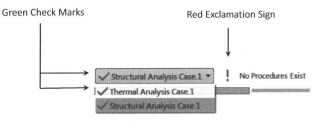

Once again, select the "Finite Element Model" icon from the action bar in the bottom row.

The resulting dialogue box is displayed on the right. In this box, select the row shown.

Immediately, the red exclamation mark in front of "Structural Analysis Case.1" turns into a green check mark.

So, the bottom left corner now appears as shown below.

At this point, you must make a decision on whether to create the "Procedures" for thermal analysis or the structural analysis first. The order that you do this in is irrelevant; however, we suggest that you select the "Thermal Analysis Case.1" first.

The bottom left corner should look like this:

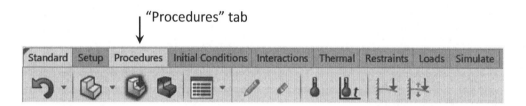

Creating a "Step" for Thermal Analysis:

Select the "Procedures" tab from the bottom row.

"Procedures" tab

Choose the "Steady-State Heat Transfer" icon from the action bar.

The "Steady State Heat Transfer " dialogue box opens. Keep in mind that the present problem deals with the linear steady state heat transfer and as a result the information on time in this dialogue box is entirely fictitious. Therefore, the default values are accepted.

Steady-State Heat Transfer Step

Configures a heat transfer analysis procedure that calculates the steady-state distribution of temperatures in a body.

❓ Press F1 for more help.

The thermal step appears in the tree.

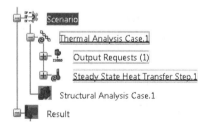

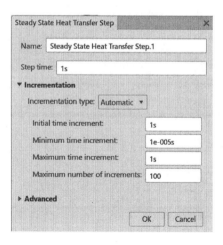

Applying the Thermal Boundary Conditions:

Select the "Thermal" tab of the action tool bar.

"Thermal" tab

Before applying the boundary condition, it is wise to change the default unit of temperature (which is Kelvin) to Celsius. The process of changing units was described in an earlier chapter but due to its importance it is repeated below. Please note that in the present run I skipped changing the units; however, it is presented if you are interested.

Place the cursor in the upper right corner of the screen, right click and select "Preferences".

In the resulting dialogue box, navigate the tree in the left margin, and select the "Parameters and Units". Find the "Temperature" and using the pulldown menu, change the units to "Celsius degree (Cdeg)". Close the window. I left the temperature in Kdeg.

Keep in mind that even without changing the units, one could have entered the data in "Cdeg" and the conversion to "Kdeg" would have been done automatically by the software. The formal change of units with "Preferences" makes the data entry process less prone to error and the temperature plots will be in "Cdeg".

Select the "Film Condition" icon [Film Condition] from the action bar. Pick the three surfaces which are responsible for convection to the ambient (outside of the fin). For "Reference temperature" use 21 Cdeg.

Since I did not change the temperature unit, you literally have to type "21Cdeg" .

Film Condition

Defines heating or cooling due to convection by surrounding fluids.

❓ Press F1 for more help.

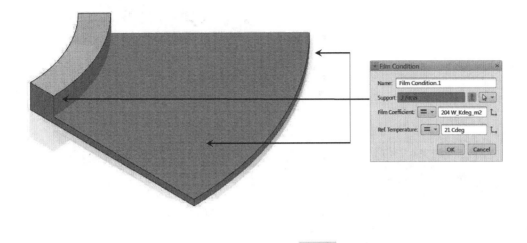

Once again, select the "Film Condition" icon ![Film Condition] from the action bar. Pick the inside surface which is responsible for convection to the fluid (hot fluid inside the fin). For "Reference temperature" use 232 Cdeg.

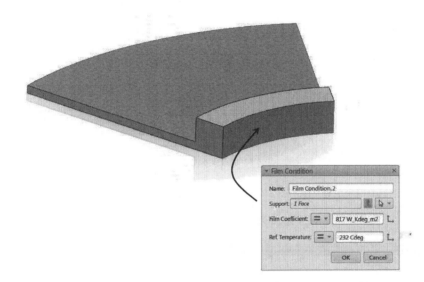

In heat transfer codes (including the one in 3DEXPERIENCE), if no boundary condition is applied to a surface, it is treated as an insulated surface. Therefore, the remaining four faces are insulated which is a result of the symmetries in the geometry.

The tree structure at this point is shown on the next page.

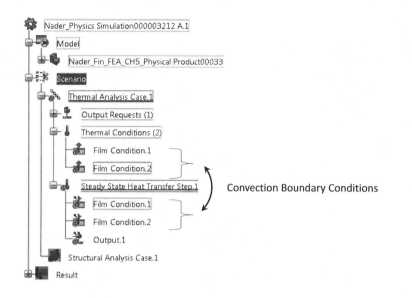

Convection Boundary Conditions

Creating a "Step" for Stress (Mechanical) Analysis:

Check the bottom middle section of the interface. The "Structural Analysis Case.1" must be selected.

Select the "Structural Analysis Case.1"

✓ Structural Analysis Case.1 ▾   ! No Procedures Exist
✓ Thermal Analysis Case.1
✓ Structural Analysis Case.1

So, your screen should have the following message on the bottom.

Select the "Procedures" tab from the bottom row.

"Procedures" tab

| Standard | Setup | Procedures | Initial Conditions | Interactions | Thermal | Restraints | Loads | Simulate | Dis |

Select the "Static Step" icon ⊢⊥ Static Step from the action bar.

The "Static Step" dialogue box opens. Keep in mind that the present problem deals with the linear static analysis; as a result, the information on time in this dialogue box is entirely fictitious. Therefore, the default values are accepted.

The static step appears in the tree.

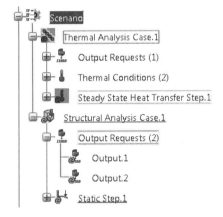

Now there are two green check marks next to the items in the bottom left corner of your interface.

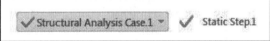

Applying the Mechanical Boundary Conditions (Restraints):

Select "Restraints" tab of the action bar.

Select the "Planar Symmetry" icon , and choose the sides indicated below. It seems that in the 3DEXPERIENCE software, multiple selection in a single dialogue box is not possible. You need to perform this operation 4 times separately.

Planar Symmetry

Imposes symmetrical displacement restraints about a selected face.

? Press F1 for more help.

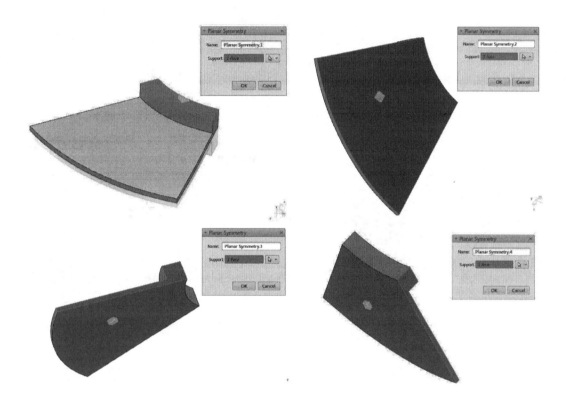

The symmetry plane boundary conditions are reflected in the tree.

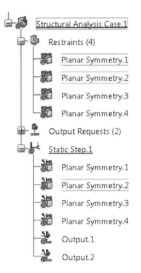

Specifying the Inputting Mode of Temperatures for Stress Analysis 🌡️ **:**

Choose the "Thermal" tab from the action bar at the bottom of the screen.

↓ "Thermal" tab

The final task is to tell the software how to receive the nodal temperatures. This task is often forgotten, resulting in no temperature effect in the stress analysis.

The bottom middle section of the screen should still be in the "Structural Analysis Case.1".

✓ Structural Analysis Case.1 ▾   ✓ Static Step.1

Select the "Prescribed

Temperature" icon 🌡️
from the action bar.
This leads to the "Prescribed
Temperature" dialogue box
shown on the extreme right.

Prescribed Temperature

Defines the temperature in a region for a structural analysis case.

❓ Press F1 for more help.

Prescribed Temperature   ×

Name: Prescribed Temperature.1

Support: No selection

Temperature: = ▾ -273.15 Cdeg

Scale factor: 1

Amplitude: Default ▾

OK   Cancel

Note that the "Support" line has a pulldown menu as shown on the right. Select the "Mesh Part". Once you do this, a second window pops up.

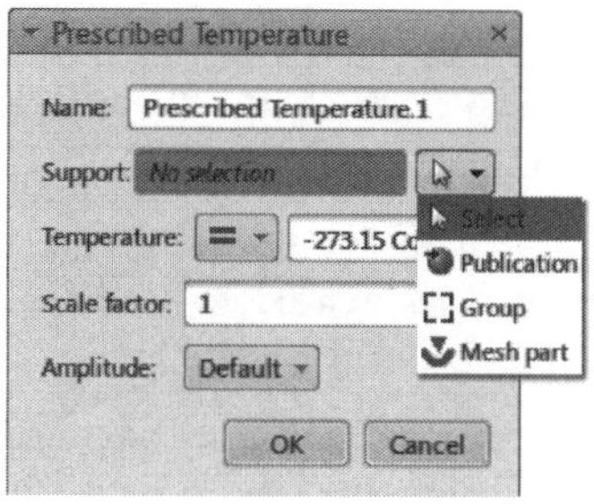

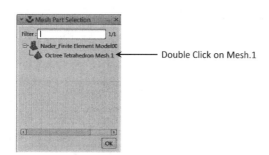

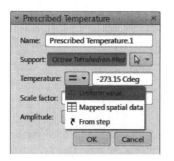

Double Click on Mesh.1

An alternative to using the "Mesh Part" is to select the "PartBody" as the support.

The result of the previous step (the content of the dialogue box) is shown below.

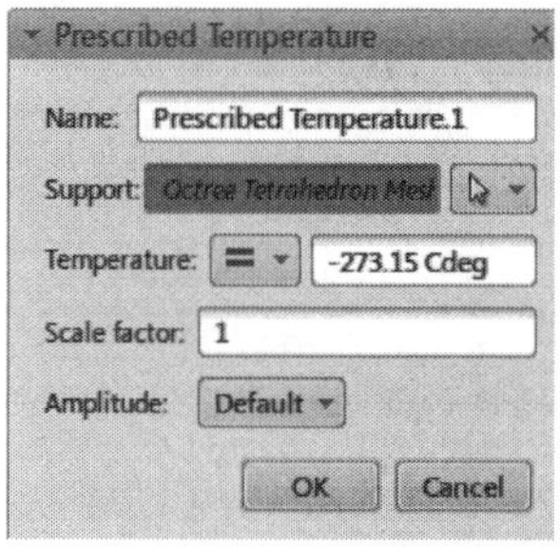

The "Temperature" section of the box has a pulldown menu.

Select "From step" From step . This means that the nodal temperatures are retrieved from the final results of the previous thermal step.

Prescribed Temperature ✕

Name: Prescribed Temperature.1

Support: *Whole Model*

Temperature: Case: Thermal Analysis Case.1 ▾

Absolute exterior tolerance: 0mm

Relative exterior tolerance: 0.5

Beginning step: Steady State Heat Transfer Step.1 ▾

Begin Increment: 1

Ending step: Steady State Heat Transfer Step.1 ▾

End Increment: last

OK   Cancel

Close the window by pressing "OK".

The bird's eye view of what was done in the last few pages is shown in the tree structure. This displays only the "Scenario.1" section of the tree.

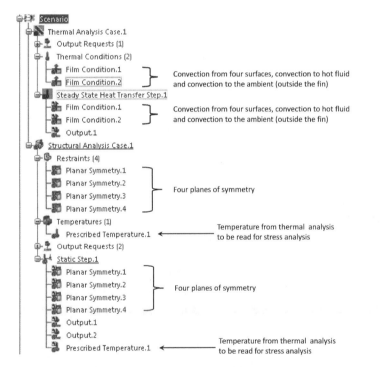

Scenario
Thermal Analysis Case.1
  Output Requests (1)
  Thermal Conditions (2)
    Film Condition.1
    Film Condition.2   — Convection from four surfaces, convection to hot fluid and convection to the ambient (outside the fin)
  Steady State Heat Transfer Step.1
    Film Condition.1
    Film Condition.2   — Convection from four surfaces, convection to hot fluid and convection to the ambient (outside the fin)
    Output.1
Structural Analysis Case.1
  Restraints (4)
    Planar Symmetry.1
    Planar Symmetry.2   — Four planes of symmetry
    Planar Symmetry.3
    Planar Symmetry.4
  Temperatures (1)
    Prescribed Temperature.1 ← Temperature from thermal analysis to be read for stress analysis
  Output Requests (2)
  Static Step.1
    Planar Symmetry.1
    Planar Symmetry.2   — Four planes of symmetry
    Planar Symmetry.3
    Planar Symmetry.4
    Output.1
    Output.2
    Prescribed Temperature.1 ← Temperature from thermal analysis to be read for stress analysis

Consistency, Model Check, and Simulation:

Select the "Simulation" tab from the bottom row of icons on your screen (i.e. from the action bar).

"Simulate" tab

Select the "Simulation Option" icon from the action bar.

This will give you the option using the server or the local machine. Use the "Server" radio button.

It is a good practice to perform the model and consistency check before submitting the work for the final run.
Select the "Model and Scenario Check" icon from the bottom row
.

The software goes through a check phase and if there are no issues, a message with a "Green" check mark is returned.

Although the Thermal and Structural consistency checks can be done independently of each other, one can choose to do them simultaneously as the window shows.

The consistency check completes without any glitches.

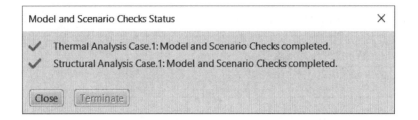

Next, select the "Simulation Checks" icon  from the bottom row of icons. Accept the number of "Cores" in the pop up box below and perform the checks simultaneously for thermal and strucural analysis.

The simulation checks for both the thermal and structural cases were successful. Close the window by pressing "Close"

Note that the "Simulation Checks" for both Thermal and Structural Cases were successful

Select the "Simulation" icon  from the bottom row.

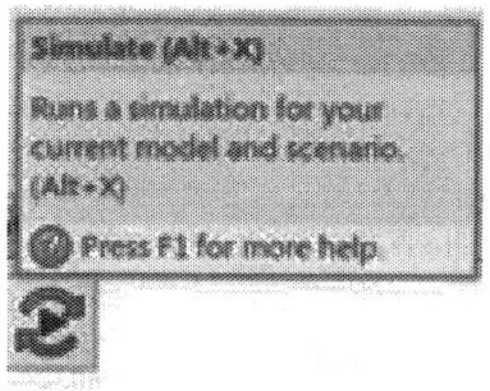

Accept the number of "cores" and perform both simulations simultaneously. Wait for the simulation to complete.

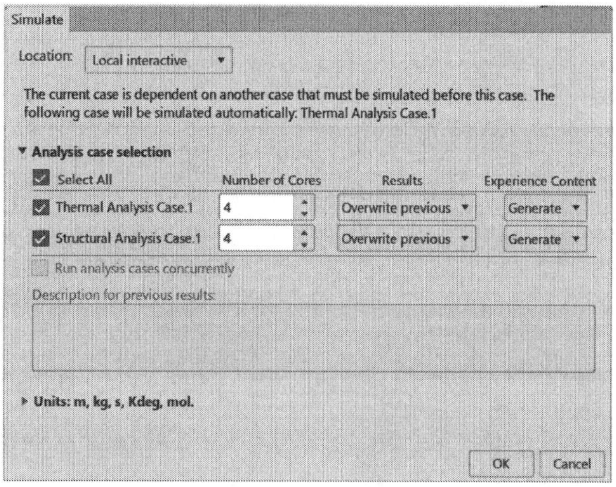

Simulate (Alt+X)

Runs a simulation for your current model and scenario. (Alt+X)

Press F1 for more help.

Both the thermal and structural analysis run without any issues and the following two dialogue boxes confirm that.

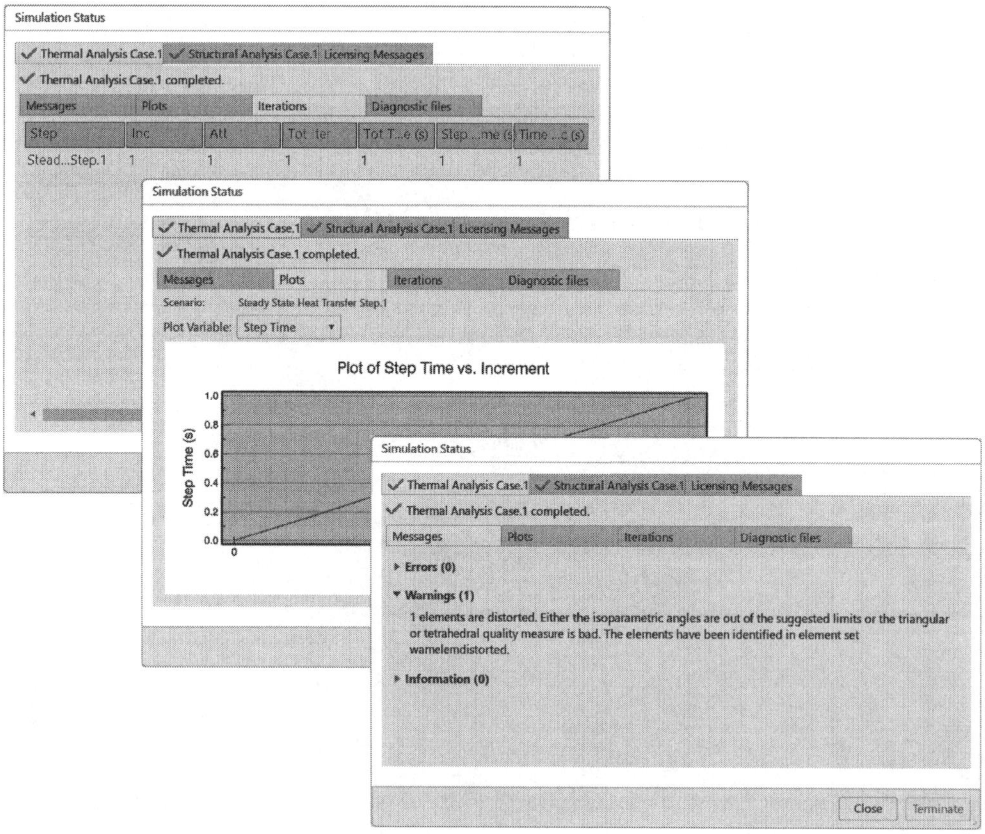

Results (Post processing):

Once you close (or move) the obstructing dialogue boxes, you must be in the "Results" section and the bottom row should appear as shown on the right.

If not, click on the "Results" icon  .

The "Plots" dialogue box is shown below. It indicates that the plot is from the thermal step and it is the second "Frame". <u>Clearly, the first frame of any analysis will produce a zero value for any quantity.</u> The distribution agrees with common sense. The fin is hottest on the inside and cooler on the outside.

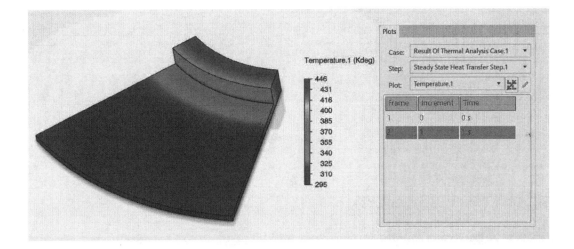

Using the pulldown menu, we can request the heat flux to be plotted. The "Vector" plot of heat flux is shown below. Once again this agrees with common sense, the energy (described by vectors) points from inside of the fin to the exterior. On the downside, the nature of the plot (vector plot), indicates a high density of the arrow symbols. This can be changed as shown in the next page. Also keep in mind that instead of a vector plot, one can request a contour heat flux plot.

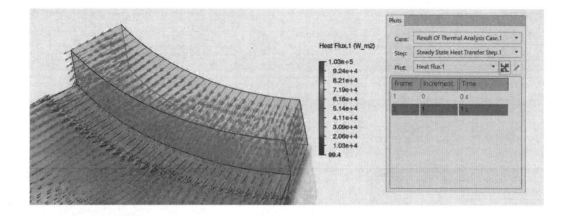

Double clicking anywhere on the arrow plot opens the dialogue box shown below. This window has three tabs. Select the middle tab with the contents displayed. At the very bottom of this window, there is a sliding bar which allows us to control the "Symbol density". Presently, it is set at "High"; this means that the arrows are plotted at every node in the model. By dragging the arrow to the left, one can control the density. The figure at the bottom of the page shows the arrow plot at the selected sliding bar location.

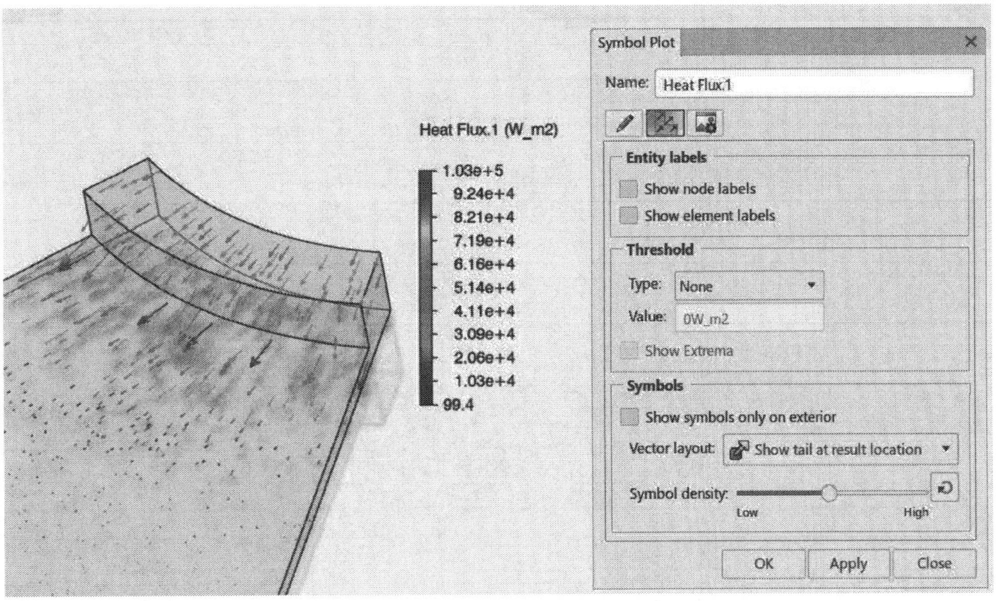

We next turn our attention to plotting the structural results. In the present analysis, only the displacement and von Mises stress are available.

Select the pulldown menu on the top of the dialogue box to change it to "Results Of Structural Analysis Case.1". For the "Plot", select "Displacement.1" and make sure that "Frame #2" is highlighted. As expected, the displacement is smallest in the vicinity of the hot fluid and larger at a point away from the core.

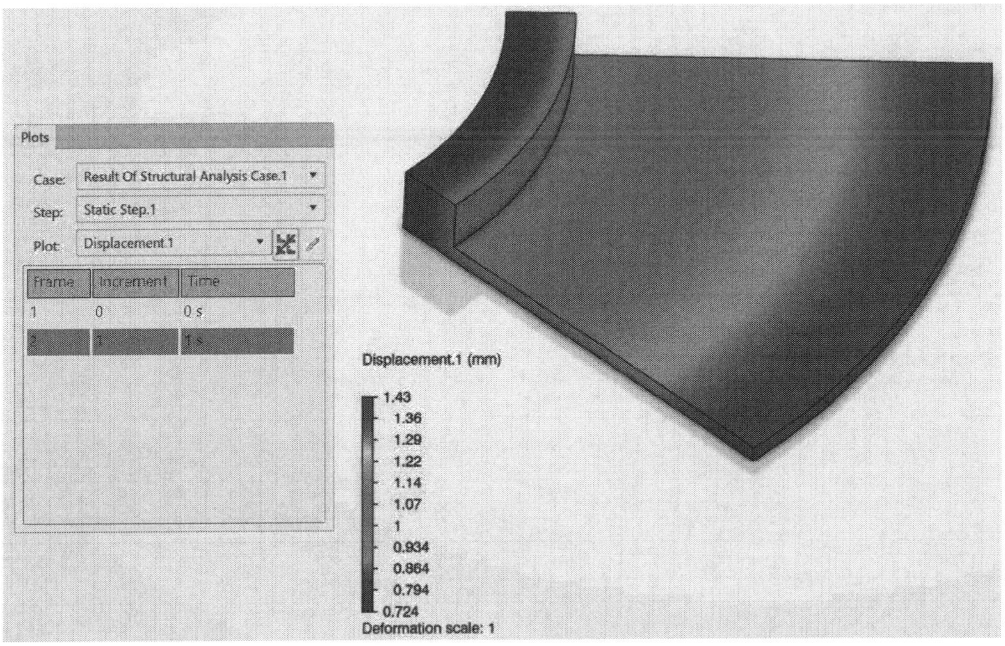

Changing the plot type to von Mises stress, the contour of this entity is shown below. Note that this is the zoomed plot where the stress is high due to the presence of the geometric discontinuity. The stress in most of the exterior fin section is very low.

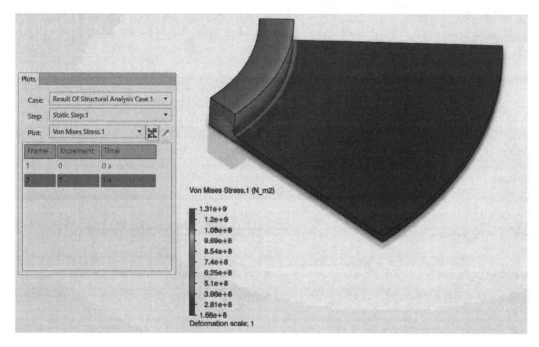

This completes the present chapter.

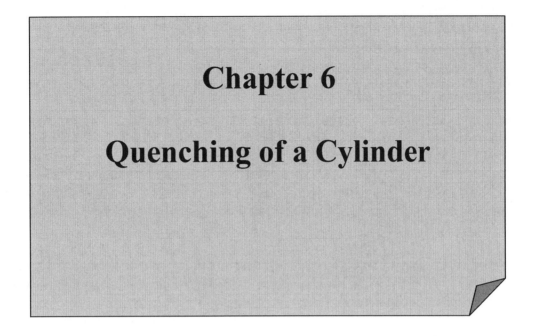

Chapter 6

Quenching of a Cylinder

Objective:

This chapter deals with residual stresses induced by quenching. During the quenching process, a heated component is dipped into a cold fluid (air, water, oil, etc.). The rate of heat loss from the surface of the component is a function of the film heat transfer coefficient and the temperature difference between the hot surface and the fluid. The non-uniform temperature distribution induces thermal stresses across the part and even leads to plastic deformation at times. Temperature dependent material properties play an important role in these types of components.

The analysis will be performed in two steps. The first step will be a transient thermal analysis and the second step will be a structural analysis that uses the thermal history data from the first step.

NOTE: It is assumed that you have basic familiarity with CAD modeling in 3DEXPERIENCE allowing you to create the simple part. If that is not the case, please consult the following tutorial book.

CAD Modeling Essentials in 3DEXPERIENCE, by Nader Zamani, SDC Publications, ISBN 978-1-63057-095-8.

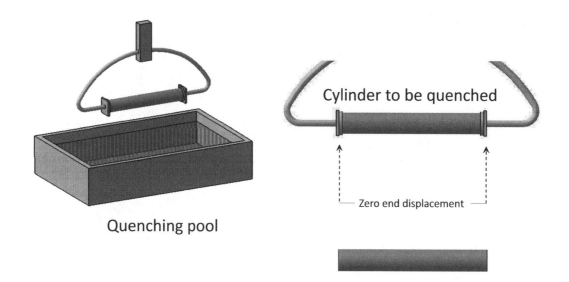

Quenching pool

Cylinder to be quenched

Zero end displacement

Problem Statement:

The geometry chosen is that of a very long cylinder where radius is assumed to be 100 mm. Because of the length of the cylinder, the heat transfer is primarily in the radial direction. Furthermore, assuming that the ends of the cylinder are restrained, the problem being considered can be assumed to be in the state of plane strain. This implies that the length of the section selected can be arbitrary. The cylinder which has an initial temperature of 1423Kdeg is subjected to convection on the curved surface. The ends are treated as being insulated. Clearly the part is under thermal stress and most probably, elastic-plastic deformation takes place.

This problem involves nonlinear elastic-plastic response which is time dependent. Therefore, the duration of simulation has been selected to be small so that it can be solved on an average PC in a reasonable length of time. The CPU requirement depends on the speed of the computer processor and the amount of RAM available.

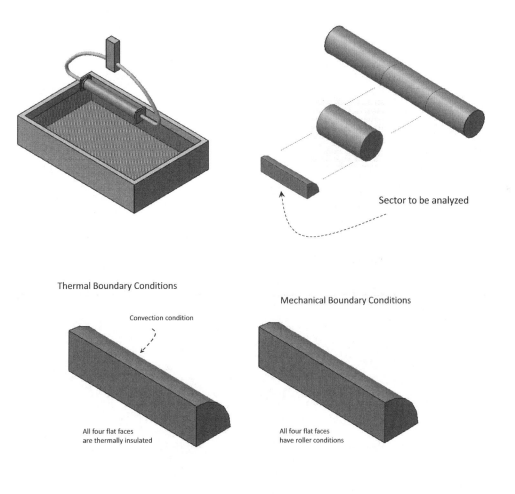

Sector to be analyzed

Thermal Boundary Conditions

Convection condition

All four flat faces
are thermally insulated

Mechanical Boundary Conditions

All four flat faces
have roller conditions

The Model and Material Properties:

First, using the Part Design App 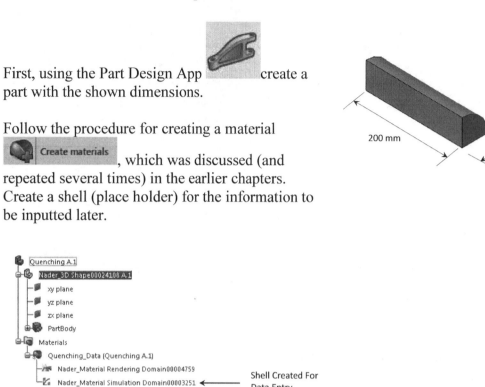 create a part with the shown dimensions.

Follow the procedure for creating a material ![Create materials], which was discussed (and repeated several times) in the earlier chapters. Create a shell (place holder) for the information to be inputted later.

The first set of data to be entered are the mass density and the coefficient of thermal expansion. Both of these are assumed to be independent of temperature. The values of $\rho = 8442 \ kg\_m^3$ and $\alpha = 1.7E - 5 \ mm\_mm\_K$. The reference temperature for α is assumed to be the room temperature of $293K$.

Double click on the second branch of the tree to open the "Material Definition, Simulation Domain" dialogue box.

Select the density box on the left side of the window and input the value.

Next, select "Mechanical" followed by the expansion box to input the data.

In this problem, the Young's modulus is assumed to be temperature dependent (The Poisson's ratio is, however, the constant of 0.32). This data in the form of a table is given below.

Young's modulus (Pa)	Poisson's ratio	Temperature (Kdeg)
1.799E+11	0.32	253
1.241E+11	0.32	923
4.723E+10	0.32	1093
3.220E+10	0.32	1203
5.516E+10	0.32	1313
5.102E+10	0.32	1423

From the same window, select "Elasticity" followed by "Elastic" boxes. Make sure that you check the box on the right hand side "Use temperature-dependent data". The elasticity model to be used is "Isotropic". These steps are graphically shown in the next page.

Note that the data can be inputted into the dialogue box table line-by-line or it can be imported as an excel table. We choose to follow the second option.

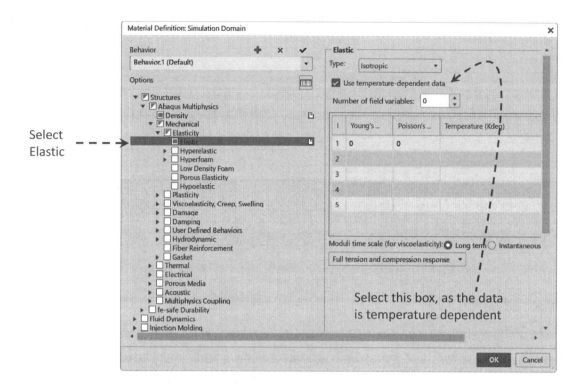

Place the cursor in the location shown, right click and select "Import".

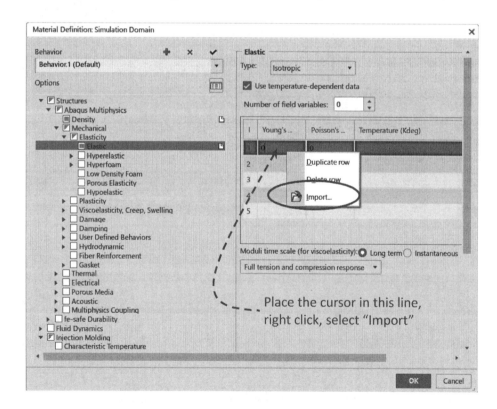

You are prompted to find the stress-strain temperature dependent data from your computer.

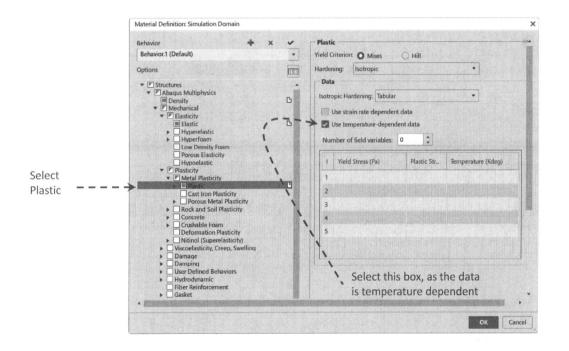

From the same window, select "Plasticity" followed by "Plastic" boxes. Make sure that you check the box on the right hand side "Use temperature-dependent data". The plasticity model to be used is "Isotropic" and the "Yield Criterion" is Mises.

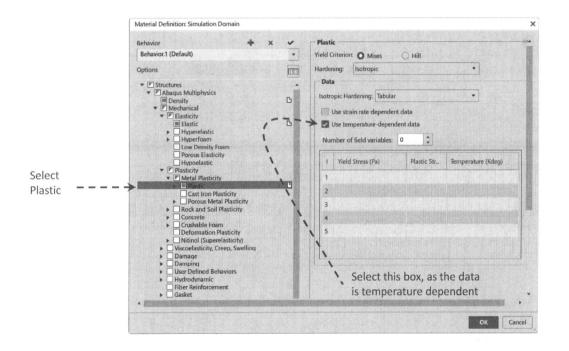

Recall that the engineering stress/engineering strain data can be converted to the true stress/true strain data through the following formulas which are valid up to the necking point.

$$\varepsilon_{true} = \ln(1 + \varepsilon_{eng})$$

$$\sigma_{true} = \sigma_{eng}(1 + \varepsilon_{eng})$$

Place the cursor in the location shown, right click and select "Import".

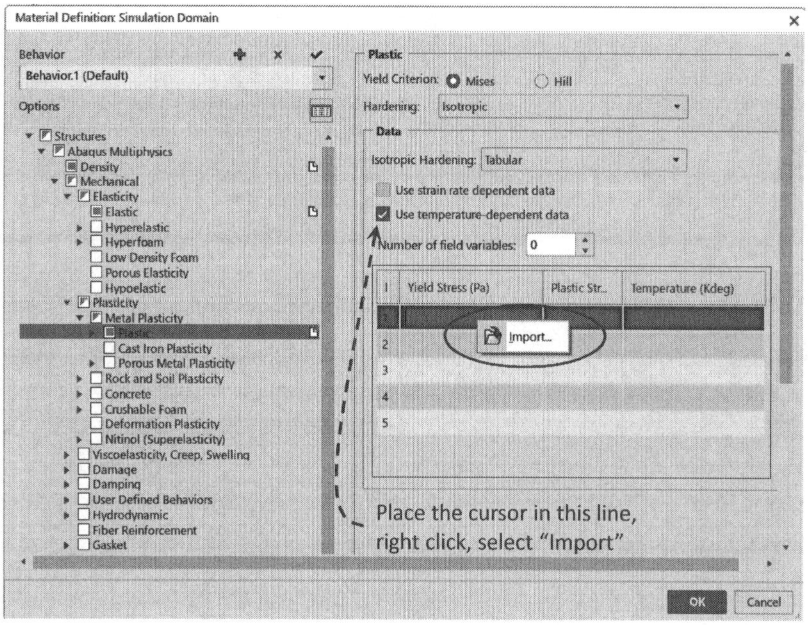

You are prompted to find the stress-strain temperature dependent data on your computer.

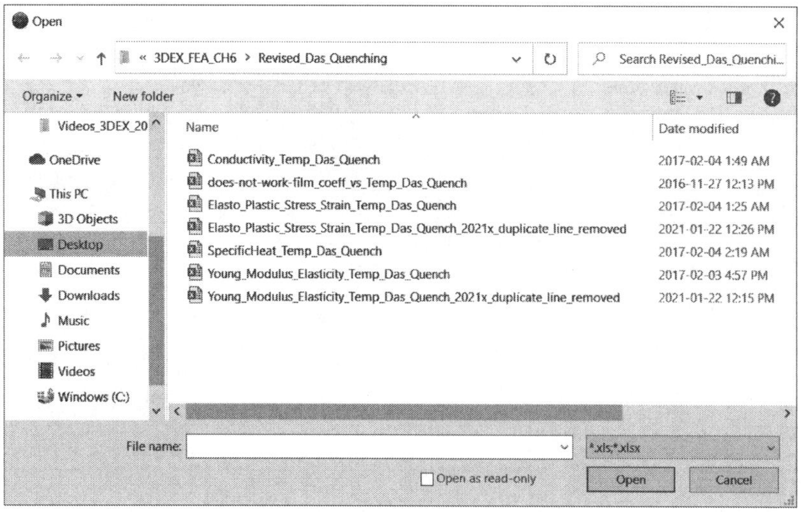

The imported data populates the table in the dialogue box.

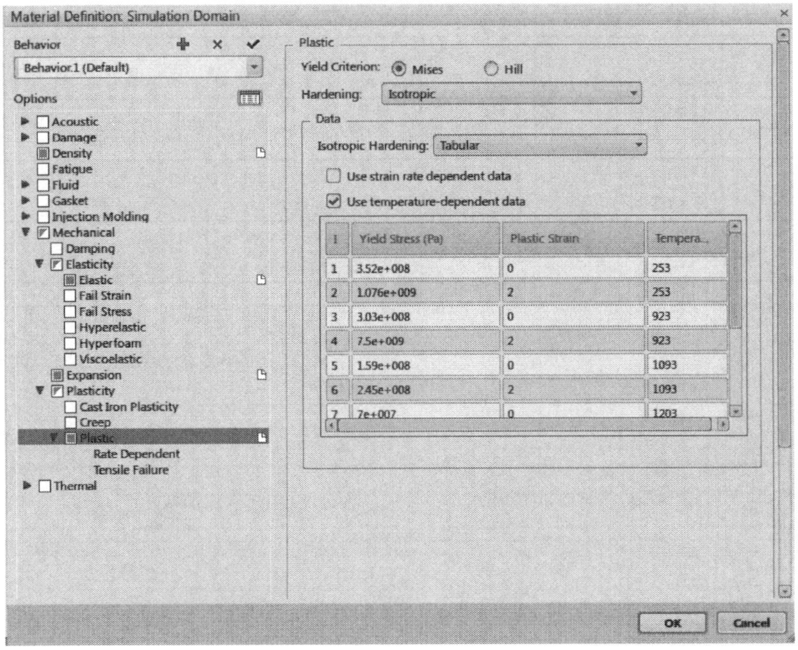

The data read into the model is shown below.

	A	B	C	D
1	Yield Strength (Pa)	Plastic Strain	Temperature (Kdeg)	
2	3.520E+08	0	253	
3	1.076E+09	2	253	
4	3.030E+08	0	923	
5	7.500E+09	2	923	
6	1.590E+08	0	1093	
7	2.450E+08	2	1093	
8	7.000E+07	0	1203	
9	2.340E+08	2	1203	
10	4.000E+07	0	1413	
11	1.380E+08	2	1413	
12	2.400E+07	0	1623	
13	8.000E+07	2	1623	
14				

The graph of this data is also shown on the next page. Notice that at the four higher temperatures, the curves cannot be distinguished from each other. Therefore, a second plot is also presented to have a better idea of the trends.
Note: The first line of the table must be yield strength at zero plastic strain, at the given temperature.

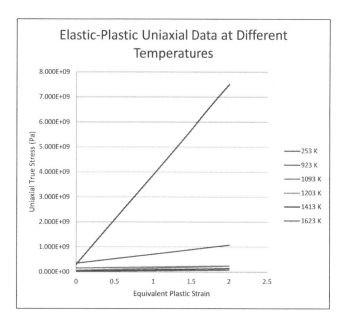

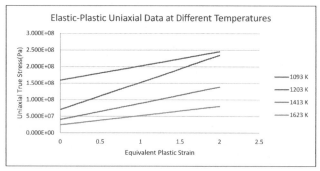

Note that the thermal expansion coefficient $\alpha = 1.7E - 5\ mm\_mm\_K$ was assumed to be constant independent of temperature. This can easily be inputted as depicted below.

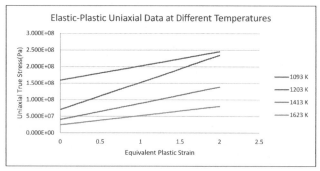

The next task is to input the thermal properties (which are also temperature dependents). From the "Material Definition, Simulation Domain", select "Thermal" followed by the "Isotropic Conductivity" boxes. Make sure that you check the box on the right hand side "Use temperature-dependent data".

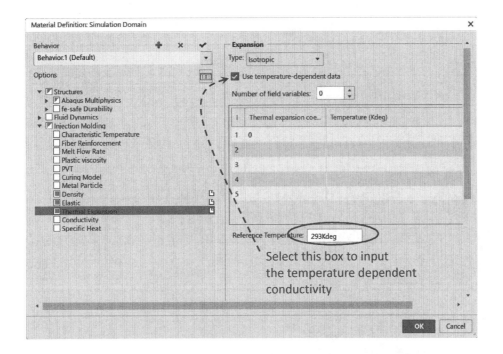

Place the cursor in the location shown below, right click and select "Import".

Find the stress-strain temperature dependent data on your computer.

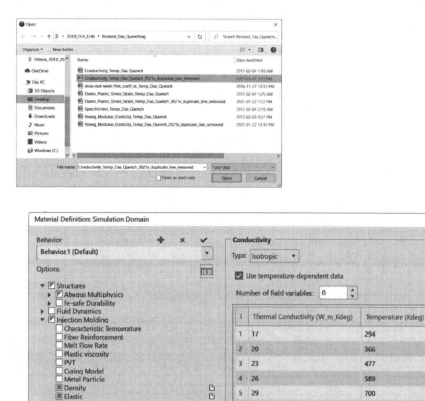

The imported data in the Excel spreadsheet is shown below.

	A	B	C
1	Conductivity (W_m_Kdeg)	Temperature (Kdeg)	
2	17	294	
3	20	366	
4	23	477	
5	26	589	
6	29	700	
7	32	811	
8	35	922	
9	38	1033	
10	41	1144	
11	44	1255	
12	46	1366	
13	49	1477	
14			

Note that the data can also be plotted by the software. The plot of thermal conductivity against the temperature, generated by the software, is shown below.

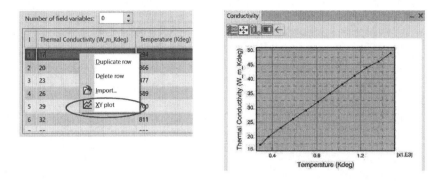

The final step is to input the temperature dependent specific heat. From the "Material Definition, Simulation Domain", select the "Specific Heat" boxes. Make sure that you check the box on the right hand side "Use temperature-dependent data".

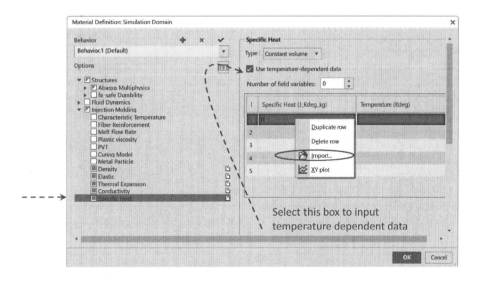

The imported Excel spreadsheet data is given below.

Specific Heat (J_Kdeg_kg)	Temperature (Kdeg)	
419	294	
448	366	
477	477	
490	589	
502	700	
523	811	
553	922	
590	1033	
657	1144	
779	1255	
900	1366	
1022	1477	

Note that the data can also be plotted by the software. The plot of specific heat against the temperature, generated by the software, is shown below.

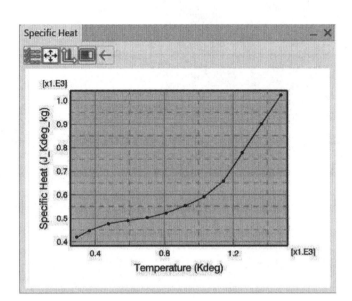

I	Specific Heat (J_Kdeg_kg)	Temperature (Kdeg)
1	419	294
2	448	366
3	477	477
4	490	589
5	502	700
6	523	811

Creating the Finite Element Model:

Locate the compass on the top left corner of the screen and select it. Scroll through the applications and select the "Structural Model

Creation" App   .

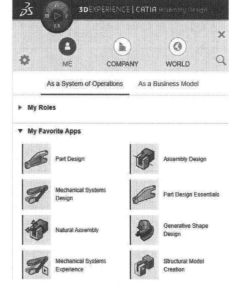

The row of icons in the bottom of your screen (action bar) changes and will appear as displayed below.

The dialogue box shown on the right, "Create Finite Element Model", appears. For now, use the "Automatic" radio button. Other options are for user control of the meshing process. In the case of "Automatic", tetrahedral elements are created.

The tree indicates that a mesh and the corresponding solid section have been created.

Mesh and section are created

Expanding the branch of the tree further indicates that the elements are of "Tetrahedron Mesh" type and the property is "Solid Section" as expected.

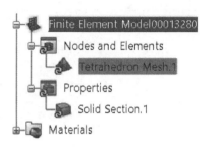

Upon double clicking on the "Tetrahedron Mesh.1" branch, the corresponding dialogue box shown on the right pops up. Here, one can change the type (linear or quadratic), the size and sag, and certain other parameters. For example, local mesh refinement can be accomplished through the "Local Specifications". Use the default settings.

There are different methods for displaying the mesh.
The instructions given below are one method of achieving that objective.

From the bottom row of icons, select the "Mesh" icon 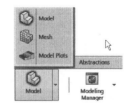 .

The bottom row's appearance now looks as shown below.

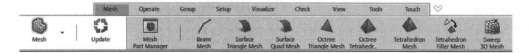

Select the "Update" icon  .
Upon updating, the mesh
appears on the screen as shown
on the right.

There are also different ways of
hiding the mesh. For example,
one can right click on the screen and from the resulting
menu choose the "Visualization Management" icon

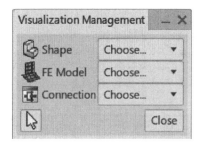

This leads to the "Visualization Management"
dialogue box shown and using the different pulldown menu options, a variety of tasks can be
achieved.

Creating a Scenario:

The nature of the analysis, namely, Static, Dynamic, Buckling, etc. is set in the "Structural Scenario Creation" App. Furthermore, the loads, restraints, and interaction are also defined in this application.

Locate the compass on the top left corner of the screen, and select it as shown on the right. Scroll through the applications and select the "Structural Scenario Creation" App

 Structural Scenario Creation

The row of icons in the bottom of your screen changes and will appear as displayed below.

| Standard | Setup | Procedures | Initial Conditions | Interactions | Thermal | Restraints | Loads | Simulate |

The pop-up window "Simulation Initialization" shown below appears on the screen. The radio button "Thermal-Structural" should be selected.

Simulation Initialization

Create Analysis Case

○ Structural
○ Thermal
● Thermal-Structural

Thermal Finite Element Model: None selected
Structural Finite Element Model: None selected

OK   Cancel

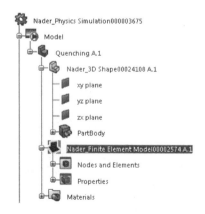

A quick glance of the tree confirms that a "Scenario" has been created.

Checking the bottom of the screen on the left side reveals that there are two red exclamation signs.
These pertain to "Thermal Analysis Case.1", "Structural Analysis Case.1" and "No Procedures Exist".

Make sure that in the bottom left margin, the "Thermal Analysis Case.1" is selected.

If you are not there, choose the "Setup" tab of the action bar.

"Setup" tab

Standard	Setup	Procedures	Initial Conditions	Interactions	Thermal	Restraints	Loads	Simulate	Display

Click the "Finite Element Model" icon  from the bottom row. This is referring to the "FE Model" which is already created. The following pop-up window appears.

Finite Element Model

Selects or creates the finite element model to use in your simulation.

Press F1 for more help.

Since a finite element model is already created, it appears in the list and make sure that you select that row.

Select the
Finite Element Model

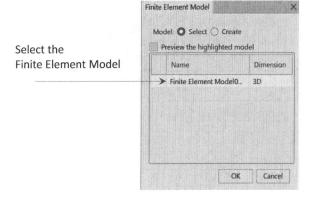

Upon pressing "OK" and closing this dialogue box, a "Green" check mark appears in front of "Thermal Analysis Case.1".

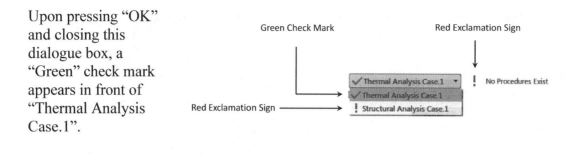

Next select the "Structural Analysis Case.1" from the list in the bottom left corner of the screen.

Therefore, the bottom left corner now appears as:

Once again, click the "Finite Element Model" icon from the bottom row. This is referring to a model which is already created. The following pop-up window appears.

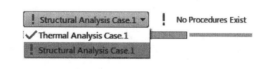

Since a finite element model is already created, it appears in the list and make sure that you select that row.

Select the
Finite Element Model

Immediately the red exclamation mark in front of "Structural Analysis Case.1" turns into a green check mark.

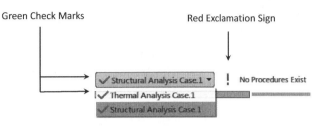

So the bottom left corner now appears as shown below.

At this point, you have to make a decision whether to create the "Procedure" for thermal analysis or the structural analysis first. The order that you do this in is irrelevant; however, we suggest that you select the "Thermal Analysis Case.1" first.

The bottom left corner should look like this:

Creating a "Step" for Thermal Analysis:

Select the "Procedures" tab from the bottom row.

Select the "Transient State Heat Transfer" icon from the action bar.

The "Transient State Heat Transfer " dialogue box opens. Make the changes shown on the right and close the dialogue box. The dialogue box is shown in the next page.

Transient Heat Transfer Step

Configures a heat transfer
analysis procedure that
calculates the static distribution
of temperatures in a body due
to conduction and boundary
radiation.

❓ Press F1 for more help.

Transient Heat Transfer Step	×

Name: Transient Heat Transfer Step.1

Step time: 2000s

▼ **Incrementation**

Incrementation type: Automatic ▾

Initial time increment:	0.02s
Minimum time increment:	1e-005s
Maximum time increment:	100s
Maximum number of increments:	1000
Maximum temperature change per increment:	20Kdeg
☐ Maximum temperature change rate for steady state:	0Kdeg_s

▶ **Advanced**

OK   Cancel

Make These Changes

The thermal step appears in the tree and you get "Green checkmarks" on the bottom of the screen.

Applying the Thermal Boundary Conditions:

Select the "Initial Condition" tab from the action bar.

"Initial Condition" Tab

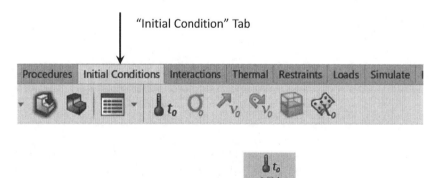

Procedures   Initial Conditions   Interactions   Thermal   Restraints   Loads   Simulate

Choose the "Initial Temperature" icon t_0 Initial Temperature.

In the "Initial Temperature" dialogue box, for the 'Support" select the "Tetrahedron Mesh.1" from the tree, and for the "Temperature" use 1423K.

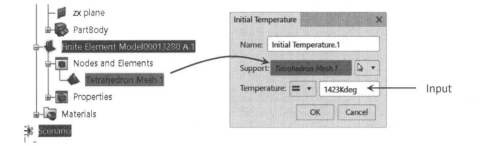

Select the "Thermal" tab of the action tool bar.

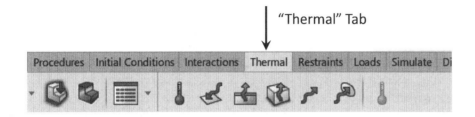

Choose the "Film Condition" icon from the action bar. As the "Support" pick the curved surface which is responsible for convection to the ambient. The "Film Coefficient" should be 5910 W_Kdeg_m2. For "Reference temperature" use 300 Kdeg. This is the temperature of the fluid in the quenching pool.

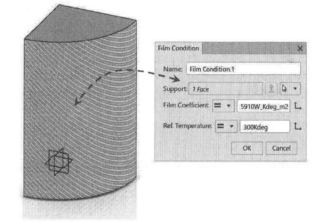

The other four surfaces that are not picked are automatically insulated.

The tree structure at this point is shown below.

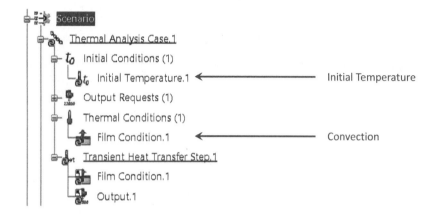

Creating a "Step" for Stress (Mechanical) Analysis:

Check the bottom left corner of the interface. The "Structural Analysis Case.1" must be selected.

Your screen should have the following message in the bottom left corner.

Select the "Procedures" tab from the bottom row.

"Procedures" Tab

Choose that "Static Step" icon 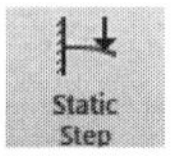 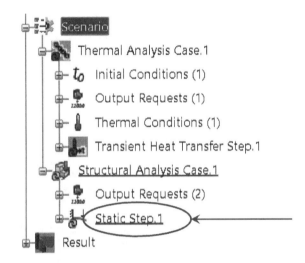 and make the changes shown below in the dialogue box. Note that the "time" plays a dummy role in a static analysis.

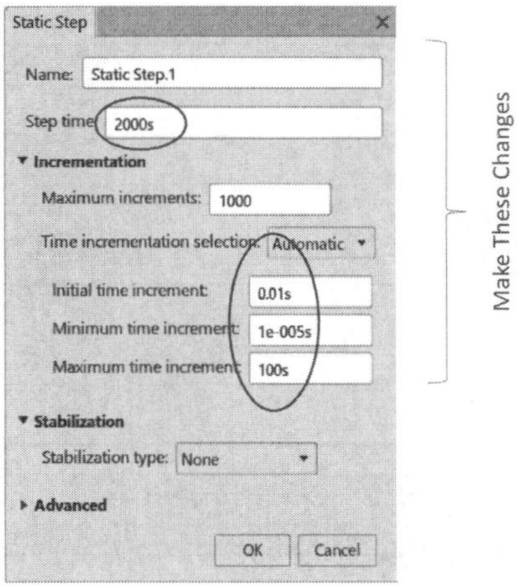

The "Static Step.1" appears in the tree.

Notice that there are two green check marks next to the items in the bottom left corner of your interface.

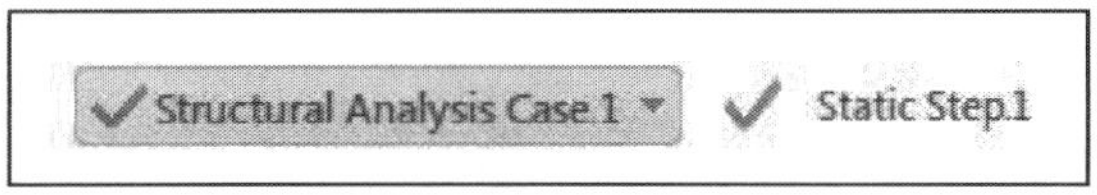

Applying the Mechanical Boundary Conditions (Restraints):

Select "Restraints" tab of the action bar.

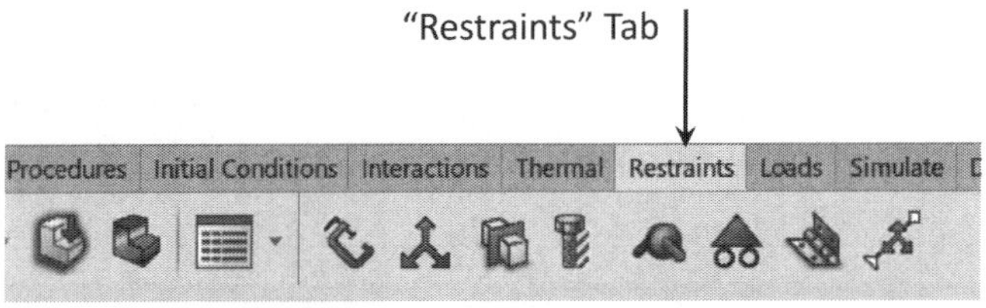

"Restraints" Tab

Choose the "Planar Symmetry" icon  from the action bar followed by selecting the faces involved. This is is done four times individually as shown below.

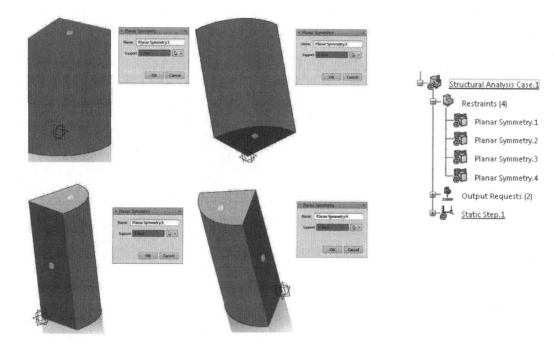

Select the "Thermal' tab from the action bar. Next choose

the "Prescribed Temperature" icon ![Prescribed Temperature] from the action bar. This leads to the "Prescribed Temperature" dialogue box on the right.

In the "Support" use the pulldown menu to select "Mesh part".

Select "Mesh part"

This leads to a pop-up window, from which you have to select "Tetrahedron Mesh.1".

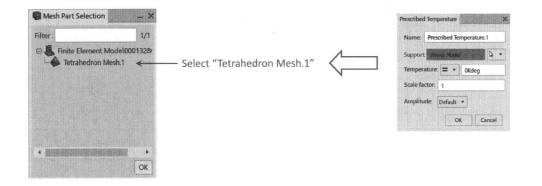

As for the "Temperature", use the pulldown menu and select "From Step ⟨ **From step** ". Notice that automatically the Thermal Step.1 selected.

Close the box by pressing "OK".

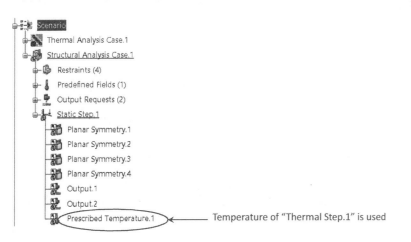

The tree at this point takes the following form.

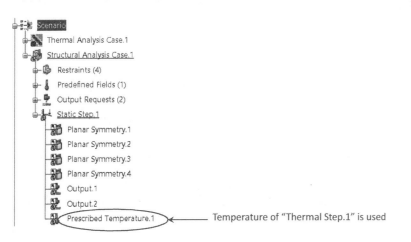

The model is now complete and ready to be simulated. However, we would like to plot the time dependent temperature variation at a point in the cylinder. In order to do so we create a group.

Select the "Model" icon from the action bar

Choose the "Group" tab from the action bar. It will land you in the environment where groups can be created.

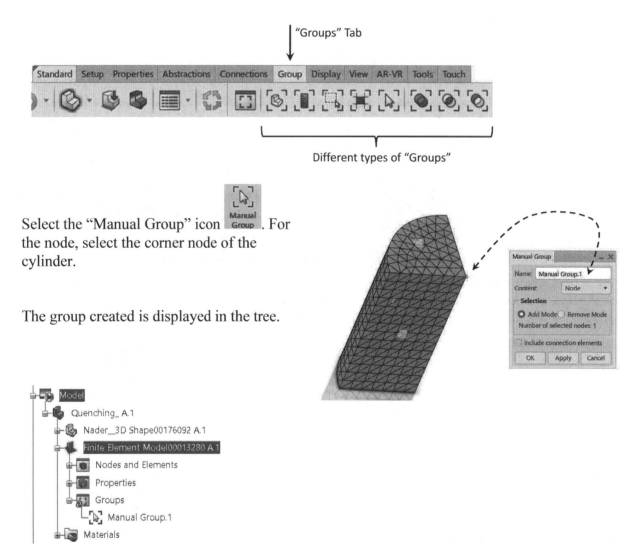

Select the "Manual Group" icon. For the node, select the corner node of the cylinder.

The group created is displayed in the tree.

Since we are interested in plotting the time history of the nodal temperature, the data must be requested. Select the "Scenario" icon to access the following action bar.

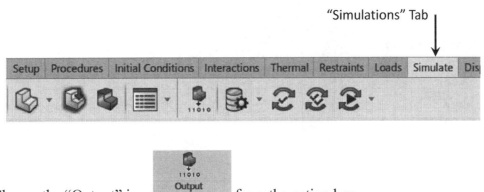

Choose the "Output" icon from the action bar.

In the resulting dialogue box, place the cursor in the location shown, and select the "Group" from the menu.

In the resulting dialogue box, double click on "Manual Group.1" from the tree, which will then place it in the "Support" placeholder.

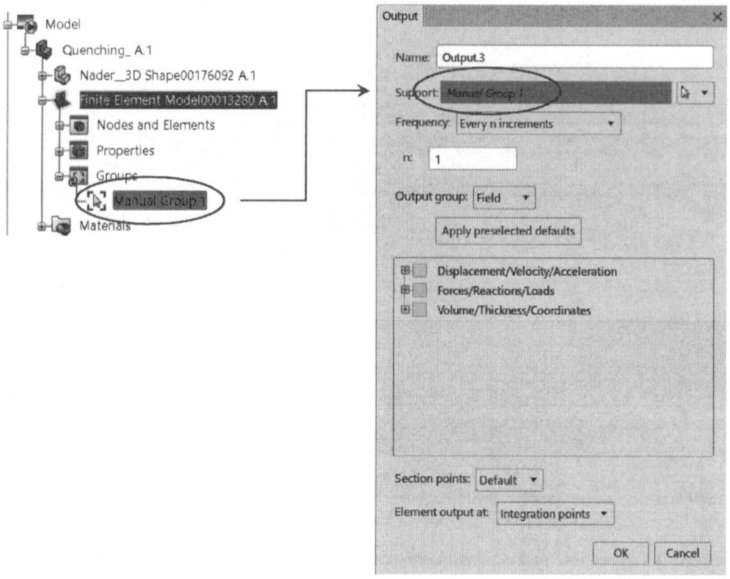

Make the selections shown in the "Output" dialogue box shown below.

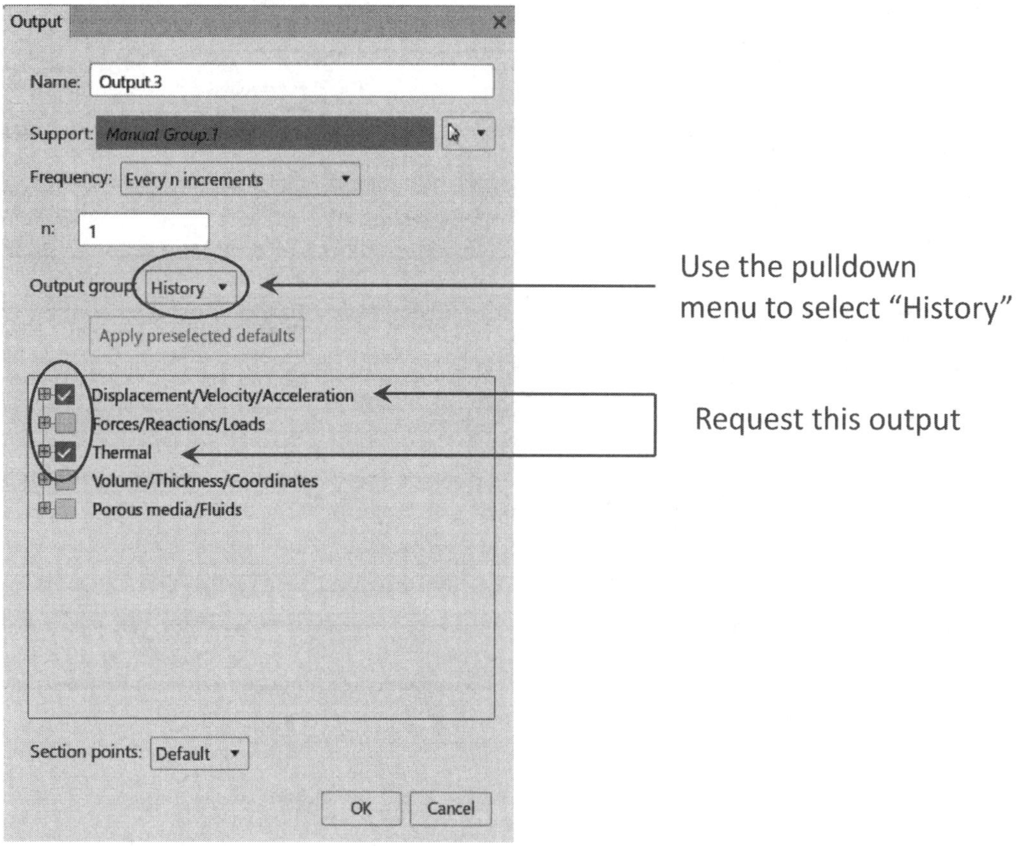

We are now able to simulate the model.

Consistency, Model Check, and Simulation:

Select the "Simulation" tab from the bottom row of icons on your screen (i.e. from the action bar).

"Simulations" Tab

It is a good practice to perform the model and consistency check before submitting the work for the final run.
Select the "Model and Scenario Check" icon from the

bottom row 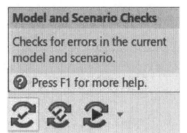.

The software goes through a check phase and if there are no issues, a message with a "Green" check mark is returned.

Although the Thermal and Structural consistency checks can be done independently of each other, one can choose to do them simultaneously as the window shows.

Model and Scenario Checks

Checks for errors in the current model and scenario.

❓ Press F1 for more help.

Model and Scenario Checks

The current case is dependent on another case that must be simulated before this case. The following case will be simulated automatically: Thermal Analysis Case.1

▼ **Analysis case selection**

☐ Select All

☑ Thermal Analysis Case.1

☑ Structural Analysis Case.1

☐ Run analysis cases concurrently

OK   Cancel

The consistency check completes without any glitches.

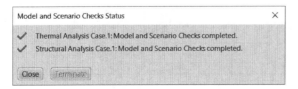

Model and Scenario Checks Status   ✕

✓ Thermal Analysis Case.1: Model and Scenario Checks completed.

✓ Structural Analysis Case.1: Model and Scenario Checks completed.

Close   Terminate

Next, select the "Simulation Checks" icon from the bottom row of icons. Accept the number of "Cores" in the pop up box below and perform the checks simultaneously for thermal and strucural analysis.

The simulation checks for both the thermal and structural cases were successful. Close the window by pressing "Close"

Select the "Simulation" icon from the bottom row.

Accept the number of "cores" and perform both simulations simultaneously. Wait for the simulation to complete.

Both the thermal and structural analysis run without any issues and the following two dialogue boxes confirm that.

Results (Post processing):

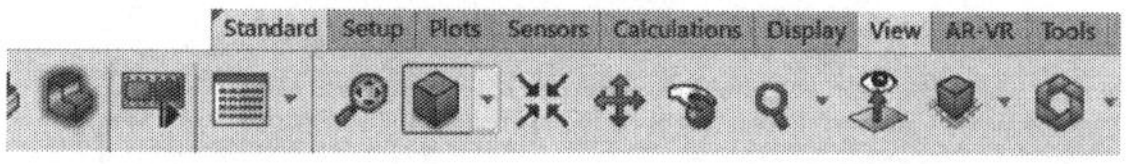

Once you close (or move) the
obstructing dialogue boxes, you must
be in the "Results" section and the
bottom row should appear as shown on the right.

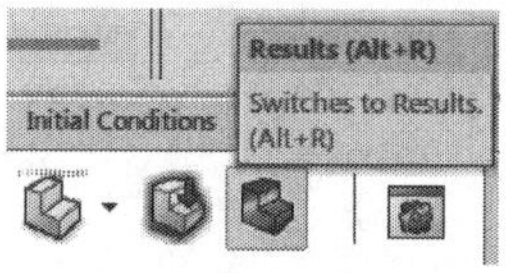

If not, click on the "Results" icon    .

The "Plots" dialogue box is shown on the next page. It indicates that the plot is from the
thermal step and it is the second "Frame". Clearly, the first frame of any analysis will
produce a zero value for any quantity. The distribution agrees with common sense. The
cylinder is hottest on the inside and cooler on the outside.

The results of temperature distribution at three different instances (3, 163, and 2000 seconds) are given below.

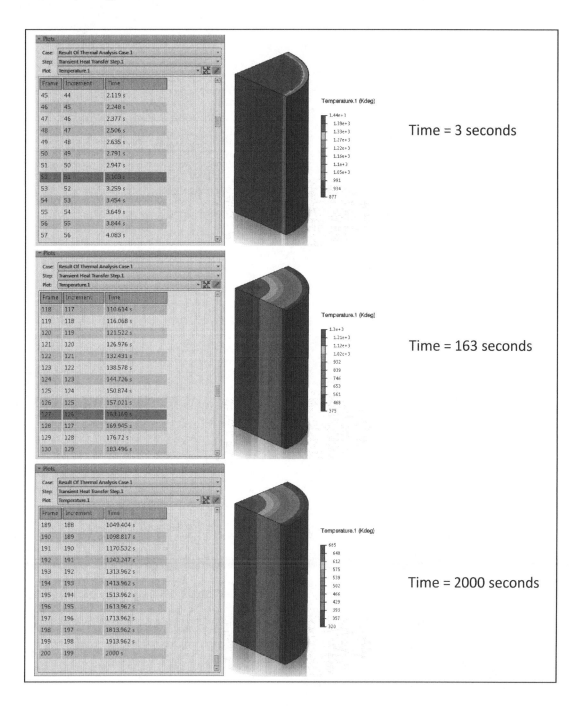

The heat flux distribution (vector rendering) at the corresponding times are also displayed below. The arrow density has been reduced for visual purposes.

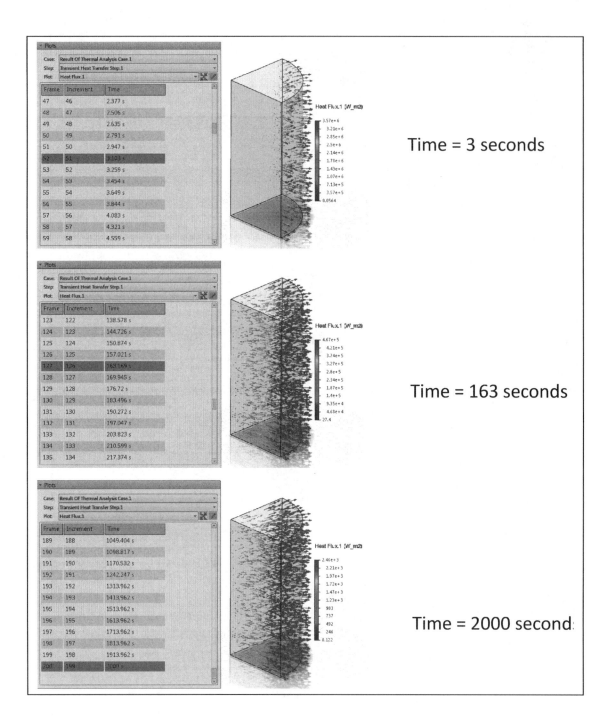

The contours of von Mises stress at the corresponding times (approximately the same times) are displayed below. Note that as the cooling takes place, stress relaxation kicks in and the von Mises stress decreases.

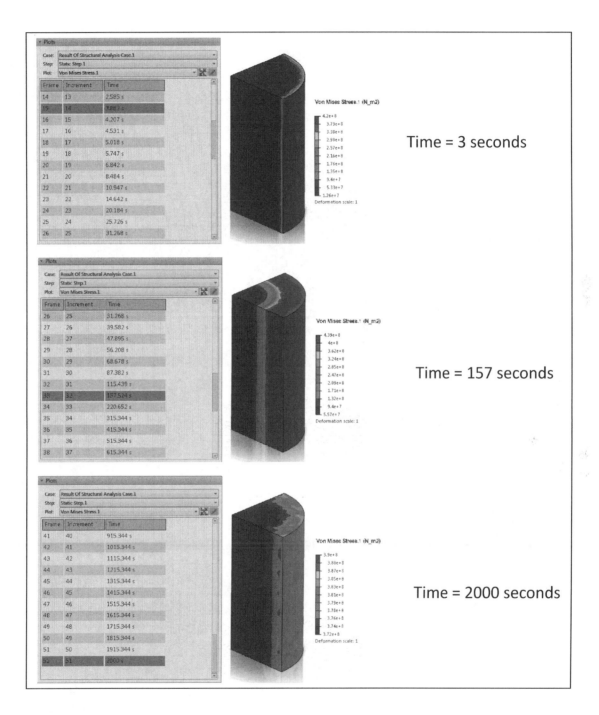

The contours of the displacement magnitudes at the corresponding times (approximately the same times) are also displayed below.

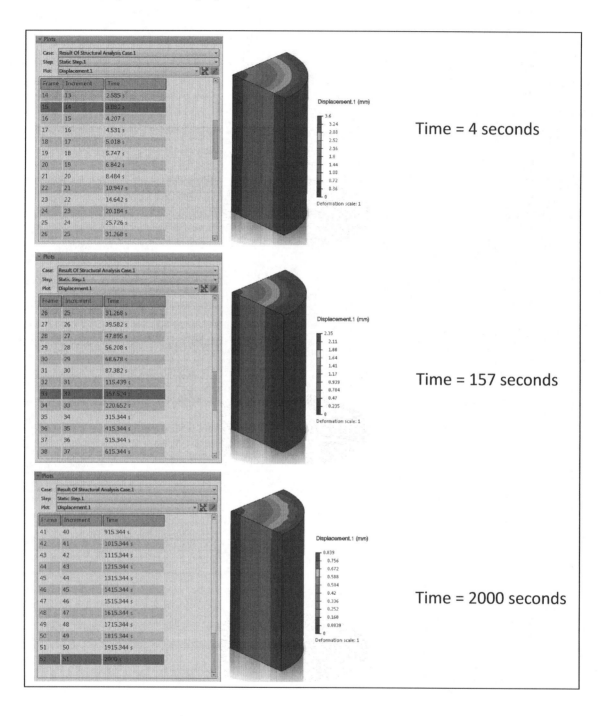

The contours of the equivalent plastic strain at the corresponding times (approximately the same times) are displayed below. Note that as the cooling takes place the plastic strain increases.

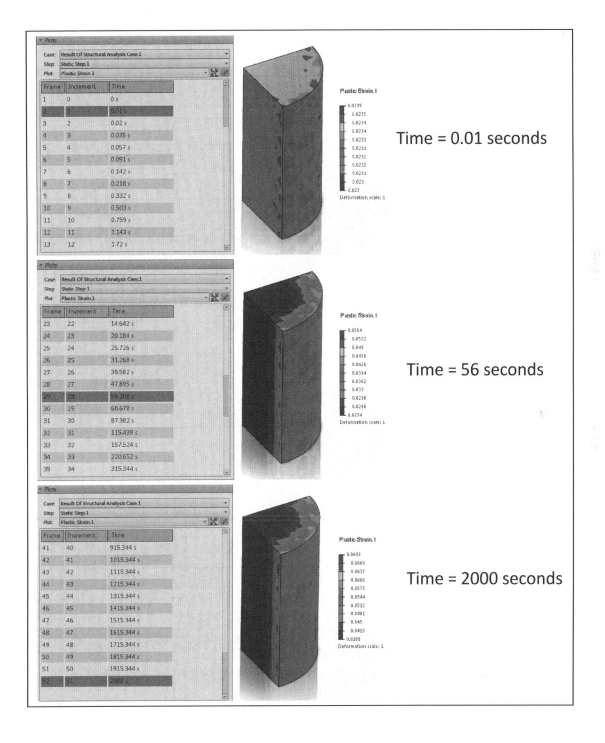

History Plot of the Temperature Distribution at the Corner Node:

Recall that the corner node of the cylinder was used to create "Manual Group.1". The purpose was to plot the temperature and displacement variation of this node as a function of time.

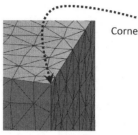

Corner Node

Select the "Plots" tab from the action bar.

"Plots" tab

From the menu, pick the "X-Y Plot from History" icon.

X-Y Plot from History

Create an X-Y plot of history output data.

? Press F1 for more help.

The following dialogue box appears.

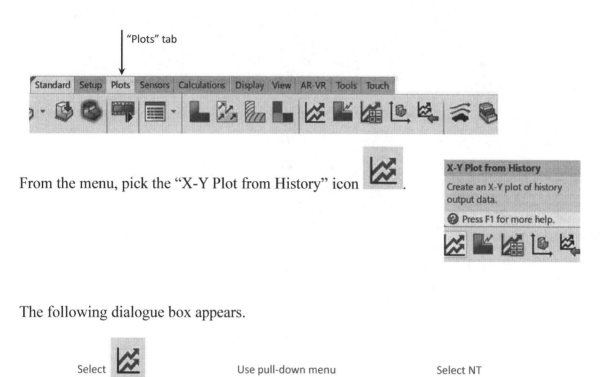

The following plot representing the temperature distribution is displayed on the screen.

Upon pressing the "Apply" button in the dialogue box, the history plot for the selected node (in the group) as a function of time appears as shown.

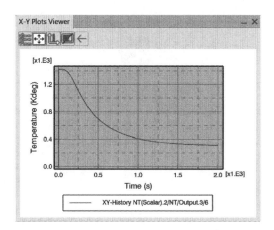

In order to plot the ***displacement*** of the node, select the "X-Y Plot from History" icon

once again. Make the following changes with the pulldown menu.

Select   Use pull-down menu   Select UT

Upon pressing the "Apply" button, the displacement history plot of the corner node appears.

Note that the generated plot is identically zero. This is not surprising as the selected point to create the group was on the axis of the cylinder. Those point do not move at all. Should we have selected a different point (node) the resulting plot would not have been identically zero.

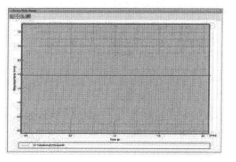

Notes:

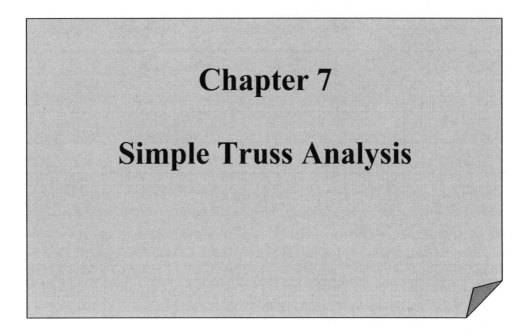

Chapter 7

Simple Truss Analysis

Objective:

In this chapter, you will be creating and analyzing a very simple truss structure. One of the roller supports in this problem is at an inclined direction. You will use a local coordinate system to implement this restraint boundary condition.

Problem Statement:

Truss structures are relatively simple to analyze in most FEA packages. However, there are some subtle points that have to be considered. These details sometimes make the truss (and frame) modeling rather cumbersome. However, because of the importance of such structures, we will devote the present tutorial to them.

Consider the three-member truss shown below. The member cross sections are square with the dimensions specified in the figure. The three members are made of steel with E = 200GPa and v = 0.3. A concentrated force of F = 1.0E6 N is horizontally applied at the point B. Although there are three joints (points) in the model, four points will be defined where the last one is for specifying the orientation of the beams which is important in the next chapter.

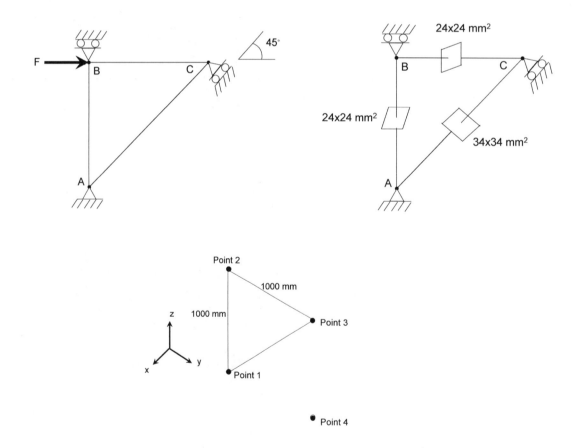

The Model and Material Properties:

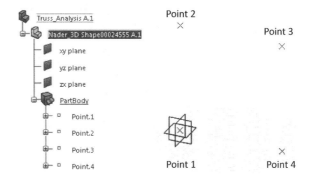

Enter the Part Design App   , and create four points with the
coordinates given below.

Point 1: (0,0,0)
Point 2: (0,0,1000)
Point 3: (0,1000,1000)
Point 4: coordinates (0,1000,0)

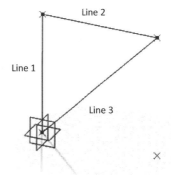

Next, create Line 1, Line 2, and Line 3 as shown.

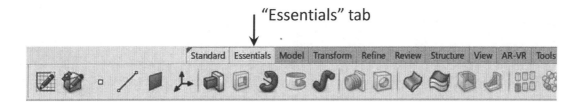

We then create a local coordinate system at Point 3 which has been rotated in the global x
direction by 45 degrees. This will be used to account for the slanted roller support.
Make sure that the Model tab of the action bar is active.

"Essentials" tab

Select the "Axis System" icon  .

This leads to the "Axis Syatem Definition" dialogue box.

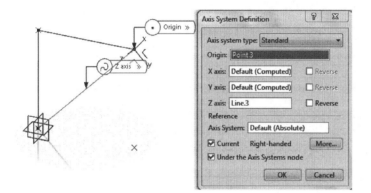

For the origin, select the point on the top right corner (ie Point3). For the "Z axis", select Line3. Close the window.

Upon closing the window, the screen displays the local coordinate system just constructed.

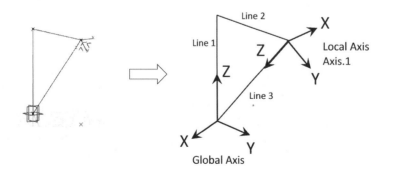

The reader should be reminded that the choice of the "Z axis" being Line3 <u>was quite</u> <u>arbitrary</u>. One could have chosen "X axis" or the "Y axis" instead. However, the choice must be taken into account when the restraints are being applied.

We will now apply the material properties of the truss structure.
The process was described in the previous chapters (see chapters 2 and 3 specifically).

Select the "Create Material" ![icon] icon to create a linear elastic material with Young's modulus of 200 GPa and Poisson's ratio of 0.3. The "Material Definition: Simulation Domain" dialogue box should look as shown below.

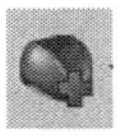

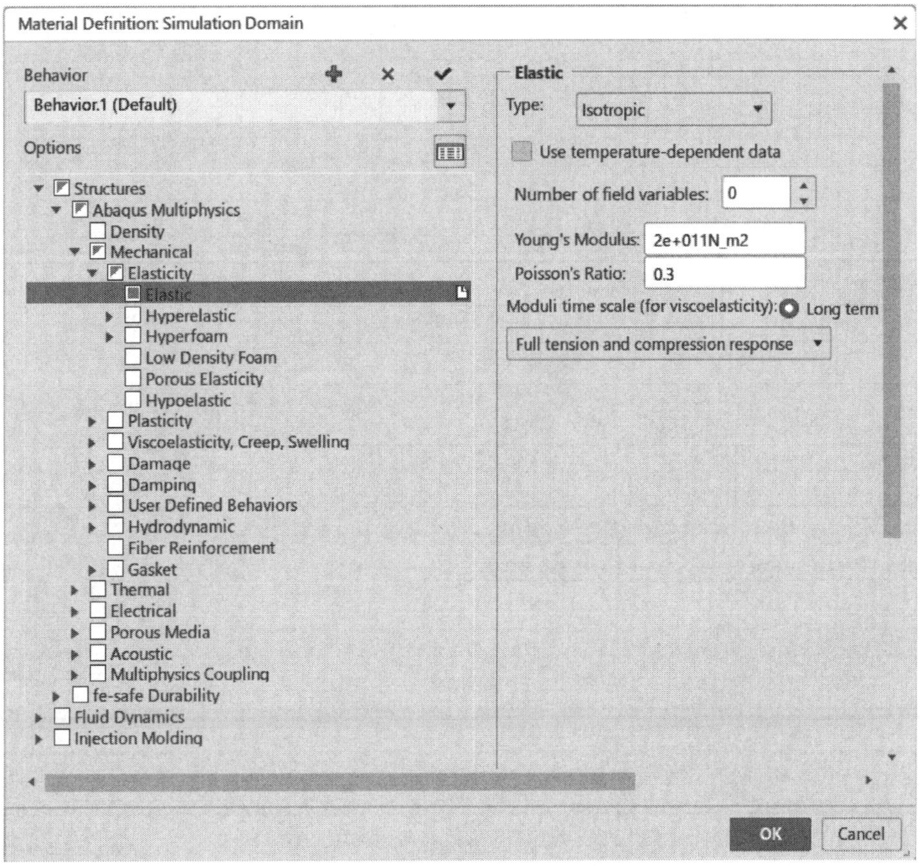

The Role of Point 4:

In the present problem where a truss structure is being analyzed, the orientation of the cross section does not play a role. This being the case, Point 4 generated will not be taking part in the model creation. However, for a frame structure, this point is responsible for the proper orientation of the beam elements and needs to be taken into account. In a later chapter, this same problem will be modeled as a frame and the role of the orientation point will be discussed.

Creating the Finite Element Model:

Locate the compass on the top left corner of the screen and click on it. Scroll through the applications and select the "Structural Model

 Structural Model Creation

Creation" App  .

The row of icons on the bottom of your screen (action bar) changes and will appear as displayed below.

The dialogue box shown on the right, "Create Finite Element Model", appears. For now, use the "Automatic" radio button. Other options are for user control of the meshing process. **Since no solid objects are involved, the beam meshing and defining the section properties must be done by the user.**

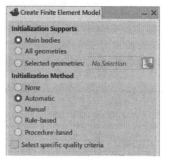

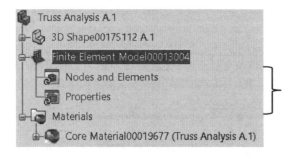 Mesh and section properties will be stored here

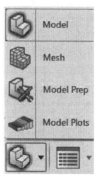

Select the Mesh icon of the action bar.

"Mesh" tab

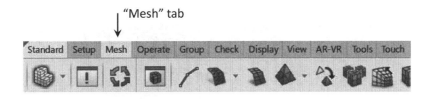

Pick the "Beam Mesh" icon 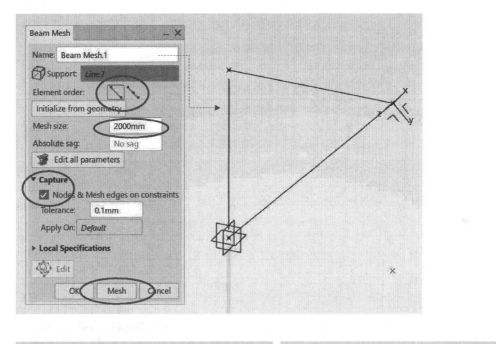. In the resulting dialogue box, select the side which was Line.1 and for size specify 2000mm. Note that the length of Line.1 is 1000 mm, therefore a single element with a length of 1000 mm is created. Repeat the process for Line.2 and Line.3. No other changes within the dialogue box need to be made. Make sure the the "Mesh" box at the bottom of the dialogue box is selected. If you skip the "Mesh" box, you will need to update the mesh later.

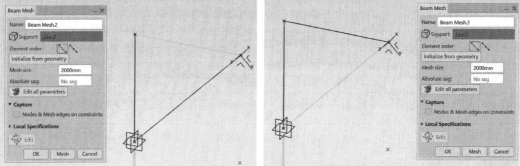

The three elements (Meshes) are created and displayed in the tree.

NOTE: It is important that the box "Automatic Mesh Capture" be checked. Otherwise, duplicate nodes are created at the junction between two lines leading to error messages.

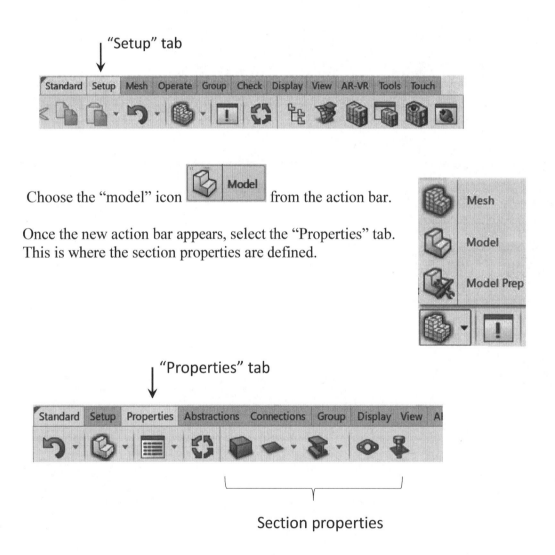

Select the "Setup" tab of the action bar.

"Setup" tab

Choose the "model" icon ⬛ Model from the action bar.

Once the new action bar appears, select the "Properties" tab. This is where the section properties are defined.

"Properties" tab

Section properties

Expand the beam section menu. From the available choices, select

the "1D Link Section" icon 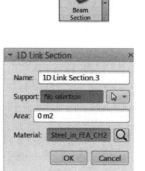.

The resulting dialogue box is shown below. Note that there is no mention of the shape of the cross section. This is understandable as for a truss element, the relevant factor is the area cross section.

One should not panic because a square cross section is displayed as a circular one.
In the resulting dialogue box, for the "Support" select the shorter lines and for the area input 576 mm2. Repeat the same process for the longer line but for area, use 1156mm2.

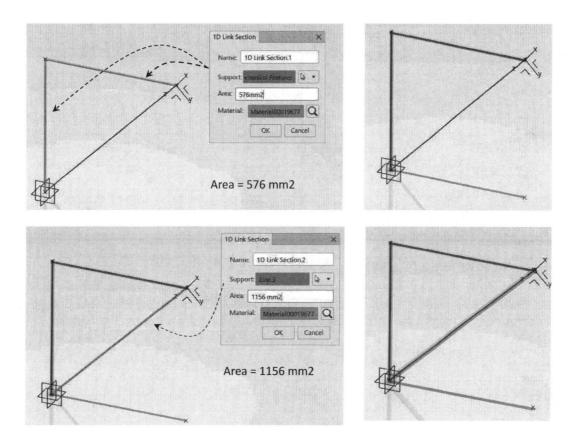

Area = 576 mm2

Area = 1156 mm2

A "zoomed in" part of the figure shows a circular cross section. This, however, is not alarming as the shape is irrelevant in simple truss analysis. In terms of magnitude, the size of the displayed area is correctly accounted for.

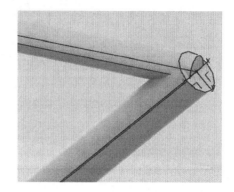

Another issue to raise here is that the "orientation Point", or point 4 constructed at the beginning of the chapter, plays no role if a truss analysis is considered. However, for a frame analysis, location of point 4 changes the orientation of the cross section and therefore the results for the entire frame.

At this point, the tree indicates that the mesh and section properties have been successfully defined. In the event that the "Green" section properties are distracting, one can place the curser on the corresponding branch, right click, and "Hide" the entities.

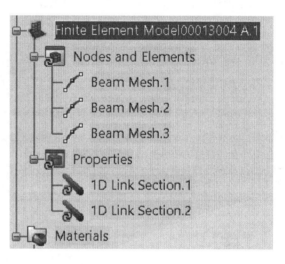

If needed (as the above tree indicates), one can update beam mesh and section properties.

Click on the "Update" icon

The updated tree is shown below.

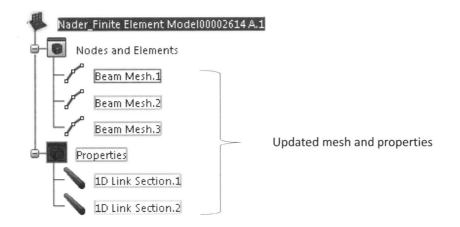

There is a very useful feature which is particularly handy in dealing with one dimensional elemens (beams and links).

a) Place the cursor on the "Properties" branch of the tree and hide it by right clicking.

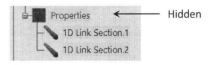

b) Activate the meshing tool bar by selecting the meshing icon.

c) Select the "Display" tab from the action bar at the bottom of the screen.

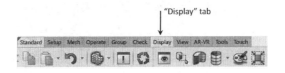

d) From the menu, select the "Visualization Management" icon and using the resulting dialogue box, hide the part.

e) From the menu, choose the "Element Shrink" icon 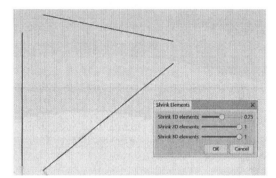 which leads to the dialogue box enabling the user to manipulate the shrink size.

Dragging the top sliding bar allows one to shrink the elements for visual inspection. The figure clearly indicates the presence of three truss elements (link elements). Furthermore, the default element colors can be changed.

Another useful information box is the "Mesh Part Manager". One way to reach this box is , right click on the screen, and scroll down to pick the appropriate line

Mesh Part Manager

Placing the cursor on one of the table entries and right clicking provides you with a variety of tasks to perform.

These features could have also been selected by right clicking on the screen!

Creating a Scenario:

The nature of the analysis, namely, Static, Dynamic, Buckling, etc. is set in the "Structural Scenario Creation" App. Furthermore, the loads, restraints, and interaction are also defined in this application.

Locate the compass on the top left corner of the screen and click. Scroll through the applications and select the "Structural Scenario Creation"

 Structural Scenario Creation

App   .

The row of icons on the bottom of your screen changes and will appear as displayed below

The pop-up window "Simulation Initialization" shown below appears on the screen. Since this is strictly a structural problem, the radio button "Structural" should be selected.

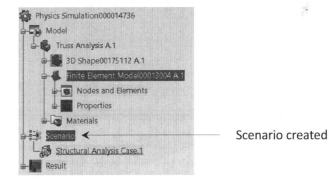

Scenario created

A quick glance of the tree confirms that a "Scenario" has been created.

Checking the bottom of the screen on the left side reveals that there are two red exclamation signs.
These pertain to "Structural Analysis Case.1" and "No Procedures Exist".

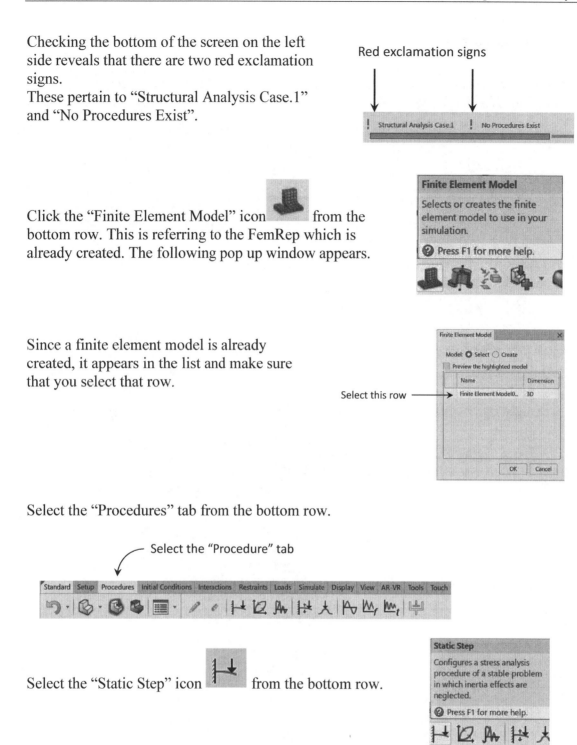

Click the "Finite Element Model" icon from the bottom row. This is referring to the FemRep which is already created. The following pop up window appears.

Since a finite element model is already created, it appears in the list and make sure that you select that row.

Select the "Procedures" tab from the bottom row.

Select the "Static Step" icon from the bottom row.

The "Static Step" dialogue box pops up. Accept all the defaults. Note that if the "Advanced" pulldown list is selected, it becomes clear that this is the point in the software where "Geometric Nonlinearities" are included, or excluded.

NLGEOM included
Not needed in this problem

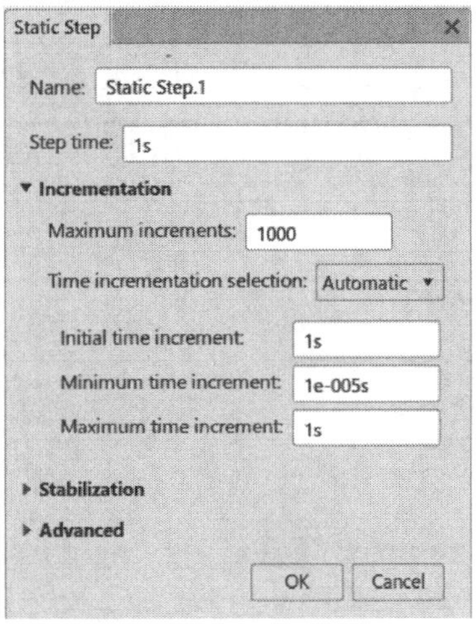

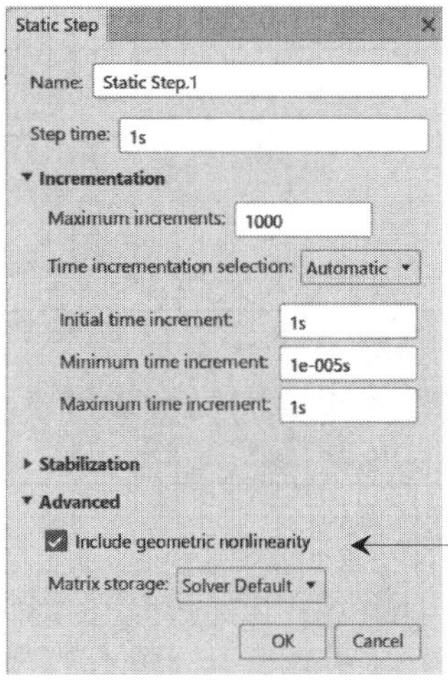

A quick glance at the bottom left corner of the screen reveals "Green" checkmarks instead of "Red" red exclamation marks.

Note the "Green" checkmarks instead of "Red" exclamations

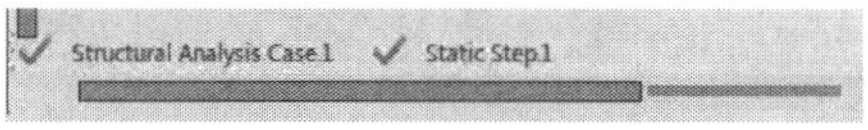

The tree indicates that "Static Step.1" has been created. There are default basic output entities that are requested upon the creation of a Step.

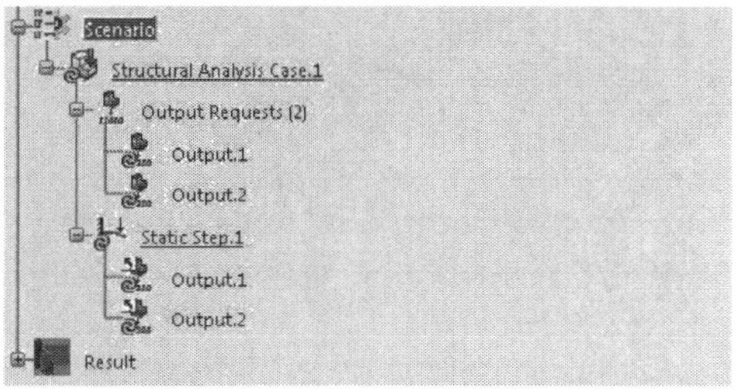

Accessing the Model, Scenario and Results Quickly:

Clearly this can be done by double clicking on the corresponding branches of the tree. However, it can also be done efficiently by selecting the appropriate icon among these three: . The first one on the left is "Model and Mesh", the middle one is "Scenario" and the one on the far right is "Results"; that is the postprocessor.

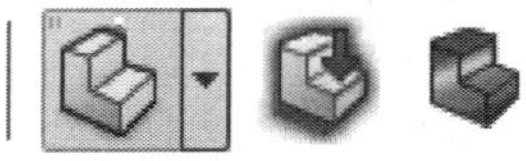

Applying the Concentrated Load:

A concentrated force of 1.0E+6 N is to be applied at the top left corner. The direction of the force is the "Global" y-direction. Note that this is a highly unrealistic load, but we ignore yielding and buckling.

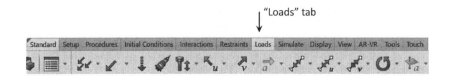

"Loads" tab

Select the "Force" icon . In the dialogue box, for the "Support" select the top left corner, and input the magnitude of the force. **Be careful**, make sure that "Point.2" is hidden first. The "Support" is not "Point.2", it is the "vertex" and can be selected only if "Point.2" is hidden. Note that the pulldown menu is set on "Global".

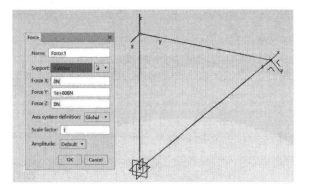

Applying the Restraints:

Once again, be careful, make sure that Point.1, Point.2, and Point.3 are hidden first. The "Support" for restraints is not these points. It is the "vertex" and can be selected only if these points are hidden.

Select the Restraints tab of the action bar.

Choose the "fixed Displacement" icon from the menu. Select the top left corner of the structure (where the force is applied). This point lies on a roller which freely moves in the y-direction. Therefore, restrain the motion in the "Global" x and z directions.

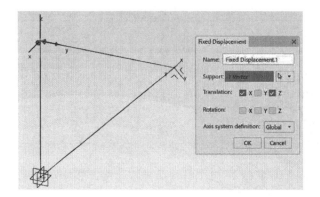

Choose the "Clamp" icon 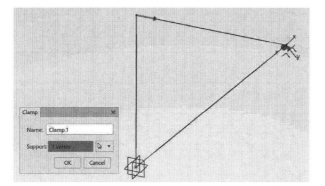 from the menu. Select the bottom left corner of the structure. This point is fixed completely.

Once again, choose the "fixed Displacement" icon from the menu. Select the top right corner of the structure. This is the point that slides along the 45° ramp. Note that the Axis system to be used is the local one. In that coordinate system, there are no displacements in the x and y directions. In the event that your local coordinate system was oriented differently, the appropriate changes have to be made.

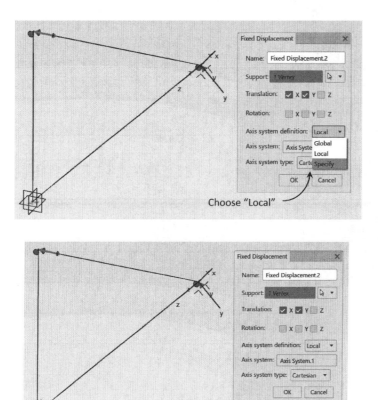

Consistency, Model Check, and Simulation:

It is a good practice to perform the consistency and consistency
check before submitting the work for the final run.
Ignoring my own advice, proceed to the "Simulation" stage.

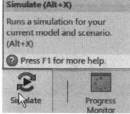

Select the "Simulation" icon ![icon] from the bottom row.

Accept the number of "cores" in the pop up box, and wait for
the simulation to complete.

The simulation completes without any glitches and one can perform the post-processing.

Simulation Checks Status

✓ Simulation checks completed.

▶ Errors (0)

▼ Warnings (1)

    For two-dimensional models, if a non-unity thickness is specified for two-dimensional solid elements and
these elements are involved in an interaction such as contact, the same thickness should be specified for
the out-of-plane thickness of the corresponding surface under *surface interaction.

▶ Information (0)

Close   Terminate

Results (Post processing):

Once you close (or move) the obstructing dialogue boxes, you must be in the "Results" section and the bottom row should appear as shown on the right.

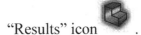

If the postprocessing (results) dialogue box does not appear automatically, click on the "Results" icon   .

If you use the "Pulldown" menu, and select von Mises stress, your view will be something resembling the depiction below.

Deformation.1
Deformation scale: 1

Make sure you select Frame 2 of the table

This is not very useful, and a few "non-trivial" steps need to be followed to make it useful.

The first step is to put it in the front view as it is a two-dimensional problem in principle. While in "Results", select the "View" tab from the action bar at the bottom of the screen.

"View" tab

Select the "Front" view leading to the configuration shown in the next page.

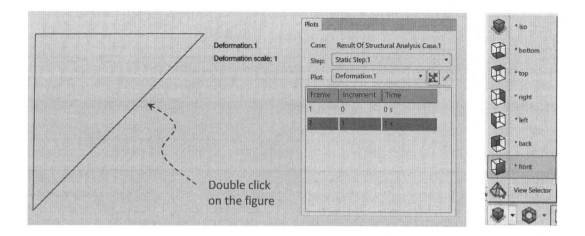

Place your cursor on the deformation shape on the screen and double click on it. This opens the dialogue box below. Change the "scale factor" to 20 and close the dialogue box. You will see that the scale of the deformation gives you a better idea of the truss final configuration.

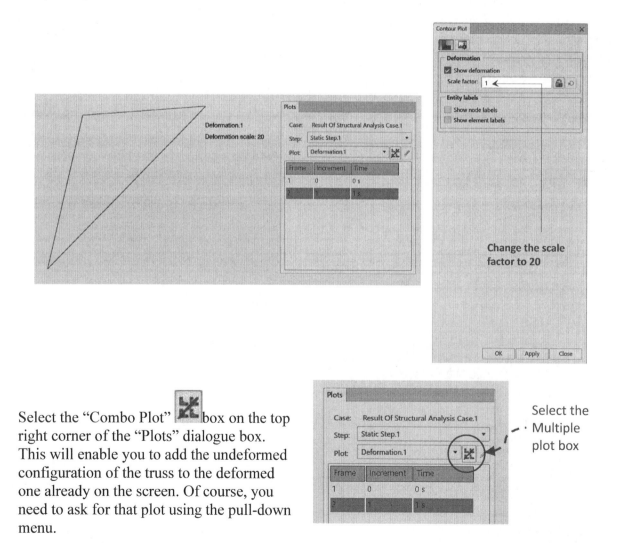

Select the "Combo Plot" box on the top right corner of the "Plots" dialogue box. This will enable you to add the undeformed configuration of the truss to the deformed one already on the screen. Of course, you need to ask for that plot using the pull-down menu.

The resulting plots (superposed) appear on the screen.

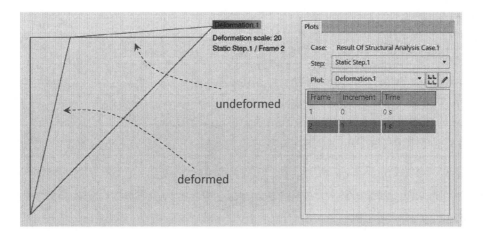

You can repeat the same steps as above, generating the displacement and the von Mises and displacement values.

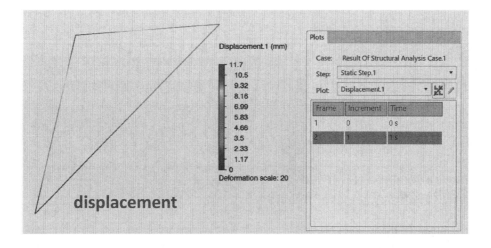

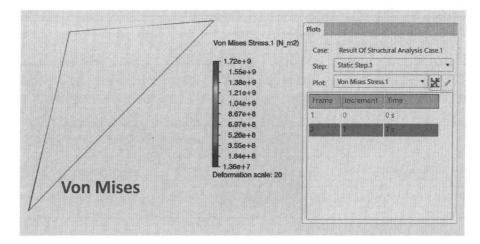

Exercise 1

Consider the two member truss structure shown below. Both members have the same cross-sectional area of 0.0006 m². They are also made of steel with Young's modulus of 210 GPa. The upward load of 1000 kN is applied at the roller support.

It is assumed that the roller supports settles by 5 cm. This means that it has a leftward horizontal displacement of 5 cm.

Model the structure in 3DEXPERIENCE, and find the upward displacement of the roller.

Answer: You should be getting 0.03369 as the answer.

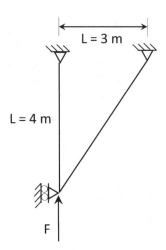

Exercise 2

The three member truss shown below is subjected to both mechanical and thermal loading. It is assumed that $L = 1m$, and that all members have the same cross-sectional area $A = 0.00001m^2$. The Young's modulus is $E = 100\ GPa$. The top member is subjected to a temperature drop of 120 °C. Given that the coefficient of thermal expansion at the room temperature of 20°C is $= 20E - 6\ m/m\_K$, find the downward deflection of the load. The applied load is $F = 10kN$.

Answer: You should be getting a downward displacement of 0.01214 m.

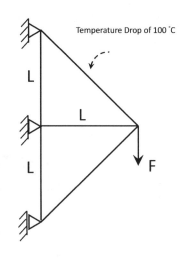

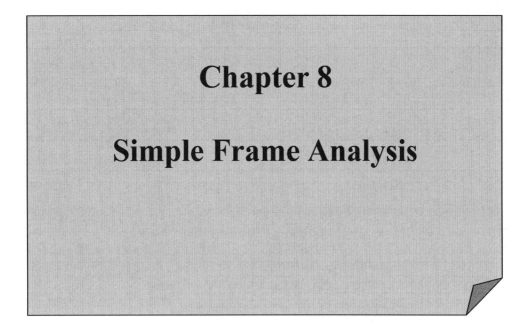

Chapter 8

Simple Frame Analysis

Objective:

In this chapter, you will modify the truss analysis from an earlier chapter to conduct frame calculations. There are very minor changes in the model to transform it into a frame and therefore, the steps that are identical are skipped. A major difference between the current analysis and the one conducted earlier is the number of elements used in each member. In the truss analysis, only three elements were sufficient to describe the overall behavior. Here, in order to display the "bending" phenomenon, fifteen beam elements on each member will be employed.

Problem Statement:

Consider the three member frame shown below. The member cross sections are square with the dimensions specified in the figure. The three members are made of steel with E = 200 GPa and ν = 0.3. A concentrated force of F = 1.0E6 N is horizontally applied at point B. Although there are three joints (points) in the model, four points will be defined where the last one is for specifying the orientation of the beams.

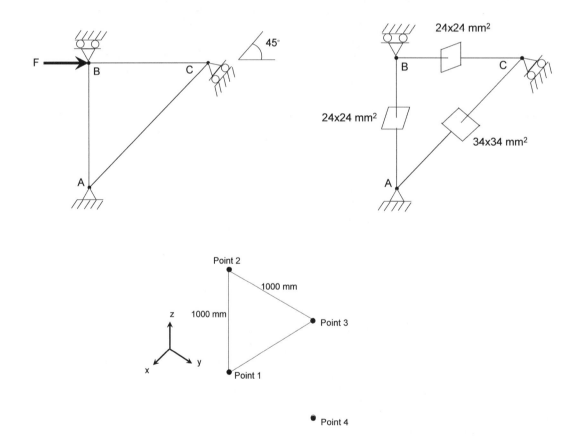

The Model and Material Properties:

This is already created in the truss problem and is
displayed below. Please consult the earlier chapter.

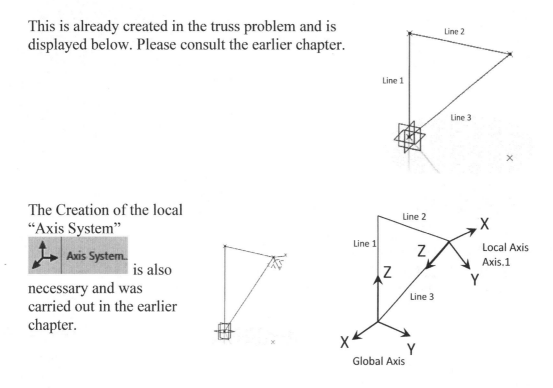

The Creation of the local
"Axis System"

 is also
necessary and was
carried out in the earlier
chapter.

The material for the frame is identical to that of the truss, namely, linear elastic with
Young's modulus of 200 GPa and Poisson's ratio of 0.3.

Creating the Finite Element Model:

Locate the compass on the top left corner of the
screen and click on it. Scroll through the
applications and select the "Structural Model

Creation" App

The dialogue box shown on the right, "Create Finite Element Model", appears. For now, use the "Automatic" radio button. Other options are for user control of the meshing process. **Since no solid objects are involved, the beam meshing and defining the section properties must be done by the user.**

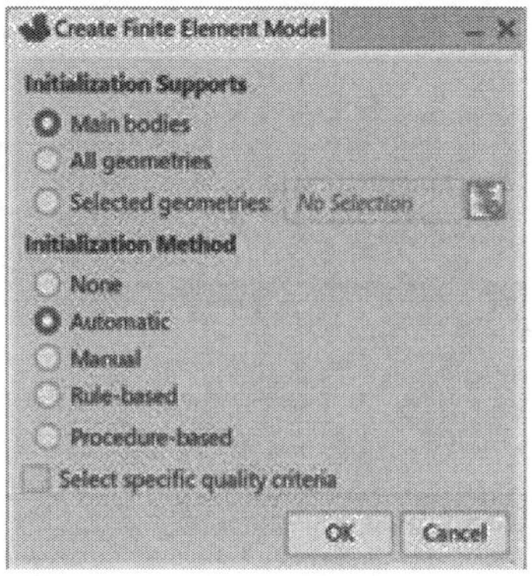

Following the process described in the truss analysis chapter, mesh the three lines with

"Beam Mesh" 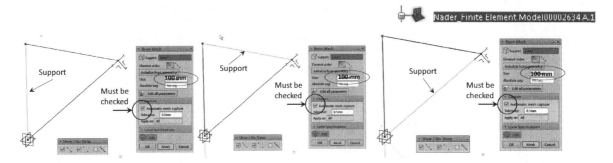 one at a time. The only **difference being** the "Size" value. **Use 100mm as the size of the element**. This gives you ten elements on the vertical and horizontal sections and approximately fourteen elements on the longest member.

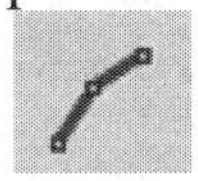

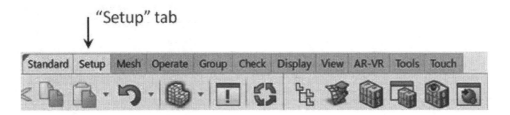

The three lines are now meshed and displayed in the tree.

NOTE: It is important that the box "Automatic Mesh Capture" be checked. Otherwise, duplicate nodes are created at the junction between two lines leading to error messages. If you find the dialogue boxes above too small to read, please check it in the chapter on "A Simple Truss Analysis".

Select the "Setup" tab.

"Setup" tab

Select the "model" icon 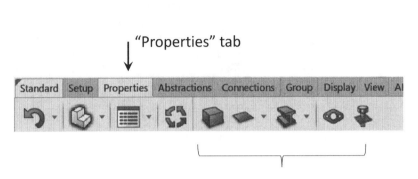 from the action bar.

Once the new action bar appears, select the Properties tab. This is where the section properties are defined.

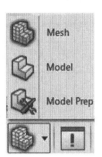

"Properties" tab

Section properties

Expand the beam section menu. From the available choices,

select the "Beam Profile" icon 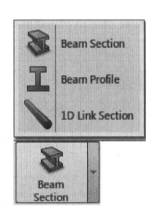.

The following "Beam Profile" dialogue box opens. From the pulldown menu select "Rectangle" and for the "Base (a)" and "Height (b)" input 24.

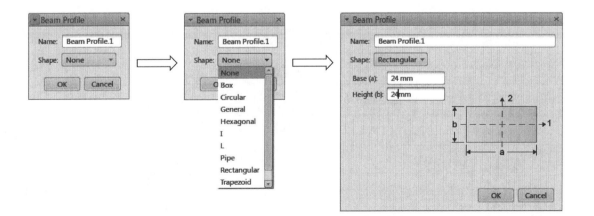

Repeat this process to create Beam Profile.2 with the information displayed below.

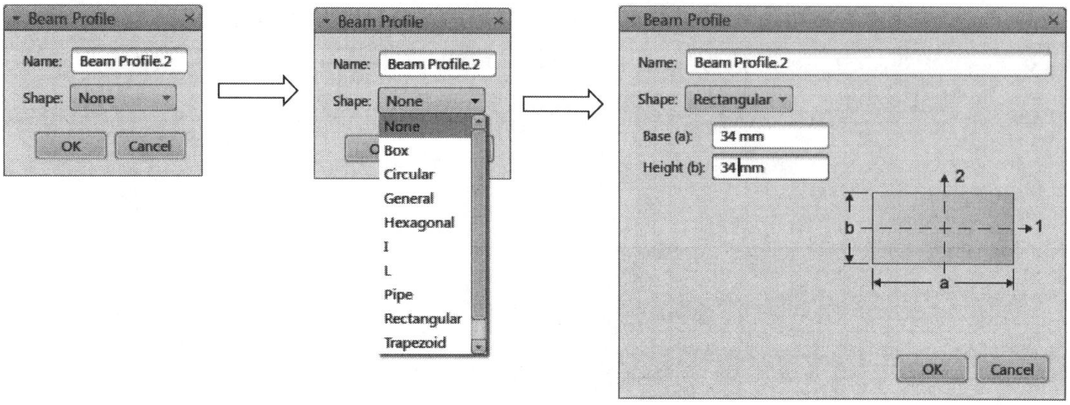

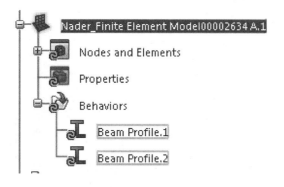

These profiles are recorded in the tree as anticipated.

The next step is to choose the "Beam Section" property.

Select the "Beam Section" icon  which leads to the dialogue box below. Note that there is a pulldown menu which allows you to select one of the two profiles. Select "Beam Profile.1".

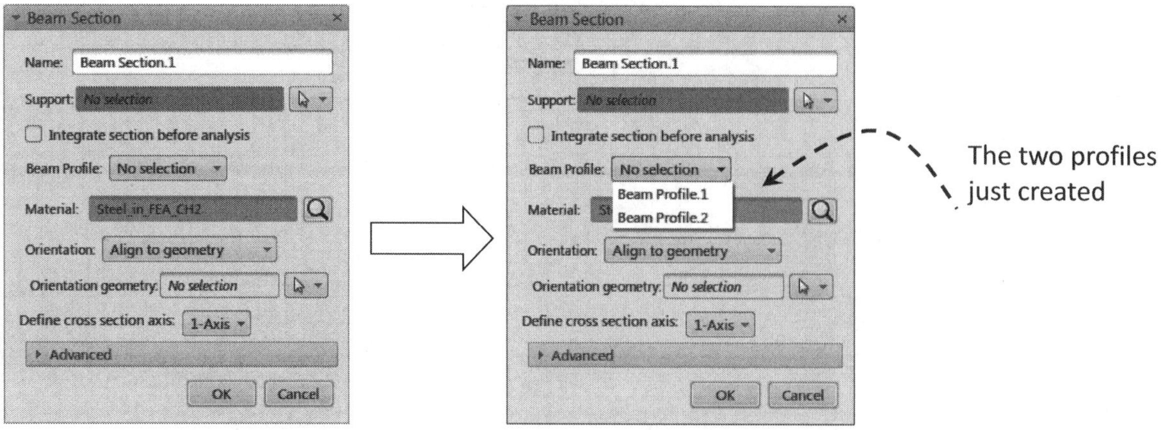

For the "Support" select the vertical left edge (Line.1). For the "Orientation Geometry", select "Point.4". **Note that multiselection (although it works), does not seem to create the appropriate sections. This means that you cannot select Line.1 and Line.2 in one shot. This is in spite of the fact that they have identical sections.**

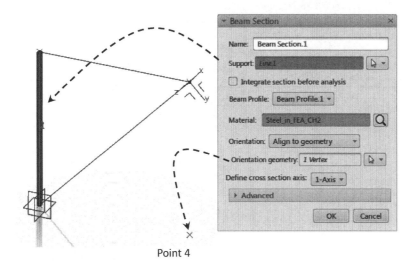

Point 4

Repeat this process for the horizontal top edge (Beam Profile.1).

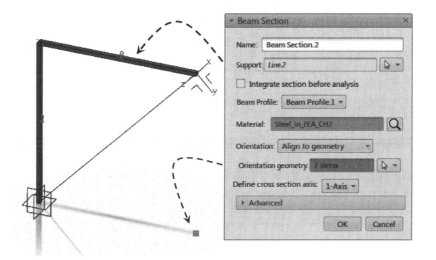

The final task in this part of the modeling is to create the beam section for the slanted line (Line.3) which is the "Profile.2".

A "zoomed in" part of the figure shows the rectangular cross sections.

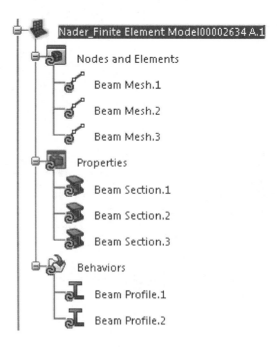

At this point, the tree indicates that the mesh and section properties have been successfully defined. If the "colored" section properties are distracting, one can place the curser on the corresponding branch, right click, and "Hide" the entities.

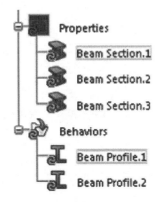

If needed (as the above tree indicates), one can update beam mesh and section properties.

"Setup" tab

Click on the "Update" icon   .

The updated tree is shown below.

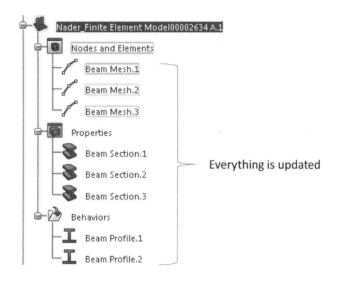

Everything is updated

There is a very useful feature which is particularly handy in dealing with one dimensional

elements (beams and links). Select the "Mesh" icon   to land in the action bar shown below.

Use the cursor to manually "Hide" the "Properties" and the "3D Shape" of the part, leaving only the one dimensional beam elements on the screen as shown on the right.

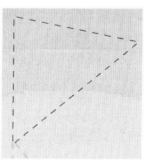

Select the "Shrink Element" icon to get the three sliding bars allowing to shrink the elements as shown below.

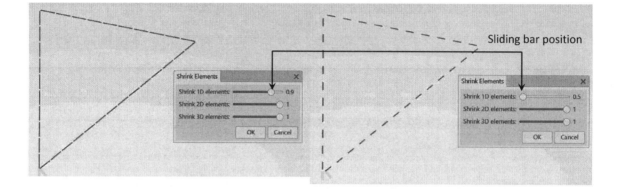

Dragging the top sliding bar allows one to shrink the elements for visual inspection. The figure clearly indicates the presence of the beam elements on the different lines. There are ten elements on the horizontal and vertical lines and fourteen on the slanted line as expected. Furthermore, the default element colors can be changed.

Creating a Scenario:

The nature of the analysis, namely, Static, Dynamic, Buckling, etc. is set in the "Structural Scenario Creation" App. Furthermore, the loads, restraints, and interaction are also defined in this application.

Locate the compass on the top left corner and click. Scroll through the applications and select the "Structural Scenario Creation" App

     Structural Scenario
                        Creation

The row of icons on the bottom of your screen changes and will appear as displayed below.

The pop up window "Simulation Type" shown below appears on the screen. Since this is strictly a structural problem, the radio button "Structural" should be selected.

Scenario created

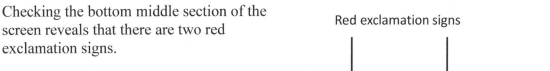

A quick glance of the tree confirms that a "Scenario" has been created.

Checking the bottom middle section of the screen reveals that there are two red exclamation signs.

These pertain to "Structural Analysis Case.1" and "No Procedures Exist".

Red exclamation signs

Click the "Finite Element Model" icon from the bottom row. This is referring to the FE model which is already created. The following pop-up window appears. Since a finite element model is already created, it appears in the list and make sure that you select that row.

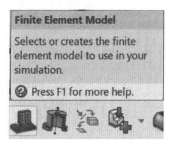

Finite Element Model

Selects or creates the finite element model to use in your simulation.

Press F1 for more help.

Select this row ───────►

Finite Element Model

Model: ⦿ Select ◯ Create

☐ Preview the highlighted model

Name	Dimension
Finite Element Model0...	3D

OK   Cancel

Choose the "Procedures" tab from the bottom row.

Select the "Procedure" tab

Standard | Setup | Procedures | Initial Conditions | Interactions | Restraints | Loads | Simulate | Display | View | AR-VR | Tools | Touch

Select the "Static Step" icon ⊢↓ from the bottom row.

Static Step

Configures a stress analysis procedure of a stable problem in which inertia effects are neglected.

❓ Press F1 for more help.

The "Static Step" dialogue box pops up. Accept all the defaults. Note that if the "Advanced" pulldown list is selected, it becomes clear that this is the point in the software where "Geometric Nonlinearities" are included, or excluded.

Static Step

Name: Static Step.1

Total time: 1 s

▾ Incrementation

Maximum increments: 1000

Time incrementation selection: Automatic ▾

Initial time increment: 1 s

Minimum time increment: 1e-005 s

Maximum time increment: 1 s

▸ Stabilization
▸ Advanced

OK   Cancel

Static Step

Name: Static Step.1

Total time: 1 s

▾ Incrementation

Maximum increments: 1000

Time incrementation selection: Automatic ▾

Initial time increment: 1 s

Minimum time increment: 1e-005 s

Maximum time increment: 1 s

▸ Stabilization
▾ Advanced

☑ Include geometric nonlinearity ◄─────── NLGEOM Included

Matrix storage: Solver Default ▾

OK   Cancel

A quick glance at the bottom left corner of the screen reveals "Green" checkmarks instead of "Red" exclamation marks.

Note the "Green" checkmarks instead of "Red" exclamations

The tree indicates that "Static Step.1" has been created. There are default basic output entities that are requested upon the creation of a Step.

Applying the Concentrated Load:

A concentrated force of 1.0E+6 N is to be applied at top left corner. The direction of the force is the "Global" y-direction. Note that this is a highly unrealistic load but we ignore yielding and buckling.

"Loads" tab

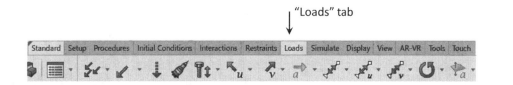

Select the "Force" icon [Force]. In the dialogue box, for the "Support" pick the top left corner, and input the magnitude of the force. **Be careful; make sure that "Point.2" is hidden first. The "Support" is not "Point.2"; it is the "vertex" and can be selected only if "Point.2" is hidden.** Note that the pulldown menu is set on "Global".

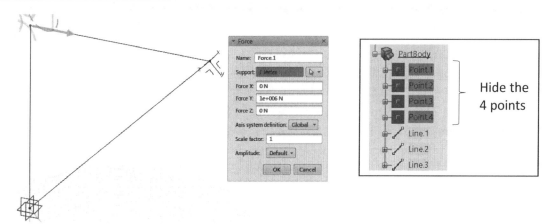

Applying the Restraints:

Be careful; make sure that Point.1, Point.2, and Point.3 are hidden first. The "Support" for restraints is not these points. It is the "vertex" and can be selected only if these points are hidden.

Select the Restraints tab of the action bar.

Choose the "fixed Displacement" icon

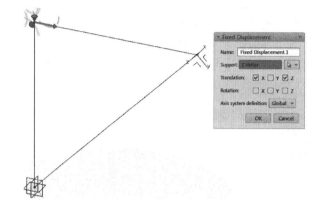

from the menu. Select the top left corner of the structure (where the force is applied). This point lies on a roller which freely moves in the y-direction. Therefore, restrain the motion in the "Global" x and z directions.

Choose the "Clamp" icon from the menu. Select the bottom left corner of the structure. This point is fixed completely.

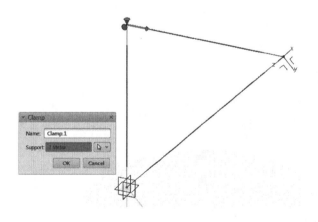

Once again, choose the "fixed Displacement" icon from the menu. Select the top right corner of the structure. This is the point that slides along the 45° ramp. Note that the Axis system to be used is the local one. In that coordinate system, there are no displacements in the x and y directions. In the event that your local coordinate system was oriented differently, the appropriate changes have to be made.

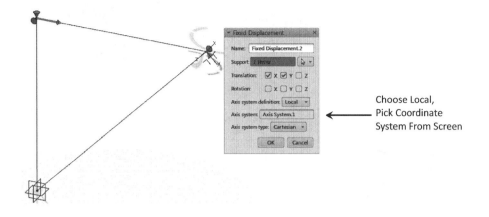

Choose Local,
Pick Coordinate
System From Screen

Consistency, Model Check, and Simulation:

Select the "Simulation" tab from the bottom row of icons on your screen.

"Simulate" tab

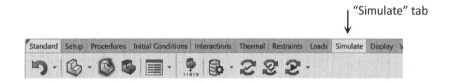

It is a good practice to perform the model and consistency check before submitting the work for the final run.
Select the "Model and Scenario Check" icon from the bottom row
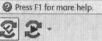.

The software goes through a check phase and if there are no issues, a message with a "Green" check mark is returned.

Simulation Checks

Complete the Model and Scenario Checks, and check the simulation for any issues likely to prevent it from running successfully.

Press F1 for more help.

Model and Scenario Checks Status	✕
✓ Model and Scenario Checks completed.	

Close   Terminate

Next select the "Simulation Checks" icon  from the bottom row of icons. Accept the number of "cores" in the pop up box below.

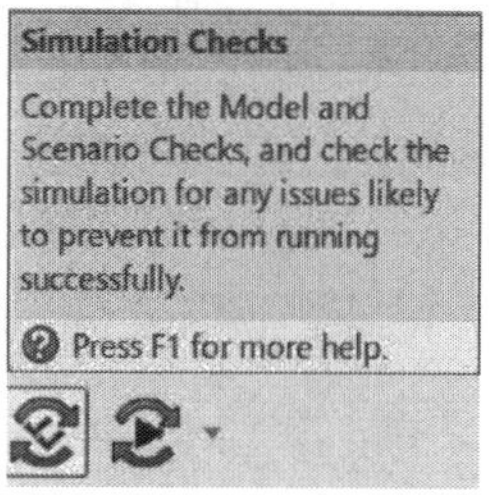

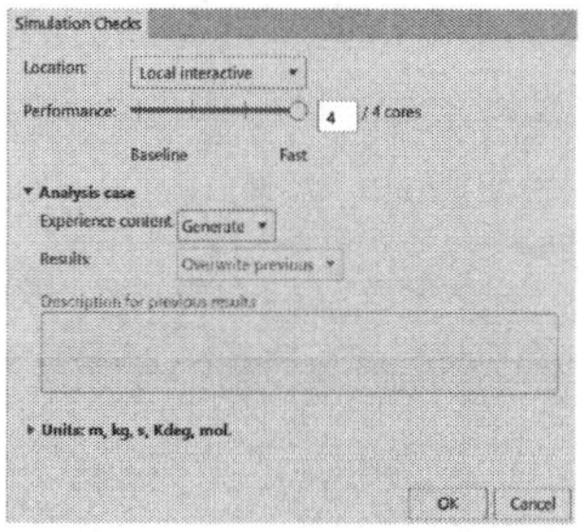

Upon the completion of the "Simulation Check", any warning messages will be available in the pop up box below.

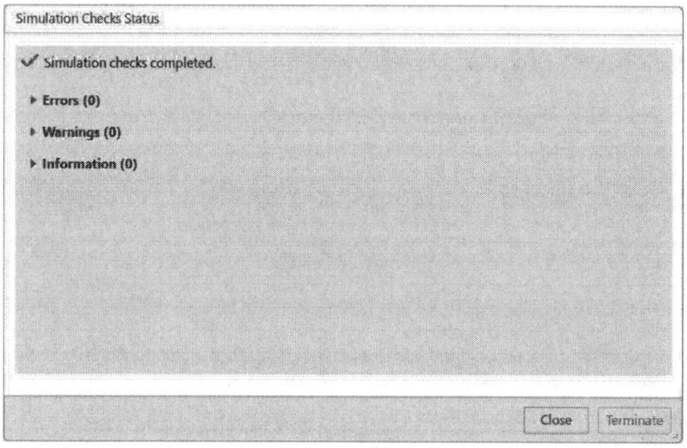

Assuming that there are no serious issues (i.e. no error messages), you are ready to submit the job for "Simulation".

Select the "Simulation" icon  from the bottom row.

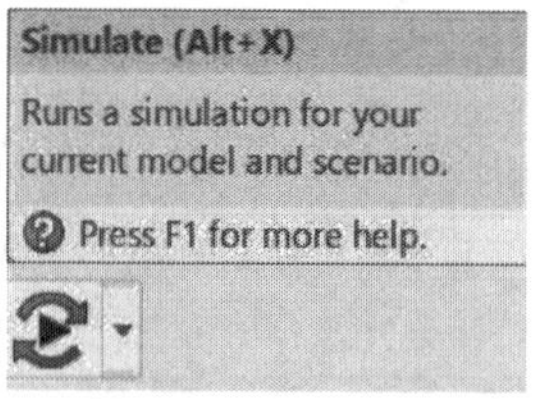

Accept the number of "cores" in the pop up box, and wait for the simulation to complete.

In the background, you should see the "Plots" dialogue box which shows the results of Frame1. Change this to Frame 2, and using the pulldown menu, plot the displacement instead. The default "Scale factor" of "1" does not display the bending of the members. In order to change the "Scale factor", double click on the displayed screen plot. In the resulting dialogue box, change the "Scale factor" to "20".

You can clearly see the bending phenomenon which was lacking in the truss analysis. The front view of the frame displacement is shown below. Note that the top right corner of the frame moves along the ramp as expected.

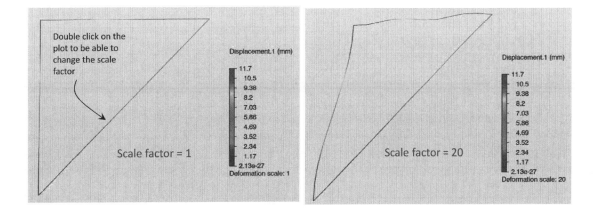

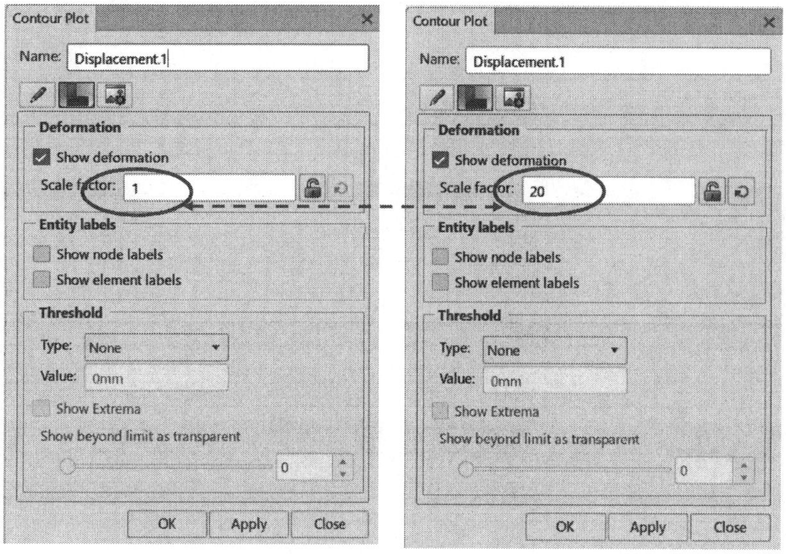
Contour Plot
Name: Displacement.1
Deformation
Show deformation
Scale factor: 1
Entity labels
Show node labels
Show element labels
Threshold
Type: None
Value: 0mm
Show Extrema
Show beyond limit as transparent
0
OK
Apply
Close
Contour Plot
Name: Displacement.1
Deformation
Show deformation
Scale factor: 20
Entity labels
Show node labels
Show element labels
Threshold
Type: None
Value: 0mm
Show Extrema
Show beyond limit as transparent
0
OK
Apply
Close

Exercise 1

Consider the frame structure shown below. Choose dimensions and material properties of your own choice, conduct an analysis on 3DEXPERIECE and compare your results with the theoretical solution below. Note that the equations given correspond to one element in the vertical and the horizontal sections. You may want to try that first.

$$\frac{EI}{L}\begin{bmatrix} \frac{A}{I}+\frac{12}{L^2} & 0 & \frac{6}{L} \\ 0 & \frac{A}{I}+\frac{12}{L^2} & -\frac{6}{L} \\ \frac{6}{L} & -\frac{6}{L} & 8 \end{bmatrix}\begin{bmatrix} u \\ v \\ \theta \end{bmatrix} = \begin{bmatrix} \alpha A\Delta T \\ 0 \\ 0 \end{bmatrix}$$

The variables $[u \quad v \quad \theta]$ correspond to the displacements and the rotation of the free point.

Exercise 2

Consider the beam shown below. Choose dimensions and material properties of your own choice, conduct an analysis on 3DEXPERIECE and compare your results with the theoretical solution below. Note that the equations given correspond to one element in the vertical and the horizontal sections. You may want to try that first.

$$\frac{EI}{L}\begin{bmatrix} \frac{12}{L^2}+\frac{A}{I} & -\frac{6}{L} \\ -\frac{6}{L} & 4 \end{bmatrix}\begin{bmatrix} v \\ \theta \end{bmatrix} = \begin{bmatrix} -F \\ 0 \end{bmatrix}$$

The variables $[u \quad \theta]$ correspond to the displacements and the rotation of the free point. It is obvious that the ramp angle implies $v = -u$

Notes:

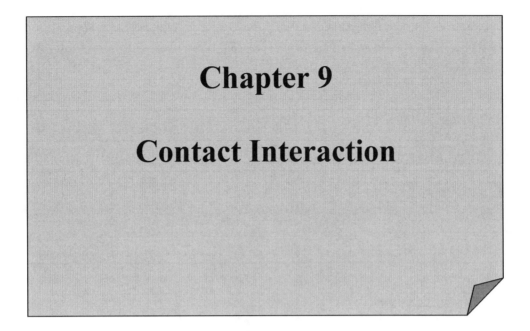

Chapter 9

Contact Interaction

Objective:

In this chapter, a contact analysis is carried out where a plate is pressing on a cylinder resulting in the bending of the plate. The analysis is in the elastic-plastic range resulting in the permanent deformation of the plate.

Problem Statement:

A rectangular plate is clamped at one end and is being pulled down by 0.5 cm in the negative "z" direction. It establishes contact with a cylindrical shaft whose ends are also clamped as shown.

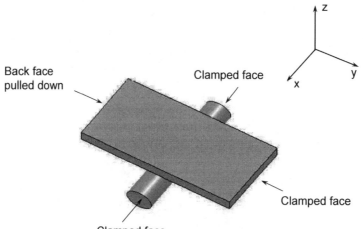

Due to symmetry, half of the assembly needs to be modeled where the planes of symmetry are assumed to have roller boundary conditions. The "half" model is displayed below.

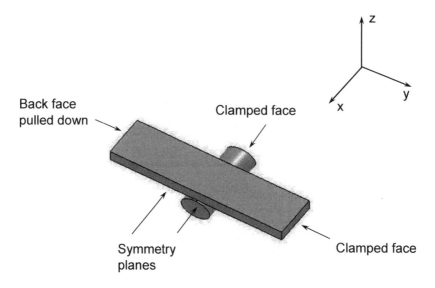

The dimensions of the half-plate and the half-cylinder are displayed in the side view and the top views below. There is an initial gap of 0.1 cm between the two parts.

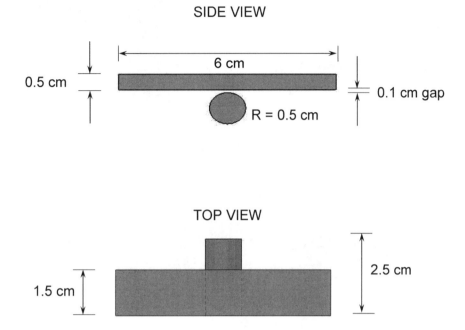

The two parts are assumed to be made of AISI 1020 hot-rolled steel. The strains are large enough to cause permanent plastic deformation. The nonlinear stress-strain data will be presented later. However, the Young's modulus and Poisson's ratio are assumed to be 200GPa and 0.3 respectively.

Creation of the Assembly

Click on the compass on the top left corner of
the screen. This will open the applications
available in 3DEXPERIENCE.

From the list, select the "Assembly Design"
App   .

It is assumed that you have already created the
two parts, the plate and the cylinder. You then
insert them into the assembly as "Existing 3D
Part" and position them properly. The
positioning can be achieved using the
"Engineering Connections" icon, if necessary.

The screen looks as shown below. Note that the symmetry condition has been used to
reduce the model.

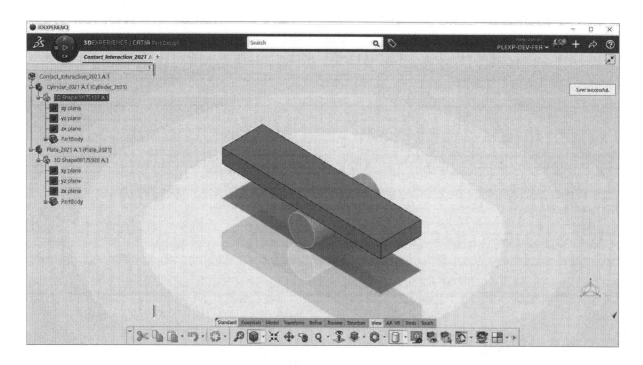

The next step is to create and apply the elastic and the elastic-plastic material data.

Applying the Material Properties:

Click on the compass on the top left corner of the screen. This will open the applications menu available in 3DEXPERIENCE.

From the list, select the "Material Definition" App.

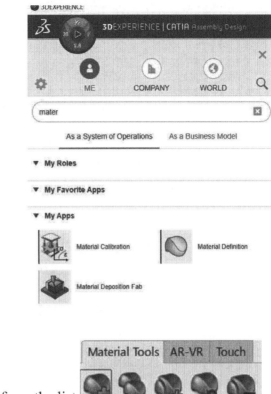

Choose the "Create Material" icon from the list.

This opens the dialogue box shown. Type the desired name and make sure that the "Simulation Domain" box is checked. This is just a "shell" and the actual data needs to be inputted later.

Type the desired name

Must be checked

Upon closing this dialogue box, you will find yourself in the material database shown in the image below. The "shell" was given the title "Contact Interaction" and you can easily find it in the top part of the database. All materials created by the user are stored in this location. We could have used one of these materials if deemed appropriate.

It may be interesting to check the creation date of your material. Use the cursor and double click on the material "shell" just created.

This "shell" was just created.
Double click on it.

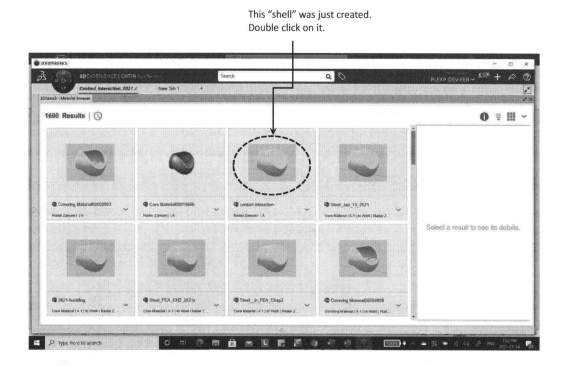

Place the cursor on the material applied to one of the parts (does not matter whether it is the "Cylinder" or the "Plate"), expand the tree, and double click on the second line, namely "Material Simulation".

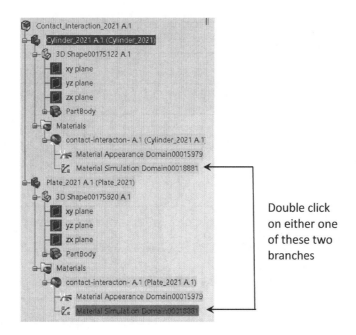

In the ensuing box, input the Young's modulus "200 GPa" and the Poisson's ratio "0.3".

Since the deformation will be significant, and the parts are to behave plastically, the stress-strain curve will be inputted in the supplied table directly or imported as an Excel spreadsheet. In the present chapter, the data is inputted directly as shown.

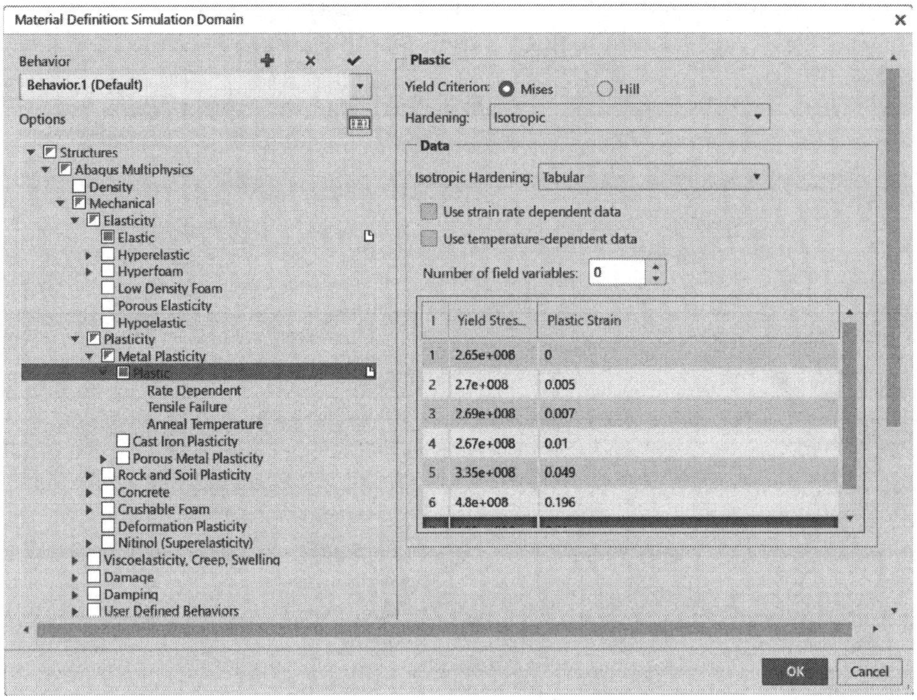

As indicated earlier, one can also upload an Excel spreadsheet with the tabulated data.

	A	B	C
1	yield stress (Pa)	plastic strain	
2	2.65E+08	0	
3	2.70E+08	0.005	
4	2.69E+08	0.007	
5	2.67E+08	0.01	
6	3.35E+08	0.049	
7	4.80E+08	0.196	
8	4.88E+08	0.21	
9			
10			

Warning:

Before you proceed to the next step, make sure that you are in the top branch of the tree, i.e., the "Assembly Design" workbench. This can be achieved by double clicking on the top branch.

Double click on the top branch to make sure that you are in "Assembly Design"

Creating the Finite Element Model:

Locate the compass on the top left corner of the screen and click on it. Scroll through the applications and select the "Structural Model

Structural Model Creation

Creation" App   .

The dialogue box shown on the right appears. For now, use the "Automatic" radio button. Other options are for user control of the meshing process. In the case of "Automatic", tetrahedral parabolic elements are created.

The entire assembly consisting of two parts
has been meshed. There two elements and two
solid sections displayed in the tree.

The main reason behind the "Warning"
statement earlier is to make sure that both
parts (Cylinder and Plate) are meshed
simultaneously.

From the bottom row of icons, select the "Mesh" icon   .

The bottom row's appearance now looks as shown below.

Select the "Update" icon   . Upon updating, the mesh appears on the screen.

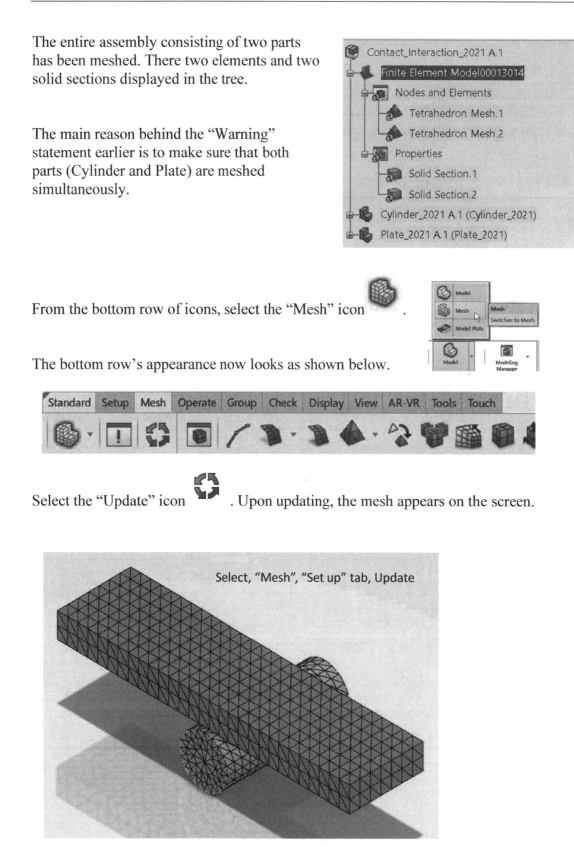

Select, "Mesh", "Set up" tab, Update

Creating a Scenario:

Locate the compass on the top left corner of the screen and click on it. Scroll through the applications and select the "Structural Scenario Creation" App

Structural Model
Creation

The row of icons on the bottom of your screen changes as shown here.

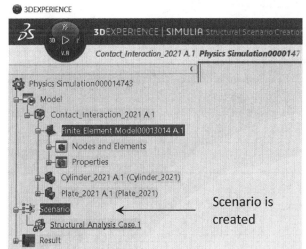

The pop-up window "Simulation Initialization" shown on the right appears on the screen. Since this is strictly a structural problem, the radio button "Structural" should be selected.

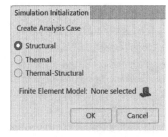

A quick glance at the tree confirms that a "Scenario" has been created.

Scenario is created

Checking the bottom middle section of the screen reveals that there are two red exclamation signs.

These pertain to "Structural Analysis Case.1" and "No Procedures Exist".

Red exclamation signs

Click the "Select the Finite Element Model" icon from the bottom row. The following pop-up window appears.

Finite Element Model

Selects or creates the finite element model to use in your simulation.

Press F1 for more help.

Since there is already a finite element model created, it appears in the list and make sure that you select that row.

Select this line

Finite Element Model

Model: Select ○ Create

Preview the highlighted model

Name	Dimension
Finite Element Model	3D

OK   Cancel

Select the "Procedures" tab from the action bar (bottom row).

Select the "Procedure" tab

Standard | Setup | Procedures | Initial Conditions | Interactions | Restraints | Loads | Simulate | Display | View | AR-VR | Tools | Touch

Select the "Static Step" icon from the bottom row.

Static Step

Configures a stress analysis procedure of a stable problem in which inertia effects are neglected.

Press F1 for more help.

The "Static Step" dialogue box pops up. Accept all the defaults. Note that if the "Advanced" pulldown list is selected, it becomes clear that this is the point in the software where "Geometric Nonlinearities" are included, or excluded.

A quick glance at the bottom middle section of the screen reveals "Green" checkmarks instead of "Red" exclamation marks.

Applying the Restraints:

Select the Restraints tab from the action bar. Choose the "Clamp" icon and use it for the two faces of the assembly as shown.

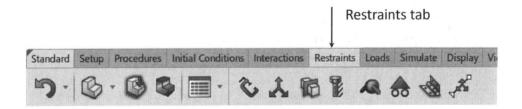

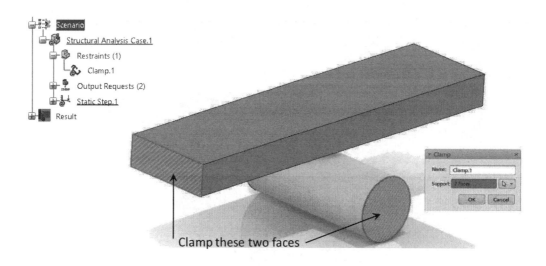

Clamp these two faces

The next task is to apply the restraints due to the symmetry considerations. Choose the "Planar Symmetry" icon 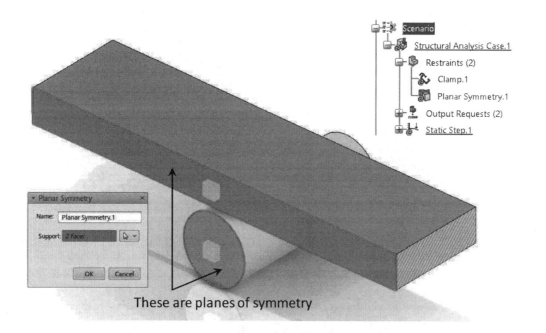 and the two faces of the parts where the symmetry cuts were made.

These are planes of symmetry

Applying the Load:

The free end face of the plate is given a downward displacement of 5mm. Needless to say, this displacement can only be the result of an applied load on the face. This being the case, choose the "Loads" tab of the action bar. Select the Restraints tab from the action bar.

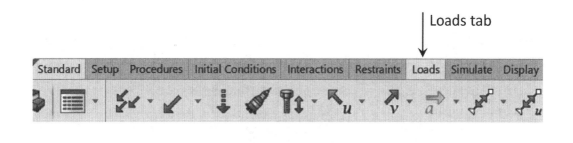

Pick the "Applied Translation" icon 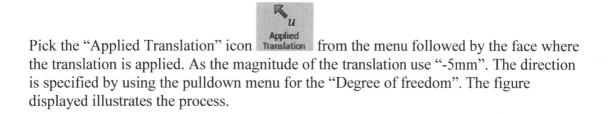 from the menu followed by the face where the translation is applied. As the magnitude of the translation use "-5mm". The direction is specified by using the pulldown menu for the "Degree of freedom". The figure displayed illustrates the process.

Defining the Contact Interaction:

Choose the "Interactions" tab from the Scenario action bar. This tab was not used in the previous chapters because they all consisted of a single part. The role of this tab is only meaningful for assemblies (or self-contact) where there are several parts interacting with each other.

Clearly, in this context, interaction means parts contacting each other.

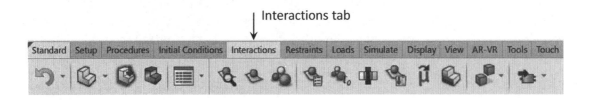

Interactions tab

Note that the name of all icons pertaining to this tab has the word "contact" associated with them. From the list, select the "Surface-based Contact" icon ![Surface-based Contact]. In the present problem, the bottom face of the plate is in direct contact with the surface of the cylinder. These two surfaces are traditionally referred to as the "Contact Pair". In these situations, one of the surfaces can be viewed as the "M" whereas the other one as the "S".

There are some guidelines for this selection. For example, the surface which has a finer mesh and/or the surface with substantial curvature is ordinarily taken as the "S". In our situation, the mesh densities are roughly the same whereas the cylinder has the curvature. Therefore, the cylinder is selected as the "S". See the figure on the next page for the present choices.

Simulation Stage:

At this point, all the preliminary work is completed, and one can simulate the problem. Select the "Simulation" tab from the action bar.

"Simulate" tab

It was pointed out earlier in the other chapters that it is a good idea to perform consistency check and scenario check before submitting the job for a full-blown simulation. These can be done by the first two icons on the left of this list below.

We will ignore this recommendation and by selecting the "Simulate" icon submit the job.

Accept the defaults in the resulting dialogue box.

A large number of warning messages are generated which is not surprising. The mesh used is very coarse and no attempt for getting a good mesh was made. Despite this, the job successfully completes as shown in the bottom figure.

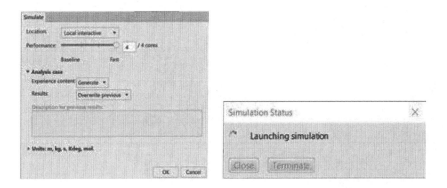

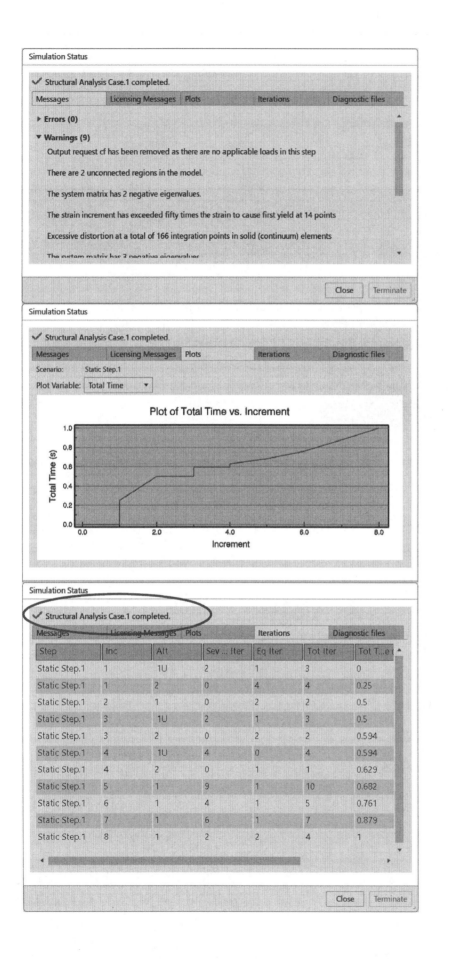

Results (Post processing):

Once you close (or move) the obstructing dialogue boxes, you must be in the "Results" section and the bottom row should appear as shown on the right.

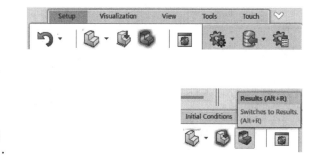

If not, click on the "Results" icon .

In the background, you should see the "Plots" dialogue box which shows the results of Frame1, and the results after the first iteration. If the first of the "Plots" dialogue box is highlighted, the value of the von Mises stress is zero as shown below.

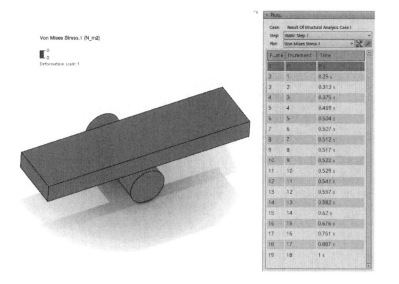

This is not surprising as the first row is before any incremental load is applied. If the load is zero, the displacement and stress are both zero. Use the cursor to select frame #10 of the "Plots" dialogue box.

The plots of von Mises stress, plastic strain, and the displacement for this frame are all given in the next page.

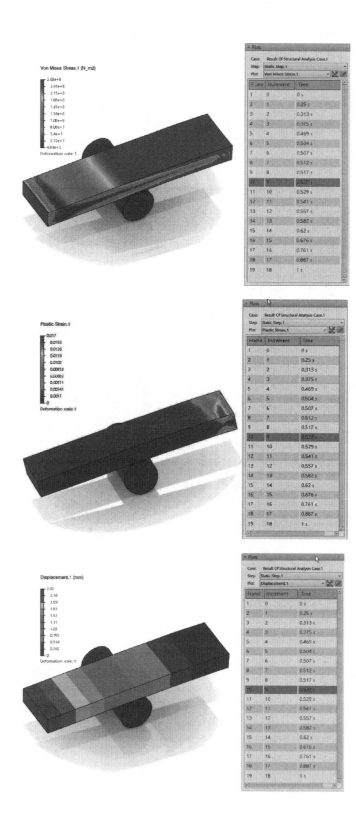

The plots for the final frame, i.e. 5mm downward displacement is provided below.

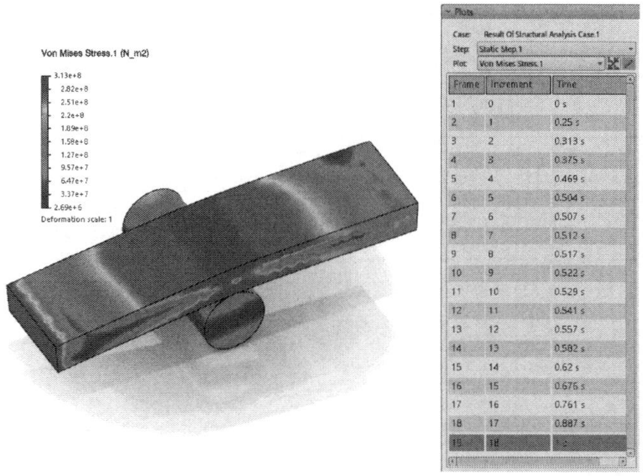

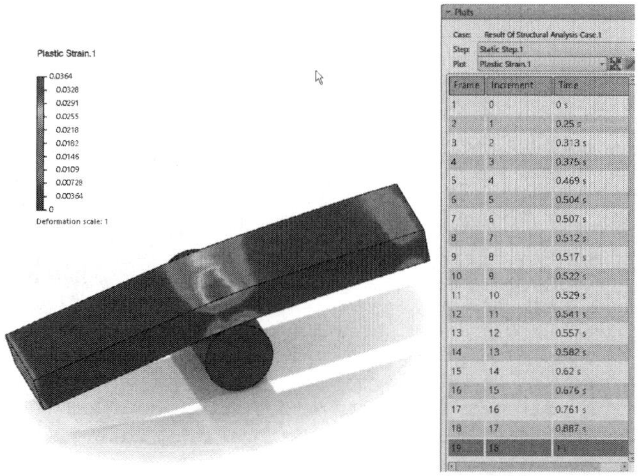

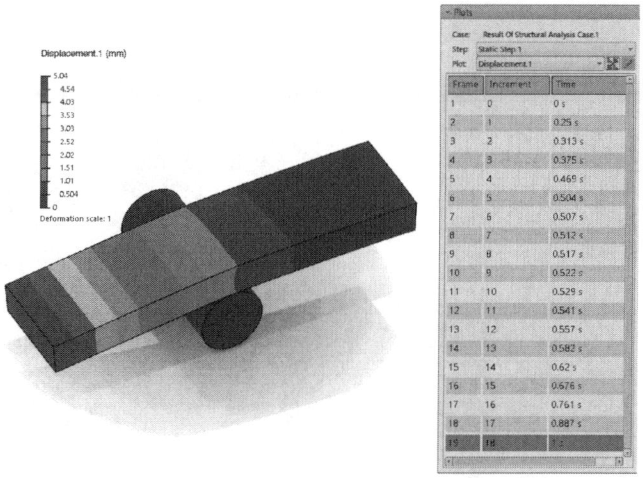

To have a better idea of the deformation magnitude (with no scaling performed), the side view of the assembly result is shown to the right.

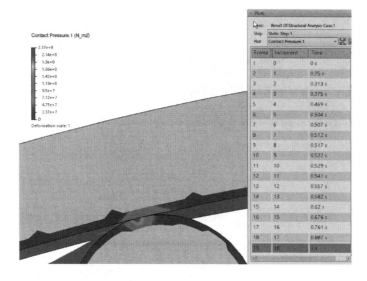

Finally, the contact pressure contour for the final frame is also displayed below.

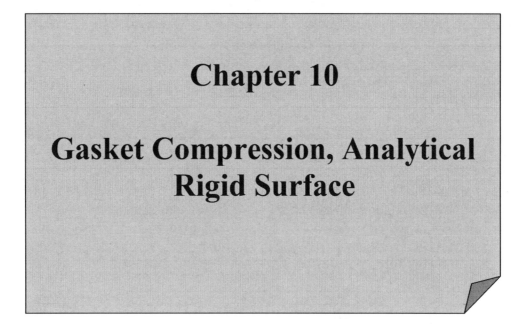

Chapter 10

Gasket Compression, Analytical Rigid Surface

Objective:

In this chapter, a hyperplastic gasket is compressed between two hard plates. The gasket is assumed to be long enough where the plane strain assumption can be justified. The plate is modeled as an analytical rigid surface available in 3DEXPERIENCE.

Problem Statement:

A very long rubber gasket is being compressed between two rigid plates as displayed below. The cross section of the gasket is a circle of radius 20 cm. Since the gasket is assumed to be long compared to its circular dimension, the problem can be represented by a plane strain condition. However, 2D plane stress/strain elements are not available in 3DEXPERIENCE, and therefore, the modeling needs to be done in 3D.
Due to symmetry, a quarter on the cross section is considered and the depth (in the longitudinal direction) is assumed to be 5 cm. This number is strictly arbitrary, as long as the resulting 3D mesh is reasonable.

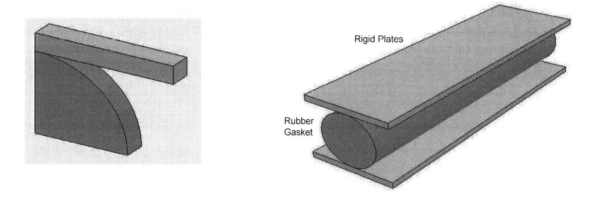

There are three options for modeling the problem which are shown below.

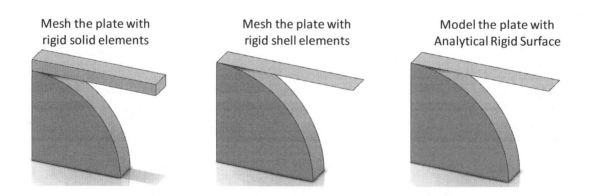

We choose to follow the last strategy. There are, however, some strict requirements when the Analytical Rigid Surface is being used. These are outlined on the next page.

Requirements "Analytical Rigid Surface:

The highlights of the requirements are provided in bullet form below.

- The rigid surface must be either "extruded" or "revolved" about an axis.
- In the event that the curve of the "extruded" curve is drawn in a sketch, the plane of the sketch must be normal to the direction of the sweep (direction of the extrusion).
- Analytical rigid surfaces are always the "master surface" in a contact pair and should be smooth to avoid convergence issues.
- The motion of the reference point associated with the surface dictates the motion of the surface.
- The surface is a part within an assembly.

Mooney-Rivlin Hyperelasticity Model:

The plate is a rigid object and therefore its properties are not used. The gasket is hyperelastic and does not require Young's modulus and Poisson's ratio.

The model selected for the gasket is the simple Mooney-Rivlin strain energy expression which is provided by

$$U = C_{10}(\bar{I}_1 - 3) + C_{01}(\bar{I}_2 - 3)$$

In this chapter, the values of the constants are taken to be $C_{10} = 0.293$ MPa and $C_{01} = 0.177$ MPa respectively. In a modified version of this model, a third parameter D appears which is assumed to be zero.

It is important to realize that because of the incompressible behavior of the gasket, the tetrahedron elements (of the gasket) used for meshing purposes have to be of the Hybrid type. Therefore, only C3D10MH or C3D10H can be used. However, the efficiency of the former is much better than the latter. It is suggested that you leave this issue to the software for default selection.

Creation of the Assembly:

 Assembly Design

Click on the compass on the top left corner of the screen. This will open the CAD applications available in 3DEXPERIENCE.

From the list, select the "Assembly

Design" App  .

It is assumed that you have already created the two parts, the plate and the gasket. You then insert them into the assembly as "Existing 3D Part" and position them properly. The positioning can be achieved using the "Engineering Connections" icon, if necessary. The screen looks as shown below. Note that the symmetry condition has been used to reduce the model.

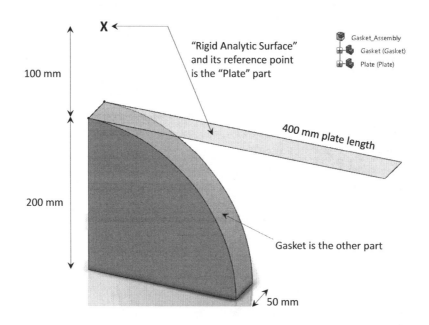

Applying the Hyperelastic Material Properties:

Choose the "Create Material" icon 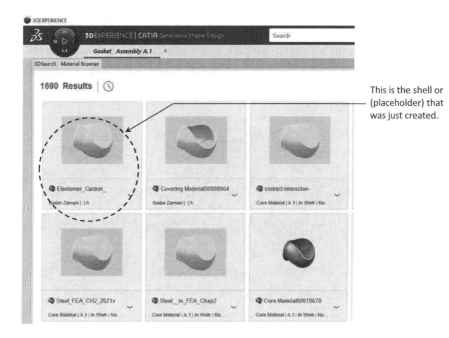 from the "Tools" tab of the action bar below.

This opens the dialogue box shown. Type the desired name and make sure that the "Simulation Domain" box is checked. This is just a "shell" and the actual data needs to be inputted later.

Upon closing this dialogue box, you will find yourself in the material database shown below. The "shell" was given the title "Elastomer_Gasket" and you can easily find it in the top part of the database. All materials created by the user are stored in this location. Place the cursor in the material "shell" that you created, right click, and select "Apply".

Upon closing the material database window above, you can left click on the "Gasket" part to apply the material. This can be confirmed by the appearance of the material branch as shown below.

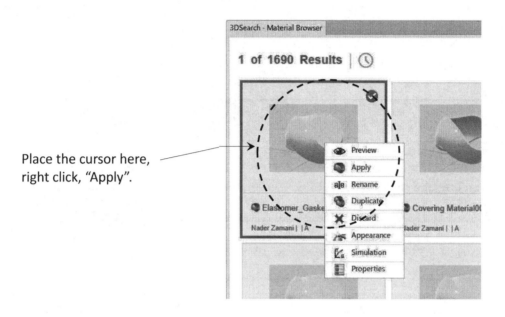

Place the cursor here, right click, "Apply".

A quick glance at the tree indicates that a "Shell" or placeholder for the material has been created. The instructions to input the material property data is given on the next page.

This is just a shell. Double click on it to input data

Double click on the branch to be able to input the data.
In the resulting dialogue box, follow the four steps outlined below.

Step 1- check "Structures"
Step 2- check "Abaqus Multiphysics"
Step 3- check "Mechanical"
Step 4- check "Elasticity"
Step 5- check "Hyperelastic"
Step 6- Use the pull-down menu to choose the "Mooney-Rivlin" model
Step 7- Input the material parameters.

$$C_{10} = 293000 \ N\_m2$$
$$C_{01} = 179000 \ N\_m2$$
$$D = 0 \ Pa$$

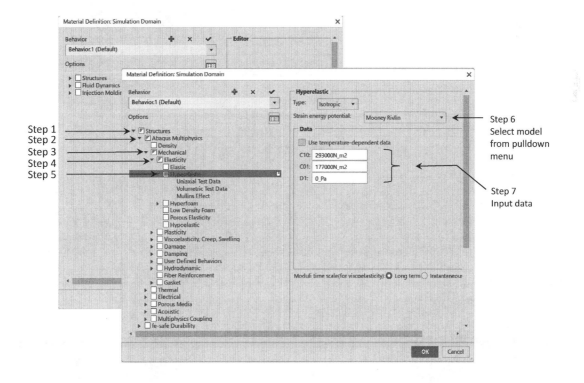

The plate is assumed to be an "Analytical Rigid Surface" and therefore, there is no material property associated with it. Before proceeding to the next step, namely entering the "Structural Model Creation" App, make sure that you are at the assembly level and not the part level. To do this, double click on the top branch.

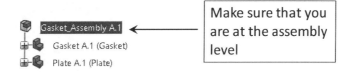

Creating the Finite Element Model:

As indicated on the previous page, before proceeding with the rest of the section, make sure that you are in the "Assembly" App. If you are not already there, double click on the top branch.

Locate the compass on the top left corner of the screen and select it. Scroll through the applications and select the "Structural Model Creation" App

The row of icons on the bottom of your screen (action bar) changes and will appear as displayed below.

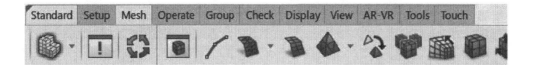

The dialogue box shown on the right, "Create Finite Element Model", appears. For now, use the "Automatic" radio button. Other options are for user control of the meshing process. In the case of "Automatic", tetrahedral parabolic elements are created.

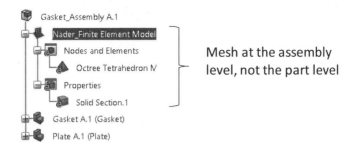

Mesh at the assembly level, not the part level

It is important that the mesh is created at the assembly level as the tree indicates. The "Analytical Rigid Surface" does not have a mesh associated with it. The mesh that appears in the tree corresponds to the Gasket.

Select the "Abstractions" tab from the action bar.

Abstractions tab

Choose the "Analytical Rigid Surface" icon

Analytical Rigid Surface from the menu.

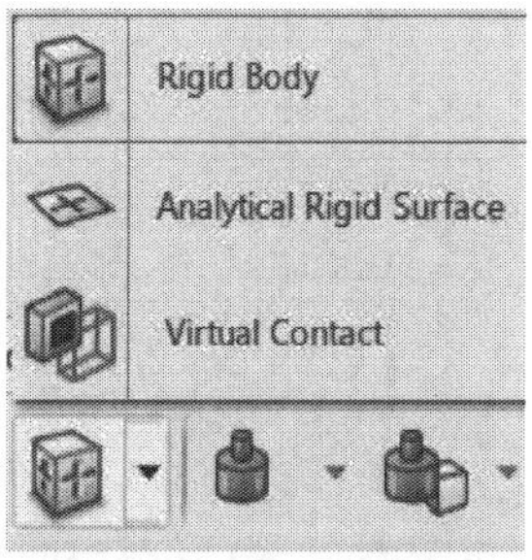

This action leads to the "Analytical Rigid Surface" dialogue box shown below.

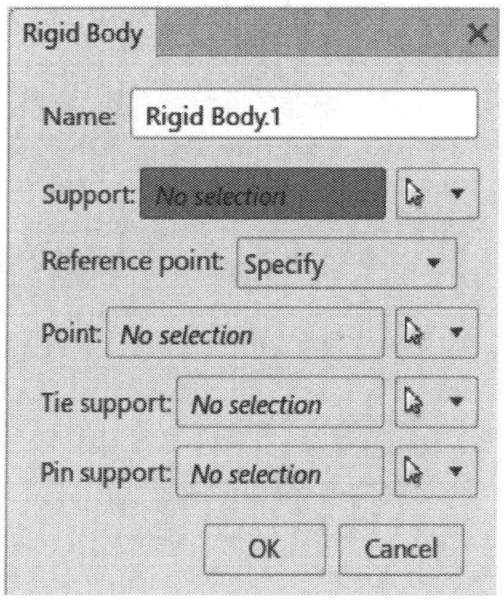

Select the extruded surface and the reference point to fully define the surface.

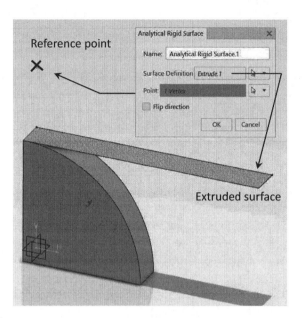

The tree reflects the creation of the analytical rigid surface.

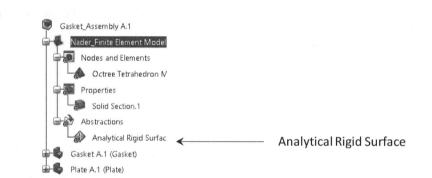

Analytical Rigid Surface

Select the meshing tab and use the "Mesh" icon 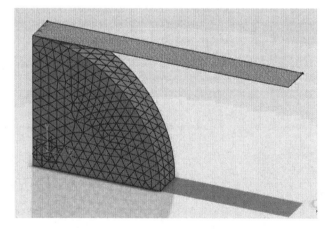 to display the mesh.

Creating a Scenario:

Locate the compass on the top left corner of the screen, and select it as shown on the right. Scroll through the applications and select the "Structural Scenario Creation" App

Structural Model
Creation

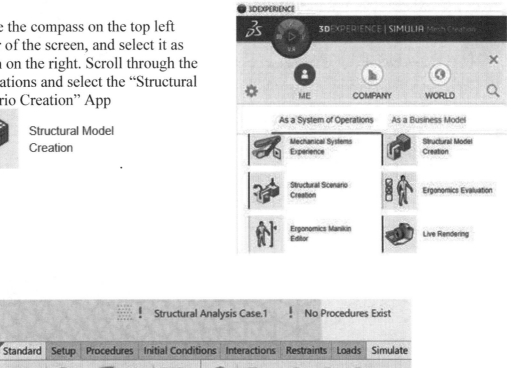

The pop-up window "Simulation Initialization" shown below appears on the screen. Since this is strictly a structural problem, the radio button "Structural" should be selected.

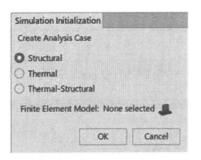

Checking the bottom middle section of the screen reveals that there are two red exclamation signs.
These pertain to "Structural Analysis Case.1" and "No Procedures Exist".

Red exclamation signs

Click the "Select the Finite Element Model" icon

from the bottom row. This is referring to the model which is already created. The following pop-up window appears.

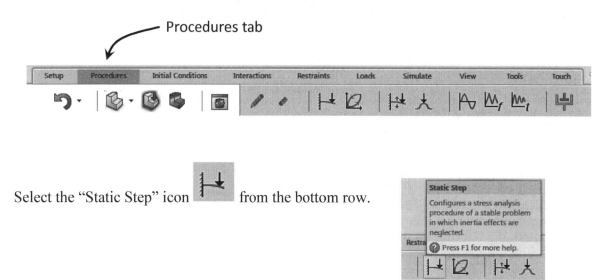

Since there is already a finite element model created, it appears in the list and make sure that you select that row.

Select this row

Select the "Procedures" tab from the action bar (bottom row).

Procedures tab

| Setup | Procedures | Initial Conditions | Interactions | Restraints | Loads | Simulate | View | Tools | Touch |

Select the "Static Step" icon from the bottom row.

The "Static Step" dialogue box pops up. Accept all the defaults. Note that if the "Advanced" pulldown list is selected, it becomes clear that this is the point in the software where "Geometric Nonlinearities" are included, or excluded.

NLGEOM included

A quick glance at the bottom of the screen reveals "Green" checkmarks instead of "Red" exclamation marks.

Note the "Green" checkmarks instead of "Red" exclamations

If the mesh is obscuring your view, you can turn it off by different methods. One way of achieving this is to right click on the screen and select the "Visualization Management" icon. In the resulting dialogue box, select the "FE Model" and choose "Hide". This will hide the mesh.

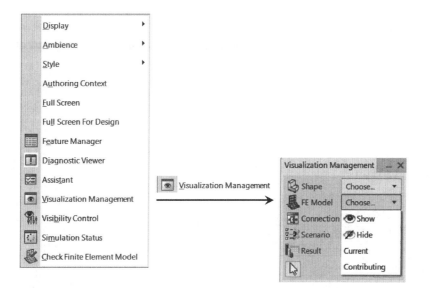

Creating the Restraints:

Select the Restraints tab from the action bar and use the "Planar Symmetry" icon Planar Symmetry ; choose the four flat sides of the Gasket as planes of symmetry. You will have to repeat these four times as shown below.

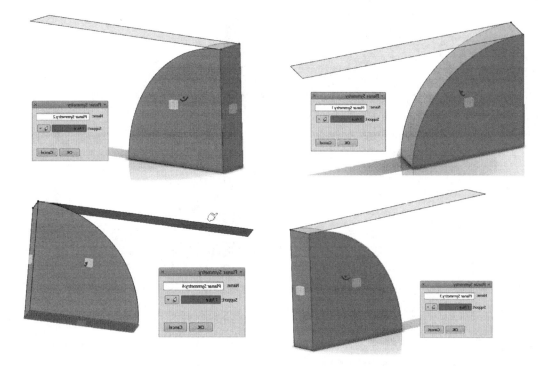

The next step is to restrain the reference point of the "Analytical Rigid Surface". Choose the "Fixed Displacement" icon from the menu. For the "Support", select the reference point as shown. The only free displacement is in the vertical direction, (namely the z-translation).

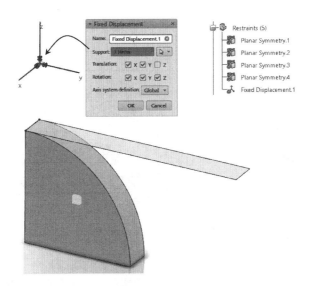

Creating the Load:

Choose the Loads tab from the action bar and use the "Applied Translation" icon ![Applied Translation] from the menu to choose the reference point as the "Support". For the "Translation" value input "-100mm". This means a downward displacement of 100 mm.

Creating Interactions:

Pick the "Interactions" tab from the action bar.

"Interactions" tab

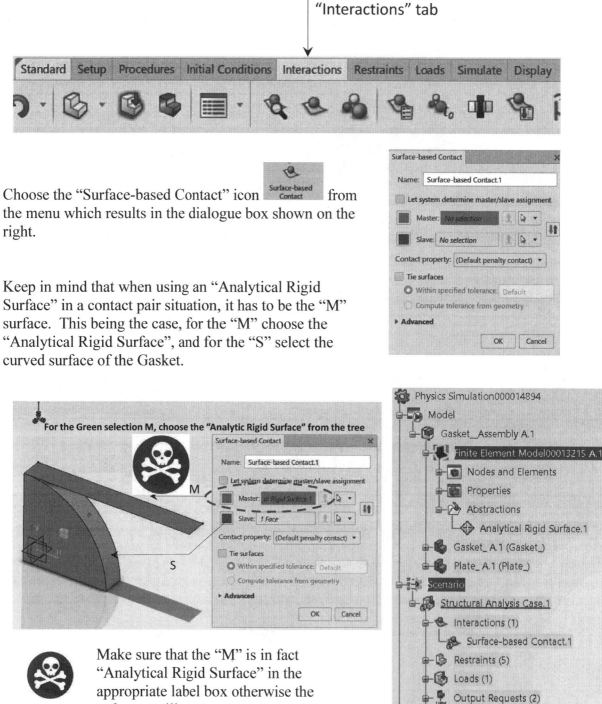

Choose the "Surface-based Contact" icon from the menu which results in the dialogue box shown on the right.

Keep in mind that when using an "Analytical Rigid Surface" in a contact pair situation, it has to be the "M" surface. This being the case, for the "M" choose the "Analytical Rigid Surface", and for the "S" select the curved surface of the Gasket.

Make sure that the "M" is in fact "Analytical Rigid Surface" in the appropriate label box otherwise the software will not run.

Simulation Stage:

At this point, all the preliminary work is completed, and one can simulate the problem. Select the "Simulation" tab from the action bar.

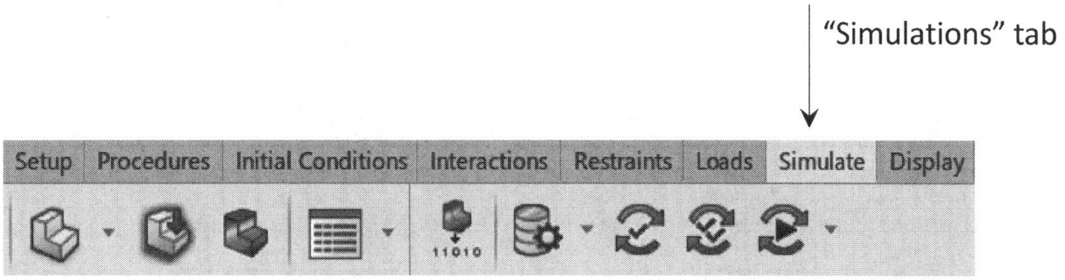

"Simulations" tab

It was pointed out earlier in the other chapters that it is a good idea to perform consistency check and scenario check before submitting the job for a full-blown simulation. These can be done by the first two icons on the left of this list below.

Select the "Model and Scenario Check" icon from the bottom row. The software goes through a check phase and if there are no issues, a message with a "Green" check mark is returned.

Next, select the "Simulation Checks" icon  from the bottom row of icons. Accept the number of "Cores" in the pop up box below and perform the checks.

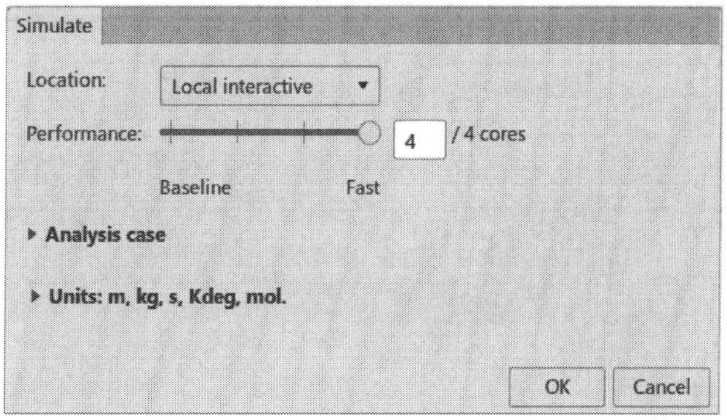

The simulation checks but some warning messages are generated which are shown on the next page.

Simulation Checks Status

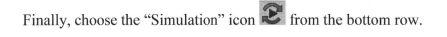

As in the past, let us ignore the above warning message and "Simulate" anyway. You will see that this leads to serious problems.

Finally, choose the "Simulation" icon 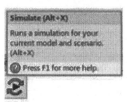 from the bottom row.

The simulation completes and the number of iterations for each increment are reflected in the resulting pop up box. The same warning appears again and the plot of the deformation indicates that the "Analytic Rigid Surface" goes through the cylinder.

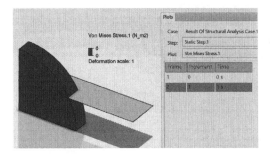

Based on the warning message, one suspects that the two contacting surfaces do not "see" each other. One way to fix this issue is to return to the definition of the "Analytic Rigid Surface" and "flip" direction.

Double click on the branch of the tree where "Analytic Rigid Surface.1" resides. This opens up the associated dialogue box.

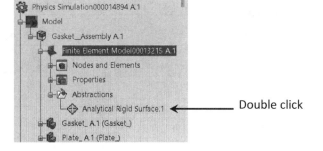

In the resulting dialogue box "Flip" the direction as shown.

Run the "Simulation" again by selecting the icon from the bottom row. This time the software will run and although there are other warning messages, the issue of the two parts seeing each other is rectified.

Results (Post processing):

Once you close (or move) the obstructing dialogue boxes, you must be in the "Results" section and the bottom row should appear as shown below.

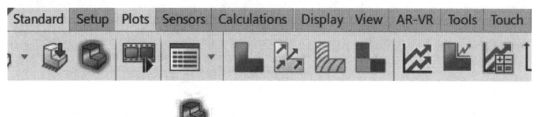

If not, click on the "Results" icon .

The deformed shape of the gasket at increments 2 and 17 are displayed below.

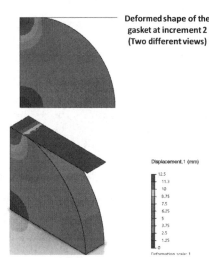

Deformed shape of the gasket at increment 2 (Two different views)

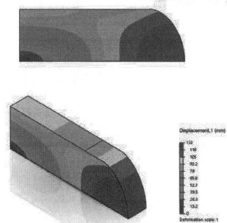

Deformed shape of the gasket at increment 17 (Two different views)

The von Mises stress distribution in the gasket at increments 2 and 17 are also displayed below.

Von Mises stress in the gasket at increment 1 (Two different views)

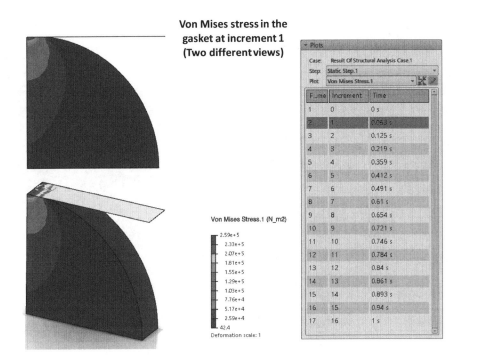

Von Mises Stress.1 (N_m2)

2.59e+5	
2.33e+5	
2.07e+5	
1.81e+5	
1.55e+5	
1.29e+5	
1.03e+5	
7.76e+4	
5.17e+4	
2.59e+4	
42.4	

Deformation scale: 1

Von Mises stress in the gasket at increment 17 (Two different views)

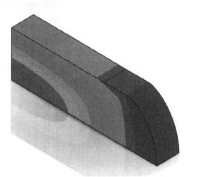

Von Mises Stress.1 (N_m2)

4.3e+6	
3.87e+6	
3.44e+6	
3.01e+6	
2.58e+6	
2.15e+6	
1.72e+6	
1.29e+6	
8.65e+5	
4.36e+5	
6.41e+3	

Deformation scale: 1

Notes:

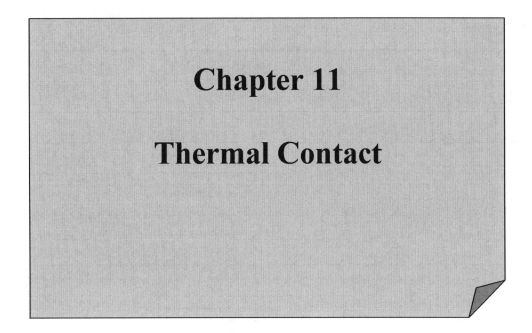

Chapter 11

Thermal Contact

Objective:

This chapter is designed to highlight the use of the thermal contact feature that is available in 3DEXPERIENCE. Thermal contact problems arise in many practical situations in which there is heat transfer accruing between two or more regions which are in imperfect contact. These types of problems are experienced in simulations involving manufacturing processes such as casting, welding, and metal forming.

Problem Statement:

The figure shows a schematic for a bonding operation that utilizes a laser to provide a constant heat flux, q, across the top of a thin, adhesive-backed, plastic film to be affixed to a metal strip. Due to the symmetry conditions, only one quarter of the assembly needs to be modeled. The sector and the appropriate dimensions are shown on the bottom of the page.

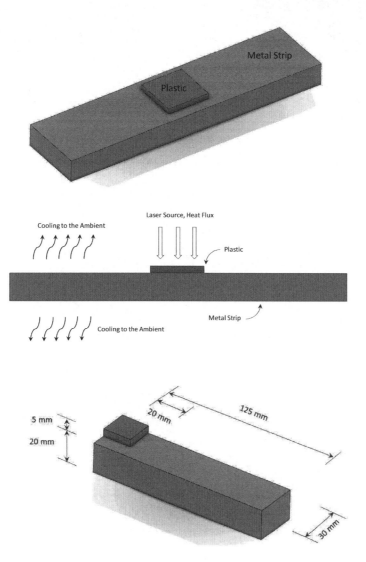

The thermophysical properties of the metal strip and the plastic are described below.

Metal Strip: Density $\rho = 2710\ kg/m^3$
               Specific heat $c_p = 220\ J/kg.K$
               Conductivity $k = 263\ W/m\,K$

Plastic Strip: Density $\rho = 1798\ kg/m^3$
               Specific heat $c_p = 200\ J/kg.K$
               Conductivity $k = 26\ W/m\,K$

The upper and the lower surfaces experience convection due to blowing air. The convection coefficient is assumed to be $h = 10\ W/m^2K$ with the ambient temperature of $T_\infty = 298\ K$.

The interface between the plastic and metal is an imperfect contact, and this will be modeled using the thermal contact option. The Gap Conductance can be defined as a function of clearance as well as a function of temperature. In this example, we are not going to use the temperature dependent variation (just to keep things simple). We arbitrarily define two values of the Gap Conductance for two levels of clearance. We will use 100000 W/m²K for 0 mm clearance and 100 W/m²K for 1 mm clearance. For this analysis, the conductance at 1mm will remain unused because there is no relative movement between the interacting surfaces. However, it is conceivable that for problems where thermal effects and displacement are calculated in a coupled analysis, this feature would be very useful.

The heat input from the laser source is 850000 W and it is applied for the first ten seconds and then turned off. The graph of the heat flux is shown below.

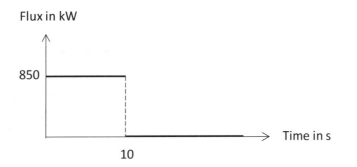

Finally, the assembly, i.e. the metal strip and the plastic strip, are at the initial temperature of $T_0 = 298\ K$.

Creation of the Assembly  :

Click on the compass on the top left corner of the screen. This will open the CAD applications available in 3DEXPERIENCE.

From the list, select the "Assembly Design" Application .

It is assumed that you have already created the two parts, the metal strip and the plastic strip, and applied the material properties at the part level prior to the assembly process. You then insert them into the assembly as "Existing 3D Part" and position them properly. The positioning can be achieved using the "Engineering Connections" icon, if necessary. The screen looks as shown below.

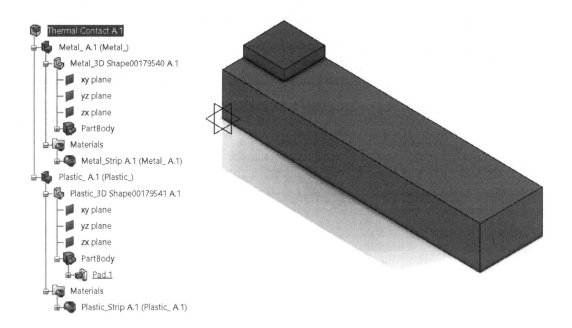

The material properties dialogue boxes for the two parts are shown on the next page.

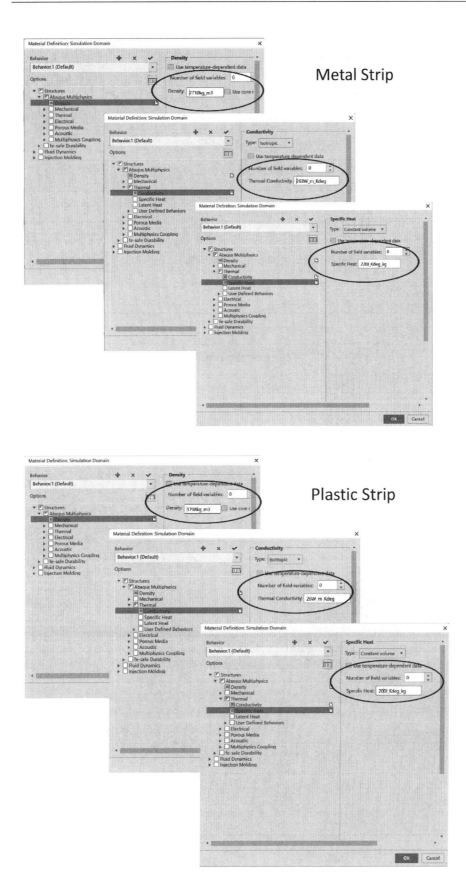

Metal Strip

Plastic Strip

At this point, there are two ways to proceed: one can take the assembly and create the mesh for the assembly, or mesh each of the two parts (at the part level) and create an assembly of meshes. For small assemblies, there is no clear advantage/disadvantage to either strategy. For large assemblies, however, the assembly of meshes may be preferable. <u>In the present problem, we will create a Mesh of the Assembly as it was done in Chapter 9.</u>

The figure below provides more information on the distinction of the two approaches.

FEM Rep Management Strategies

i)   Meshes of an assembly (**MOA**)
     Meshes and associated properties
     for all parts are created at the
     global (i.e. assembly) level.

ii) Assembly of Meshes (**AOM**)
     Part-level FEM Reps containing
     mesh parts and associated properties
     are linked to a global FEM Rep.

Note: One can also create a FEM Rep using
      a combination of the above strategies

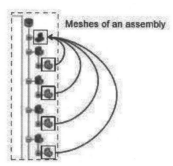

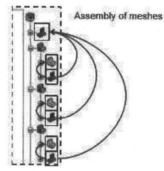

Warning:

Before you proceed to the next step, make sure that you are in the top branch of the tree, i.e., the "Assembly Design" workbench. This can be achieved by double clicking on the top branch.

Double click on the top branch to make
sure that you are at "Assembly Design"
level

Creating the Finite Element Model:

Locate the compass on the top left corner of the screen and select it. Scroll through the applications and select the "Structural Model Creation" App 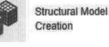 .

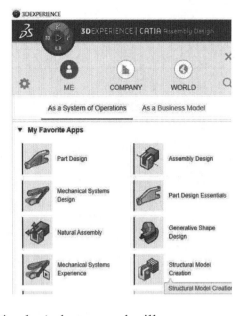

The row of icons on the bottom of your screen (action bar) changes and will appear as displayed below.

The dialogue box shown on the right "Create Finite Element Model" appears. For now, use the "Automatic" radio button. Other options are for a user control of the meshing process. In the case of "Automatic", tetrahedral parabolic elements are created.

The entire assembly consisting of two parts has been meshed. There are two elements and two solid sections displayed in the tree.

Notice that the appropriate material properties have been picked up by the software.

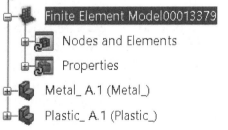

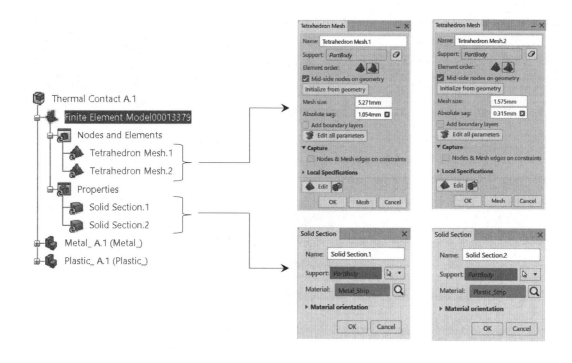

To see the mesh, click on the "Update" icon .

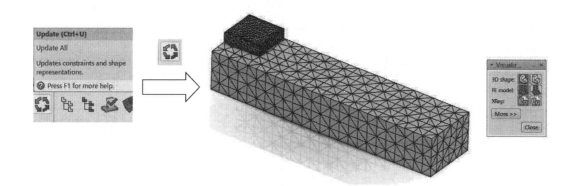

The size of the elements is much smaller in the plastic strip. One can change these sizes by double clicking on the appropriate branches of the tree. For the heat transfer problems, the element size is not very critical if it is reasonable. The present problem uses the "parabolic" elements; therefore, there is more than meets the eye in the above discretization. Needless to say, the quad elements are generally preferred over tetrahedron elements, but once again, for thermal problems, this is not an issue.
The next step is to create a "Scenario".

Creating a Scenario:

Locate the compass on the top left corner of the screen and select it. Scroll through the applications and select the "Structural Scenario

Creation" App  .

The row of icons on the bottom of your screen changes and will appear as displayed below.

The pop up window "Simulation Initialization" shown here appears on the screen. Since this is strictly a "Thermal Problem", the radio button **"Thermal"** should be selected.

A quick glance at the tree confirms that a "Scenario" has been created.

Checking the bottom of the screen on the left side reveals that there are two red exclamation signs. These pertain to "Thermal Analysis Case.1" and "No Procedures Exist".

Red "Exclamation" marks

Click the "Finite Element Model" icon ![icon] from the bottom row. This is referring to the FE model which is already created. The following pop up window appears.

Since there is already a finite element model created, it appears in the list and make sure that you select that row.

Select this row ⟶

| Finite Element Model | | × |

Model: ● Select ○ Create

☐ Preview the highlighted model

Name	Dimension
Finite Element Model0...	3D

OK   Cancel

Select the "Procedures" tab from the action bar (bottom row).

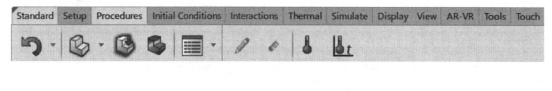

Select the "Transient Heat Transfer Step" icon ![icon Transient Heat Transfer...] from the bottom row. When the "Transient Heat Transfer Step" dialogue box appears, make the changes shown.

Transient Heat Transfer Step   ×

Name: Transient Heat Transfer Step.1

Step time: 100s   ⟵   Total simulation time (real time) 100 seconds

▼ **Incrementation**

Incrementation type: Automatic ▼

Initial time increment: 0.01s

Minimum time increment: 1e-005s

Maximum time increment: 1s   ⟵ Make these changes

Maximum number of increments: 1000

Maximum temperature change per increment: 100Kdeg

☐ Maximum temperature change rate for steady state: 0Kdeg_s

▶ **Advanced**

OK   Cancel

         ✓ Thermal Analysis Case.1   ✓ Transient Heat Transfer Step.1

Creating Interactions:

Select the "Interactions" tab from the action bar. Then from the menu, choose the "Surface-based Contact"icon .

"Interactions" tab

This leads to the "Surface-based Contact" dialogue box shown on the right. Although the present problem is a thermal one, this dialogue box has the same format already visited in structural contact problems. The difference may be in the fact that the choice of "M" and "S" surfaces is not as critical.

For the "M" and the "S" surfaces, choose the ones shown below.

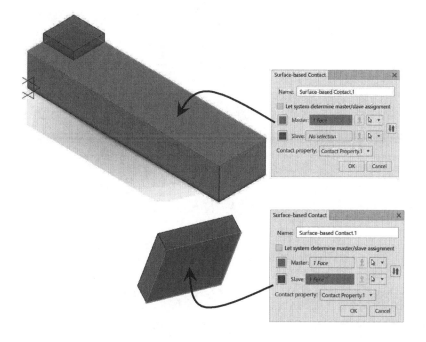

The interesting point is that as soon as the above icon is selected, a "Contact Property" branch is also created in the tree. Double click on the branch to open the appropriate dialogue box where the "Gap Conductance" data can be supplied.

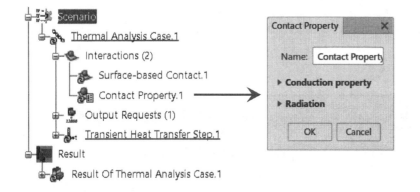

Use the pull-down menu labeled "Conduction Property" to enter the data shown below.

We will use 100000 W/m^{2}K for 0 mm clearance and 100 W/m^{2}K for 1 mm clearance. For this analysis, the conductance at 1mm will remain unused because there is no relative movement between the interacting surfaces. However, it is conceivable that for problems where thermal effects and displacement are calculated in a coupled analysis, this feature would be very useful.

Specifying the Flux Data:

First select the "Setup" tab followed by the "Tabular Amplitude" icon from the action bar.

In the resulting dialogue box, input the data which approximates the desired amplitude.

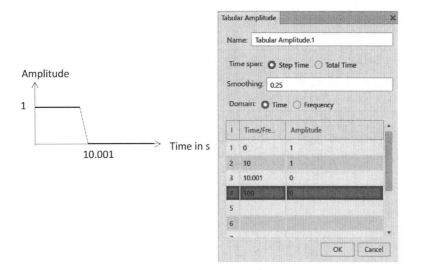

Next, choose the "Thermal" tab from the action bar.

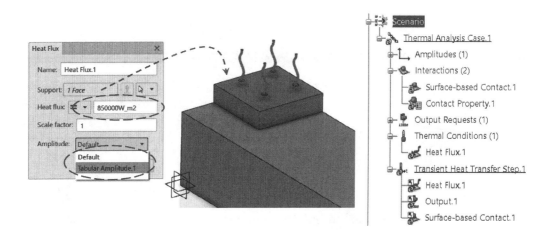

Use the "Heat flux" icon to access the corresponding dialogue box. In the resulting window, use the pull-down menu to choose the Tabular Amplitude.1 and input 850000 W for the flux value. The "Support" is the top face of the plastic strip.

Convection Boundary Conditions:

Use the "Film Condition" icon 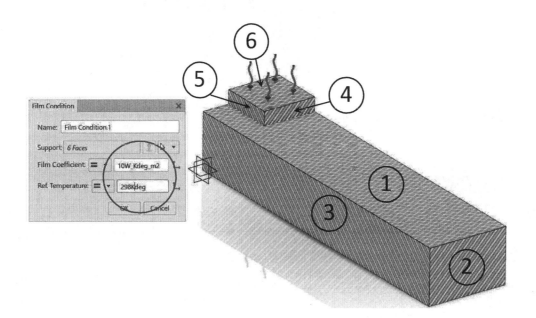 to access the corresponding dialogue box. For the "Support", pick the six faces of the plastic and the metal strips as shown. These are the faces that are subject to convection due to the blowing air. Note that in the first 10 seconds, the top face of the plastic part is subject to the heat flux and it is only after that period that it is convectiong. The "Film Coefficient" is 10 W_Kdeg_m2 and the "Ref. Temperature" is 298 Kdeg.

Applying Initial Conditions:

Select the "Initial Conditions" tab from the action bar.

From the resulting menu, pick the "Initial Temperature" icon. This immediately leads to the dialogue box shown below. For the "Support", use the pull-down menu and choose the "Mesh Part".

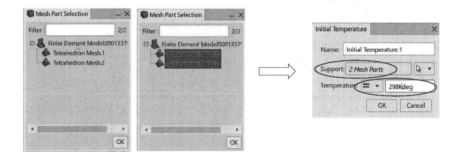

In doing so, you will be asked to select the meshes where the initial condition is to be applied. Using the Ctrl key (or the Shift key) for multiple selection, choose both Tetrahedral Mesh.1 and Tetrahedral Mesh.2 as indicated below. Finally, for the "Temperature" input 298 Kdeg.

The tree structure at the point in the model preparation is also shown below.

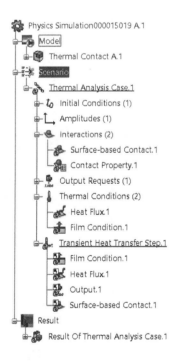

Creating a Group and Requesting for Additional Output:

One of the objectives of this example is to plot the temperature variation of the middle point of the plastic part (on the top face) as a function of time. In other words, we need to generate a history plot at that location. To do so, we create a group which is primarily made of that point. Select the "Group" tab from the action bar.

First make sure that you are in the "Model" action bar by choosing 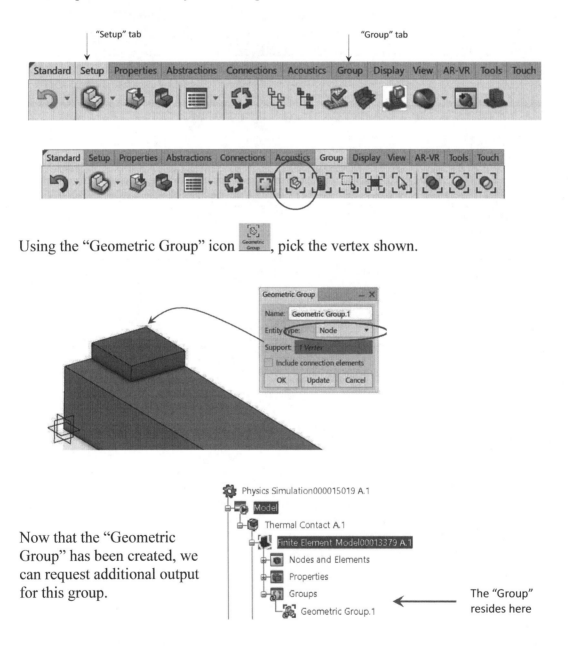. Next select the "Setup" tab followed by the "Group" tab.

"Setup" tab   "Group" tab

| Standard | Setup | Properties | Abstractions | Connections | Acoustics | Group | Display | View | AR-VR | Tools | Touch |

| Standard | Setup | Properties | Abstractions | Connections | Acoustics | Group | Display | View | AR-VR | Tools | Touch |

Using the "Geometric Group" icon , pick the vertex shown.

Now that the "Geometric Group" has been created, we can request additional output for this group.

The "Group" resides here

To do so, we should return to the "Scenario" action bar.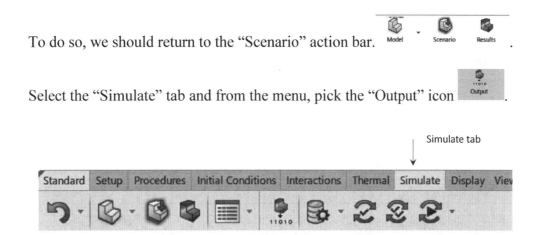

Select the "Simulate" tab and from the menu, pick the "Output" icon .

This leads to the "Output" dialogue box shown below. For the "Support", use the pull-down menu and choose the "Group" from the list. This gives you a secondary menu which allows you to pick the "Geometric Group" that was created earlier. Also, use the pull-down menu to choose "History" for the "Output group".

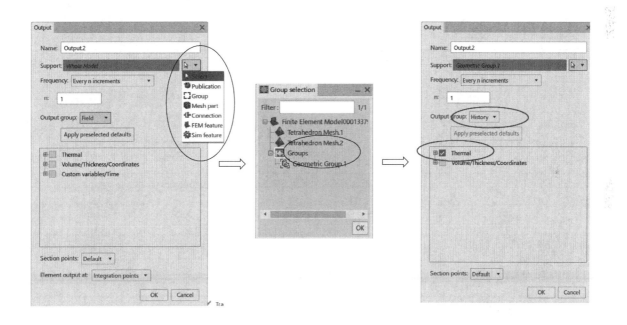

Simulation Stage:

At this point, all the preliminary work is completed and one can simulate the problem. Select the "Simulation" tab from the action bar.

Simulate tab

It was pointed out earlier in the other chapters that it is a good idea to perform consistency check and scenario check before submitting the job for a full-blown simulation. These can be done by the first two icons on the left of this list below.

We will ignore this recommendation and by selecting the "Simulate" icon submit the job.

Accept the defaults in the resulting dialogue box.

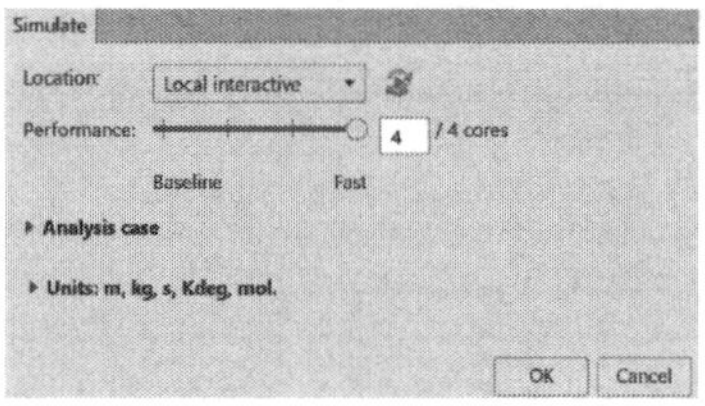

The simulation runs successfully as shown below.

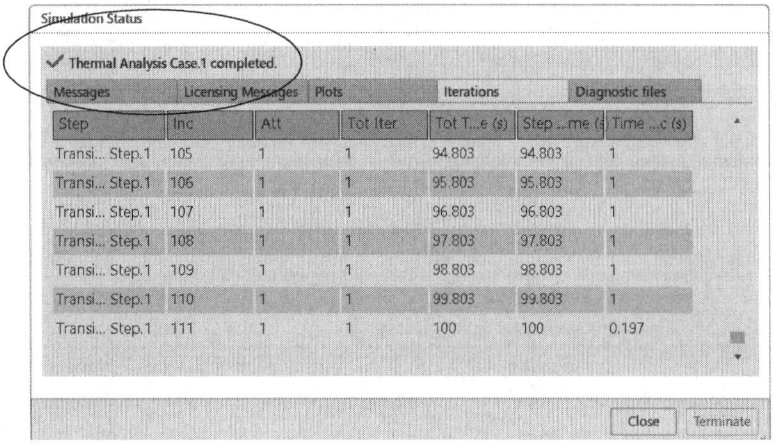

	Simulate	
Location:	Local interactive ▾	
Performance:	——————○	4 / 4 cores
	Baseline Fast	
▸ Analysis case		
▸ Units: m, kg, s, Kdeg, mol.		
		OK Cancel

Simulation Status

✓ Thermal Analysis Case.1 completed.

Messages	Licensing Messages	Plots		Iterations		Diagnostic files	
Step	Inc	Att	Tot Iter	Tot T...e (s)	Step ...me (s)	Time ...c (s)	
Transi... Step.1	105	1	1	94.803	94.803	1	
Transi... Step.1	106	1	1	95.803	95.803	1	
Transi... Step.1	107	1	1	96.803	96.803	1	
Transi... Step.1	108	1	1	97.803	97.803	1	
Transi... Step.1	109	1	1	98.803	98.803	1	
Transi... Step.1	110	1	1	99.803	99.803	1	
Transi... Step.1	111	1	1	100	100	0.197	

Close Terminate

Results (Post processing):

Once you close (or move) the
obstructing dialogue boxes, you must
be in the "Results" section and the
bottom row should appear as shown on
the right.

If not, click on the "Results" icon   .

In the background, you should see the "Plots" dialogue box which shows the results of
Frame1, and the initial results and the results after the first iteration. If the first of the
"Plots" dialogue box is highlighted, the value of the temperature is the constant ambient
temperature This is not surprising as no thermal load is applied in Frame 1.

The second frame describes the temperature distribution at t = 0.01s. It clearly shows that
the plastic heated by the metal strip has not been affected yet. The temperature
distribution at two other times are also displayed (please see the next page).

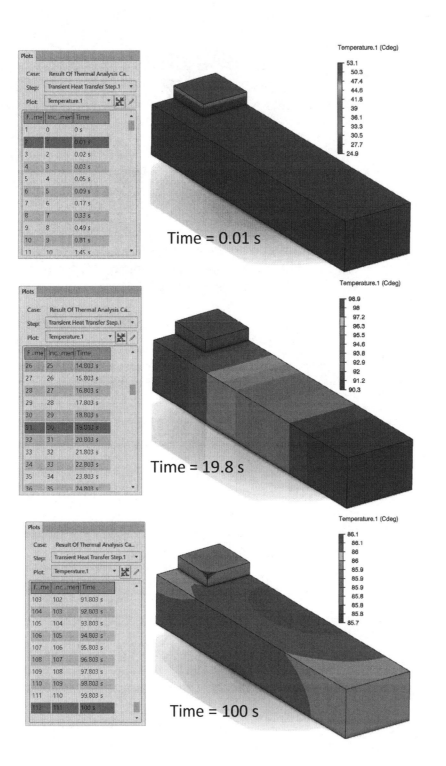

Let us try to plot the heat flux distribution in the assembly.

Select the "Symbol Plot" icon 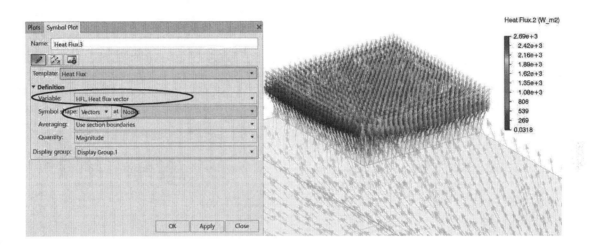 from the menu.

In the resulting dialogue box, use the pull-down menu to pick the "HFL, Heat flux vector".

For the "Symbol shape", choose "vectors"; finally click on "Apply" to get the plot. This is for time t = 0.01 s and therefore just about all the flux is into the plastic strip.

Since there are too many arrows in the above plot, we have to reduce the density of the symbols. Select the middle tab of the "Symbol Plot" window and drag the sliding bar to modify the symbol density.

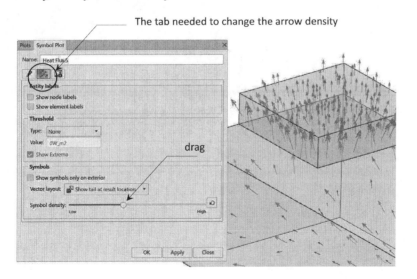

The flux distribution at a late time t = 32.8 s clearly indicates the cooling effect of the assembly.

Time History Plot:

The final task in this chapter is to plot the temperature variation of the selected vertex as a function of time. Select the "Display" tab from the action bar.

"Display" tab

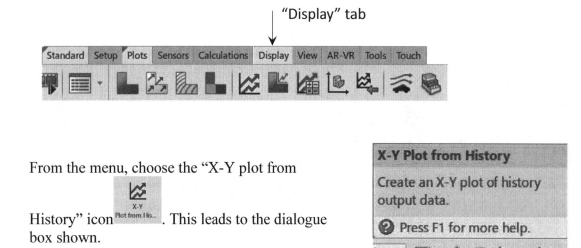

From the menu, choose the "X-Y plot from History" icon . This leads to the dialogue box shown.

Upon clicking on the "**Apply**" button in this window, the desired plot shown on the next page is generated.

This completes chapter 11.

Chapter 12

Hybrid Model, Solid/Shell/Beam Combination

Objective:

In this chapter, you will create an FEA model involving a combination of solid, shell and beam elements. We refer to such models as a "Hybrid". There are two ways to model this problem, as an "Assembly" or as a "Single Part". <u>We will adopt the second approach and show the highlights of the steps to create the needed part.</u>

Problem Statement

The model shown on the right is pressure loaded. It is made of steel with the Young's modulus $E = 200\ GPa$ and Poisson's ratio 0.3. Clearly, it is unwise to mesh all the parts with solid elements. Solid elements are suitable for meshing the upright cylinder. The horizontal plate is best represented by shell elements, and the two supporting vertical parts should be meshed with beam elements. The surface is subjected to a downward pressure of 1000 Pa.

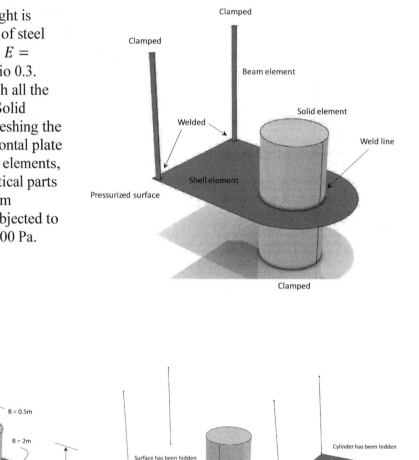

The key in this exercise is to ensure that duplicate nodes are not created at the interfaces. This will be illustrated at the meshing stage.

Detailed Steps to Create the Part:

First create the cylinder.

Enter the Part Design workbench 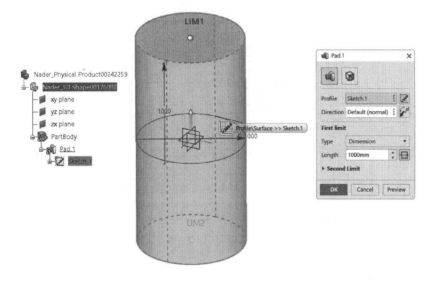 . Draw a sketch of a circle of radius of

0.5m center at the origin and pad it symmetrically (up and down) by a total length of 2m.

Next create the "Geometrical Set" containing the surface and the two vertical lines.

In Part design, create a "Geometrical Set" and switch to the "Generative Shape

Design" workbench. . On the xy plane, make the sketch shown below where the center of the circular arc is at the origin of the sketcher coordinate system. This sketch and the follow up vertical lines must reside in the Geometrical Set. Note that the solid cylinder was hidden for your visual aid.

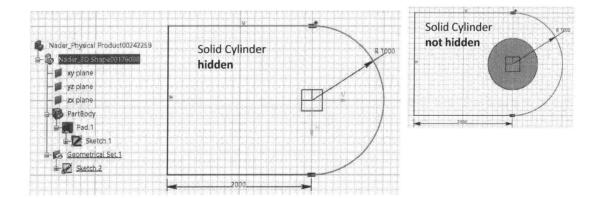

Now, exit the sketcher and use the "Fill" icon 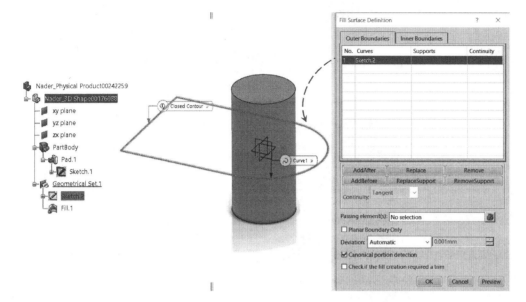 to create a surface on this sketch.2.

The surface is now created; however, the solid cylinder goes right through it as shown below. We need to create an opening in the surface through which the solid cylinder passes.

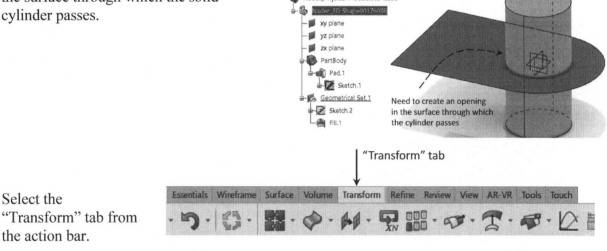

"Transform" tab

Select the "Transform" tab from the action bar.

Next choose the "Split" icon  from the list. Keep in mind that there is also a "Split" icon availabe in the Part Design workbench but that cannot be used for splitting surfaces.

For the "Element to cut", select Fill.1 from the tree or the surface displayed on the screen. For the "Cutting element", choose "Sketch.1" which was used to create the solid cylinder.

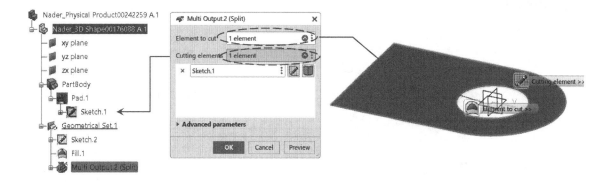

The result is shown below.

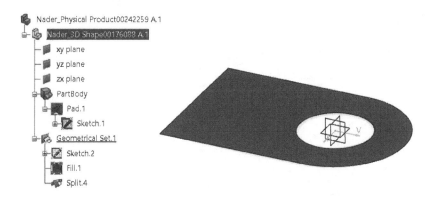

You will next create the two vertical lines and they will reside in the "Geometrical Set.1'

"Wireframe" tab

Using the "Line" icon ![line icon], create the two vertical lines. There are different methods of doing this. On the next page, I have outlines of the process graphically for Line.1. For the second line proceed exactly the same way except for the choice of the "Point".

Line

Creates a line.

Select the line creation method and specify the necessary inputs.

? Press F1 for more help.

For the method to be used, select "Normal to Surface"; for the actual "surface", pick the "Split" explained on the previous page. For the "Point", use one vertex of the surface as depicted. Finally, for the "Offset" type 2000mm. Repeat the same process for other lines.

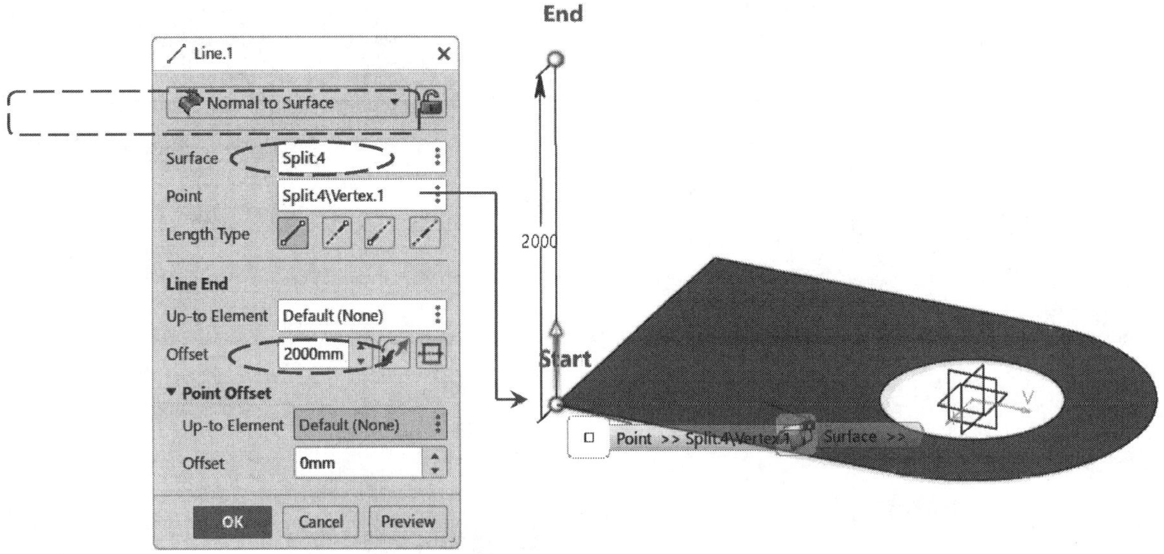

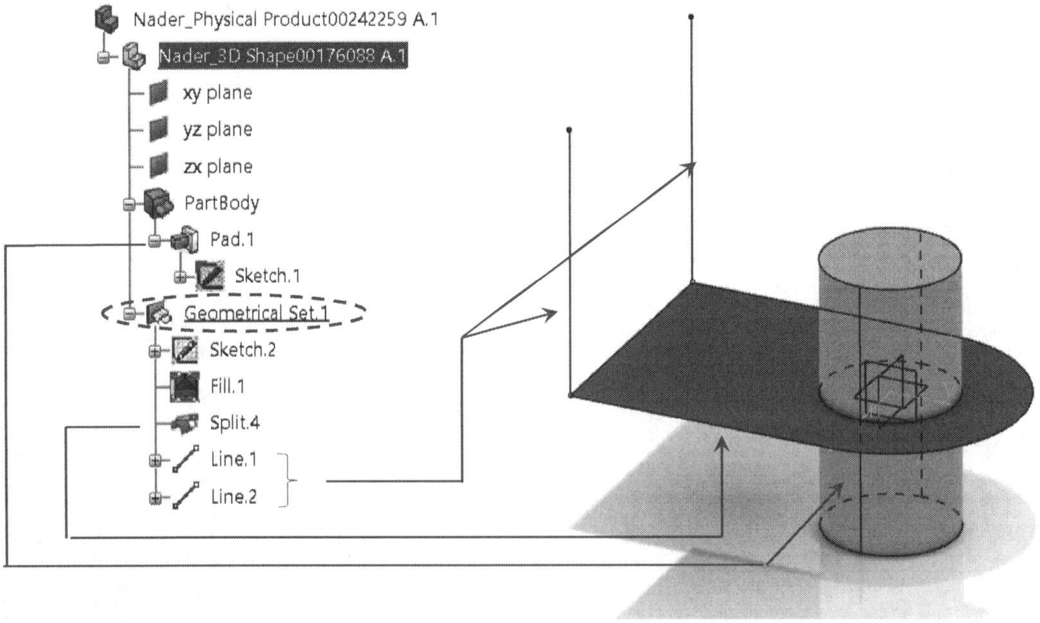

The Model and Material Properties:

Select the "Create Material"  icon to apply the properties to the entire part. The density is not needed for the present problem.

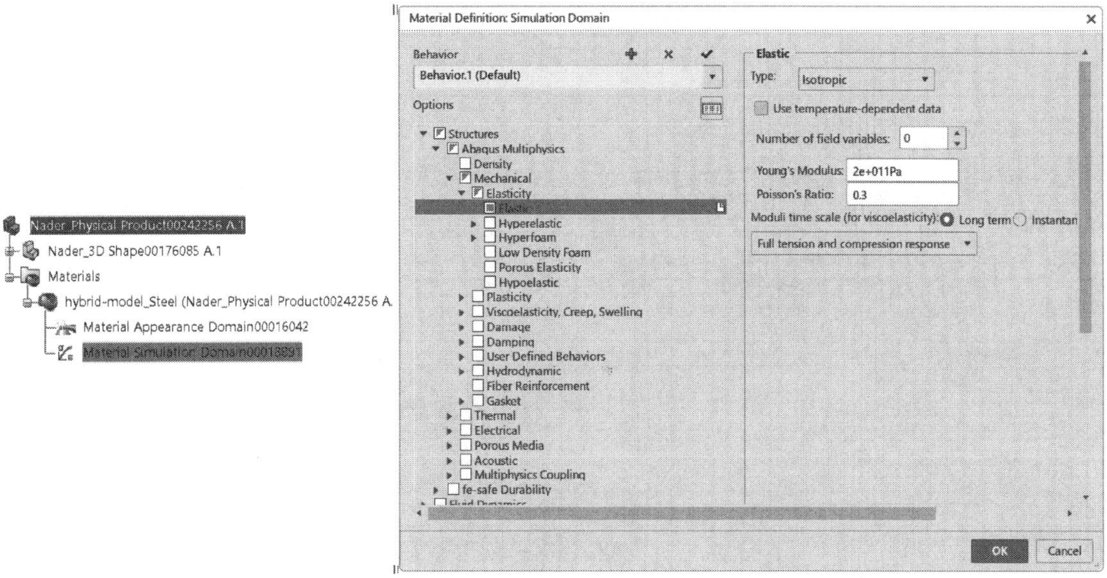

Creating the Finite Element Model:

Locate the compass on the top left corner of the screen as shown on the right and select it. Scroll through the applications and select the "Structural Model Creation" App

The appropriate branches are created in the tree; however, only the cylinder is meshed automatically. Both the line and surface must be meshed manually by the user.

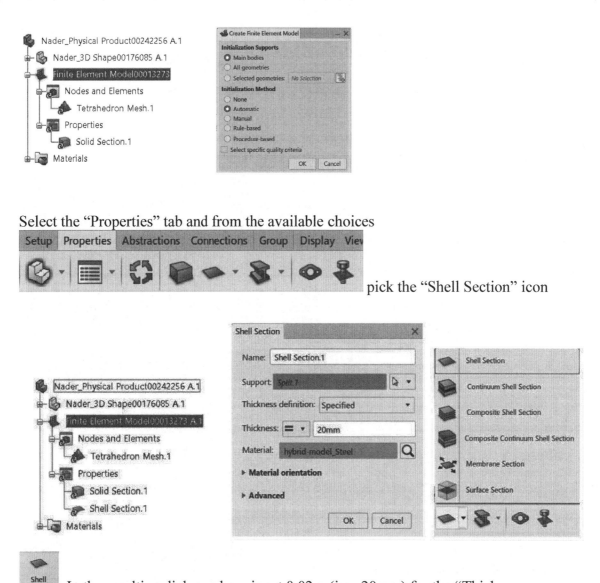

Select the "Properties" tab and from the available choices

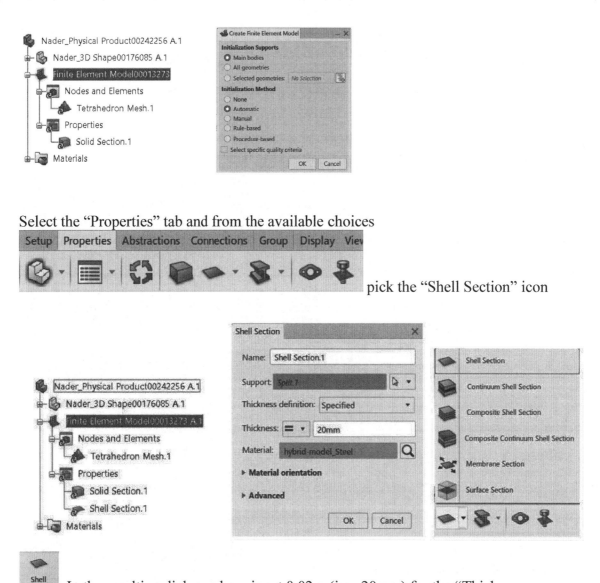 pick the "Shell Section" icon

. In the resulting dialogue box, input 0.02m (i.e., 20mm) for the "Thickness definition" of the plate.

Next, select the "Beam Profile" icon from the list . Using the pull-down menu, choose a "Circular" profile and input a radius of 10mm for the cross section.

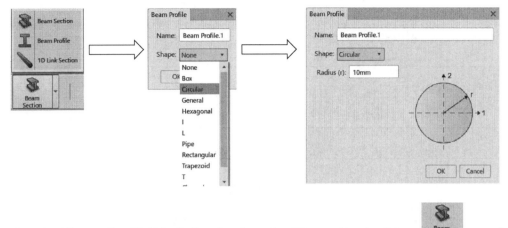

After the "Beam Profile" is defined, select the "Beam Section" icon , use the pull-down menu to choose the "Profile.1" just constructed. Finally, select the two lines "individually" to assign the section properties.

At this point, the section properties are defined, and the meshing can be initiated. Select the "Mesh" icon 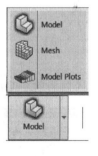 from the list.

Mesh tab

Choose the "Surface Quad Mesh" icon from the menu. In the resulting dialogue box, make the changes shown and pick the surface for the "Support".

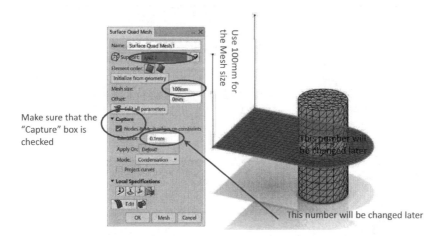

The checking of the two boxes shown above is critical to avoid getting duplicate nodes at the interface between the lines, the surface, and the solid cylinder. However, the "Tolerance" value is also playing the role. The default value shown is too small to account for this issue. It will be changed later.

Press the "Mesh" button in the dialogue box, and the mesh will appear on the screen.

Use the "Beam Mesh" icon  and make the changes indicated in the dialogue box below. The two lines are then meshed.

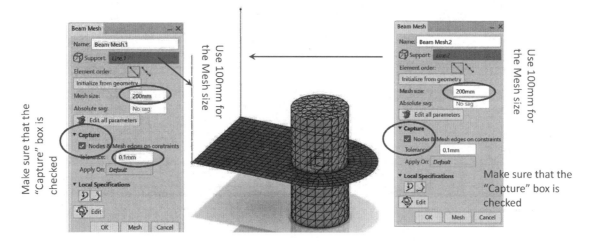

Right clicking on the screen allows you to access the "Mesh Visualization" dialogue box which is quite useful in displaying the mesh on the screen.

Select the "Display" tab from the action bar.

"Display" tab

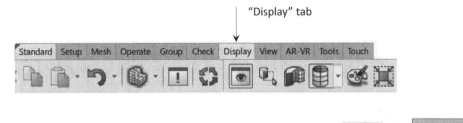

From the menu choices, pick the "Element Shrink" icon .

This leads to the dialogue box with three sliding bars. By dragging the sliding bars, you can shrink the three types of element for visual inspection as shown.

Element Shrink

Displays elements at a reduced percentage of their original size.

Press F1 for more help.

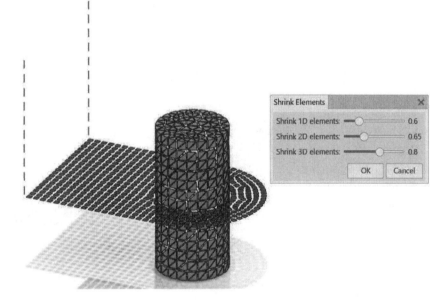

If some elements are not displayed, use the "Update" icon [Update] from the action bar. Returning the sliding bars to the original positions shows the default display of the three types of elements in the mesh. The "Visualization Management" icon [Visualization Management] allows you to toggle back and forth between the different display options. The "Hide" and "Show" feature enables you to do such operations on the fly without referring to the tree.

Shape is "Hide"   Shape is "Show"
FE Model is "Show"   FE Model is "Hide"

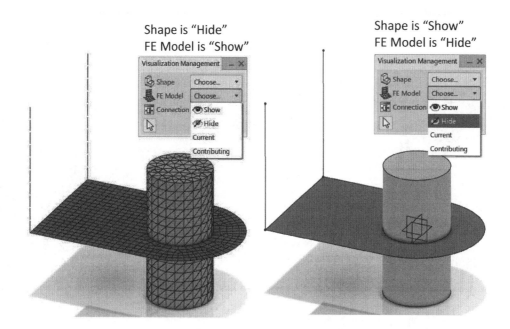

The Issue of Incompatible Mesh, or Duplicate Nodes:

A closer look at the interface between the shell and solid elements indicates that the nodes of these elements do not coincide. This is related to the "Tolerance" issue already alluded to.

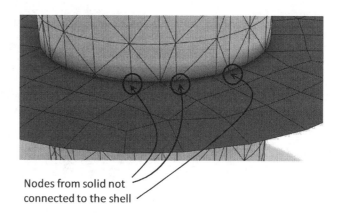

Nodes from solid not connected to the shell

To fix this matter, double click on the branch of the three labeled "Surface Quad Mesh.1". This opens the dialogue box seen earlier where some changes were already made.

For the "Tolerance" enter a new value of 0.3m (or 300mm). This implies that any two nodes from two different regions which are within 30cm of each other are readjusted to merge into a single node. For the "Tolerance" enter a new value of 0.03m (or 30mm). This implies that any two nodes from two different regions which are within 30mm of each other are readjusted to merge into a single node.

The effect is displayed below.

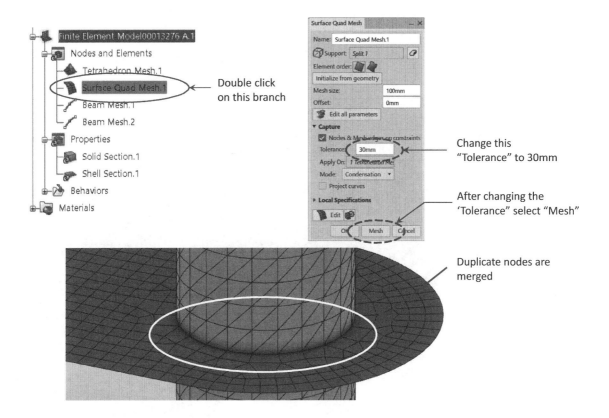

A close look at the interface between the surface and the cylinder clearly indicates that the orphan nodes have disappeared and merged with others. It is clear here that the shell element nodes have been readjusted to take care of the problem. There are no issues with the interface between the beam and shell elements.

Upon right clicking of the mouse and selecting "Mesh Part Manager", you can view more information about the mesh generated. Note that the solid elements are quadratic, whereas the shell elements are linear. This, however, does not lead to "error" messages.

Mesh Part List	A	C	C	P	U	St.	Size	Sag	Order		Elements	No..	Quality
Finite Element Model00013276 A.1											2007	3411	
Tetrahedron Mesh.1		●		3D		OK	145.306mm	29.061mm	Quadratic		1513	3411	
Surface Quad Mesh.1		●		2D		OK	100mm		Linear		474	527	
Beam Mesh.1		●		1D		OK	200mm	No Sag	Linear		10	11	
Beam Mesh.2		●		1D		OK	200mm	No Sag	Linear		10	11	3411

Assigning the "Beam Section":

An inspection of the tree clearly indicates that the "Beam Section" is missing.

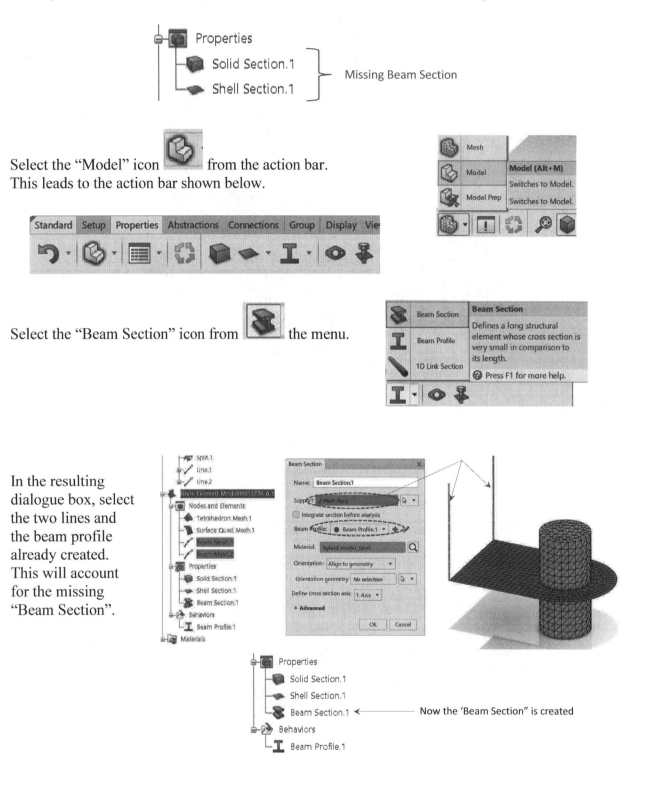

Select the "Model" icon ![Model icon] from the action bar.
This leads to the action bar shown below.

Select the "Beam Section" icon from ![Beam Section icon] the menu.

In the resulting
dialogue box, select
the two lines and
the beam profile
already created.
This will account
for the missing
"Beam Section".

Locate the compass on the top left corner of
the screen and select it. Scroll through the
applications and select the "Structural
Scenario Creation" App

Structural Scenario
Creation

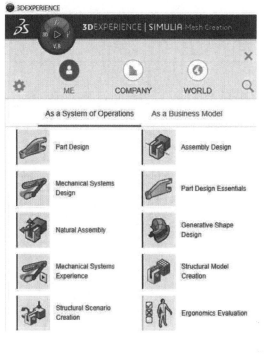

The pop-up window "Simulation
Initialization" shown below appears on the
screen. Since this is strictly a structural
problem, the radio button "Structural" should
be selected.

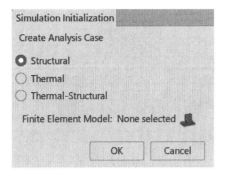

Click the "Finite Element Model" icon from the bottom row. This is referring to
the Finite Element model which is already created. The following pop-up window
appears.

Since there is already a finite
element model created, it appears
in the list and make sure that you
select that row.

Select this row ⟶

Finite Element Model	✕

Model: ● Select ○ Create

☐ Preview the highlighted model

Name	Dimension
Finite Element Model0...	3D

OK   Cancel

Choose the "Procedures" tab from the action bar (bottom row).

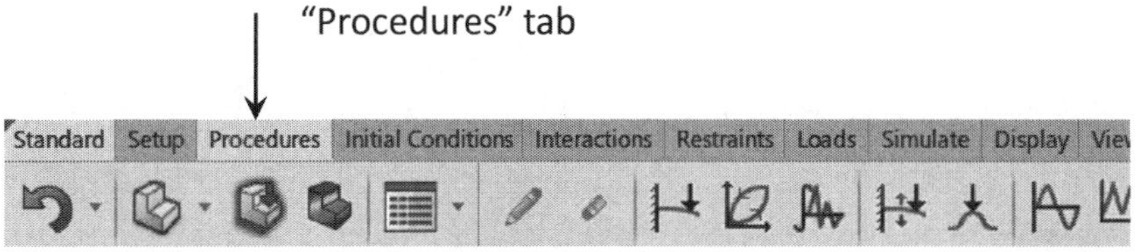

"Procedures" tab

Select the "Static Step" icon [Static Step] from the bottom row.

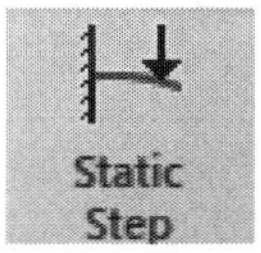

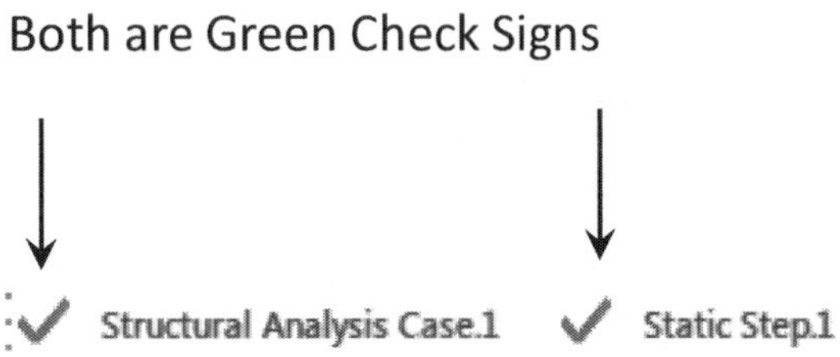

Both are Green Check Signs

✓ Structural Analysis Case.1   ✓ Static Step.1

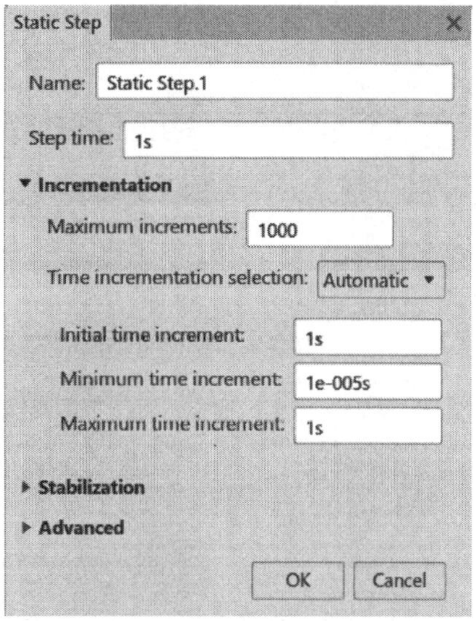

Applying the Restraints:

Pick the "Restraints" tab from the action bar.

"Restraints" tab

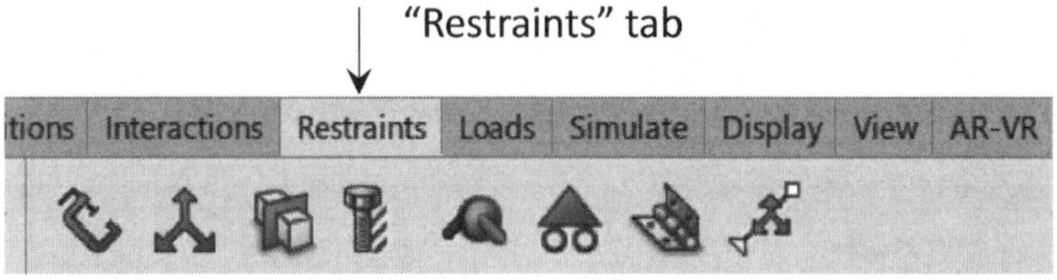

Choose the "Clamp" icon 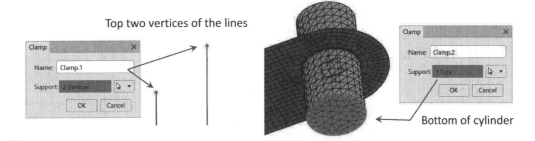 and in two tries, select the top two vertices of the lines in the model, and the bottom face of the cylinder.

Top two vertices of the lines

Bottom of cylinder

Applying the Load:

Pick the "Loads" tab from the action bar and choose the "Pressure" icon from the menu.

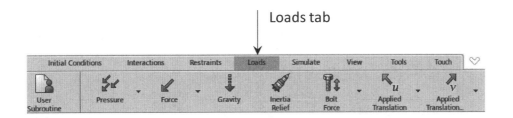

Loads tab

For the "Support" pick the surface in the part and specify 1000 Pa for the value.

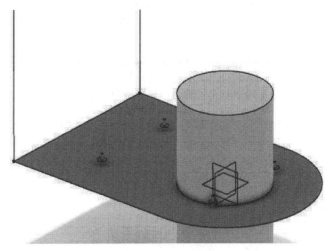

The complete tree for the "Scenario" created is displayed below.

```
⚙ Nader_Physics Simulation000000005_1B28E5B6-0000-69CC-58EA4,
├─▶ Model
│   └─ Nader_Physical Product00049718 A.1
├─ Scenario
    └─ Structural Analysis Case.1
        ├─ Restraints (2)
        │   ├─ Clamp.1
        │   └─ Clamp.2
        ├─ Loads (1)
        │   └─ Pressure.1
        ├─ Output Requests (2)
        └─ Static Step.1
└─ Result
```

Consistency, Model Check, and Simulation:

Select the "Simulation" tab from the bottom row of icons on your screen (i.e., from the action bar).

"Simulate" tab

| Setup | Procedures | Initial Conditions | Interactions | Restraints | Loads | Simulate | Display |

It is a good practice to perform the model and consistency check before submitting the work for the final run.
Select the "Model and Scenario Check" icon from the bottom row.

The software goes through a check phase and if there are no issues, a message with a "Green" check mark is returned.

Simulation Checks

Complete the Model and Scenario Checks, and check the simulation for any issues likely to prevent it from running successfully.

ⓘ Press F1 for more help.

Model and Scenario Checks Status   ✕
  ✓ Model and Scenario Checks completed.

  Close   Terminate

Next select the "Simulation Checks" icon 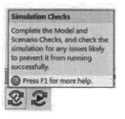 from the bottom row of icons. Accept the number of "cores" in the pop-up box below.

The "Simulation Check" runs successfully.

Simulation Checks Status

✓ Simulation checks completed.

▶ Errors (0)

▶ Warnings (1)

▶ Information (0)

Choose the "Simulation" icon 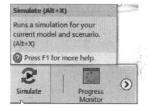 from the bottom row.

Accept the number of "cores" in the pop up box, and wait for the simulation to complete.

The program successfully runs, and no messages are reported.

Simulation Status

✓ Structural Analysis Case.1 completed.

Messages	Licensing Messages	Plots	Iterations	Diagnostic files

▶ Errors (0)

▶ Warnings (1)

▶ Information (0)

Results (Post processing):

Once you close (or move) the obstructing dialogue boxes, you must be in the "Results" section and the bottom row should appear as shown on the right.

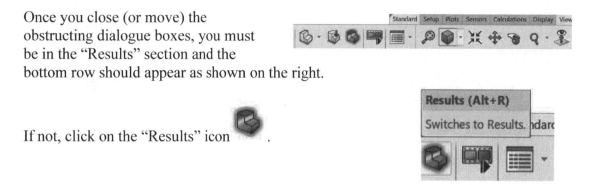

If not, click on the "Results" icon 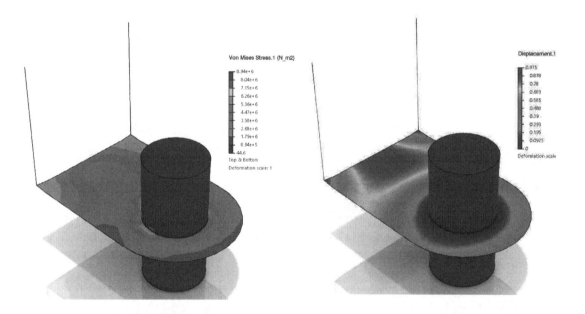 .

In the background, you should see the "Plots" dialogue box which shows the results of Frame1, and the initial results and the results after the first iteration. If the first of the "Plots" dialogue box is highlighted, the value of the von Mises stress is zero. This is not surprising as the first row is before any incremental load is applied. If the load is zero, the displacement and stress are both zero. Use the cursor to select the second row of the "Plots" dialogue box. One can then see the von Mises stress distribution in the part.

You can use the pull-down menu to plot the displacement also. These are shown side by side down below.

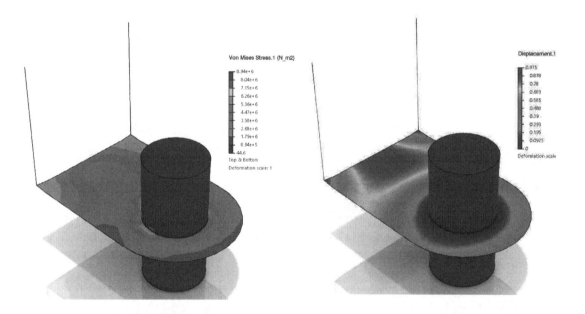

Recall that one can change the scale factor in the plot to have a more dramatic view of the deformation. To do this, double click on the contour plot and in the resulting dialogue box, change the scale factor. Here it was changed to 1000 times.

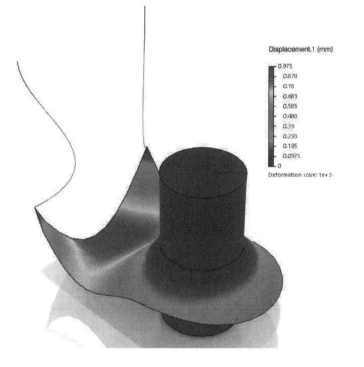

The outcome is quite pronounced, and the deformed shape is displayed below.

This operation completes the chapter.

Exercise 1: Hybrid Model

Consider the steel structure shown below. The beams have the same cross section, the cylinder is centered, and all components are perfectly welded together. The thickness of the plate is 0.1 in. The entire structure is given an acceleration of 10g, i.e., 98 m/s^2 in the direction shown.
Model the structure in 3DEXPERIENCE and run an FEA analysis.

Exercise 2: Hybrid Model

Consider the steel structure shown below. The rods have the same cross section, the block is centered, and all components are perfectly welded together. The thickness of the plate is 0.1 in. The face of the block is subject to a total force of F = 500 lbf in the direction of the arrow as shown.
Model the structure in EDEXPERIENCE and run an FEA analysis.

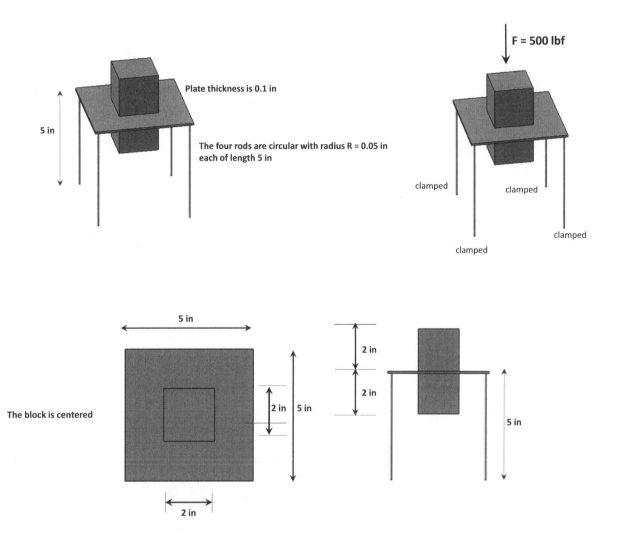

Exercise 3: Hybrid Model

The steel structure shown on the next page is sagging under its own weight. Model the problem with the most appropriate elements and run it.

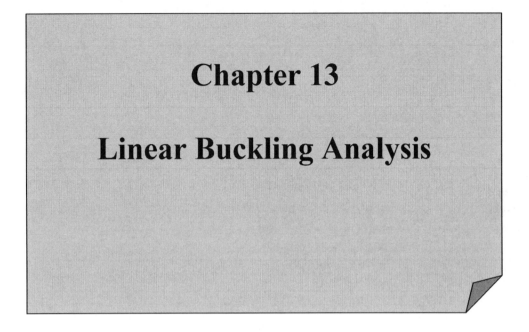

Chapter 13

Linear Buckling Analysis

Objective:

In this tutorial, the buckling analysis of a plane frame is performed. An approximate analytical solution is available which is used to assess the quality of the FEA predictions.

Problem Statement:

The frame structure shown on the right-hand side is made of aluminum with Young's modulus $E = 1.015E + 7$ psi and Poisson's ratio 0.3. The two members have a 1x1 in^2 cross section and a nominal length of $L = 10$ in.
The axial loads P could lead to the buckling of the structure. Although this problem is best suited for beam elements, solid elements will be used to predict the buckling load. The solid and FEA models are displayed below.

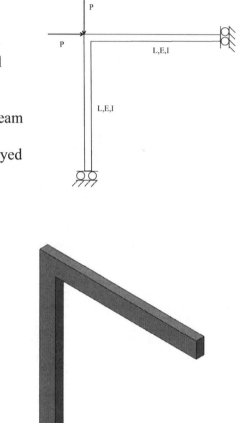

Buckled Frame

Note that, to best represent the problem, only half of the cross section is used. However, this requires imposing a symmetry condition as a restraint.

Elementary theory of strength of materials provides an estimate of the smallest buckling load from the formula $P_{cr} = \dfrac{\pi^2 EI}{4L^2}$. In this expression, $I = \dfrac{1}{12}$ in^4 and $L = 9.5$ in.
The length L has been adjusted to take into account the thickness.

The critical load, based on these values and Young's modulus, is 23125 lb. Keep in mind that this estimate uses beam theory for prediction purposes.

The Model and Material Properties:

Using the Part Design App

Part Design

, create the geometry shown.

Note that the pad length is 0.5 in to account for the symmetry.

Apply the linear elastic material properties with Young's modulus of 1.01E+7 psi and Poisson's ratio of 0.3.

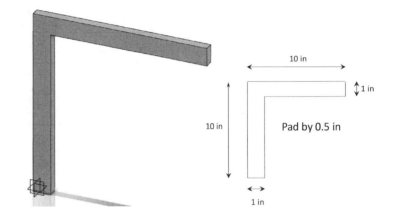

Creating the Finite Element Model:

Locate the compass on the top left corner of the screen and click. Scroll through the applications and select the "Structural Model

 Structural Model Creation

Creation" App   .

The mesh is shown below.

Creating a Scenario:

Locate the compass on the top left corner of the screen and click. Scroll through the applications and select the "Structural Scenario Creation"

 Structural Scenario Creation

App   .

The pop-up window "Simulation Initialization" shown below appears on the screen. Since this is strictly a structural problem, the radio button "Structural" should be selected.

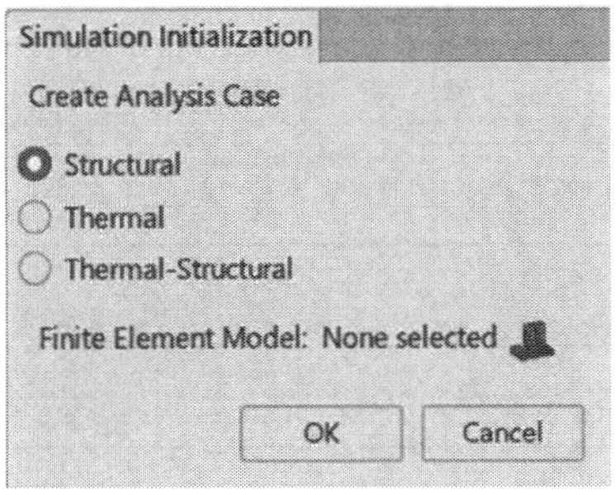

Click the "Select the Finite Element Model" icon from the bottom row. This is referring to the FE model which is already created. The following pop up window appears.

Since there is already a finite element model created, it appears in the list and make sure that you select that row.

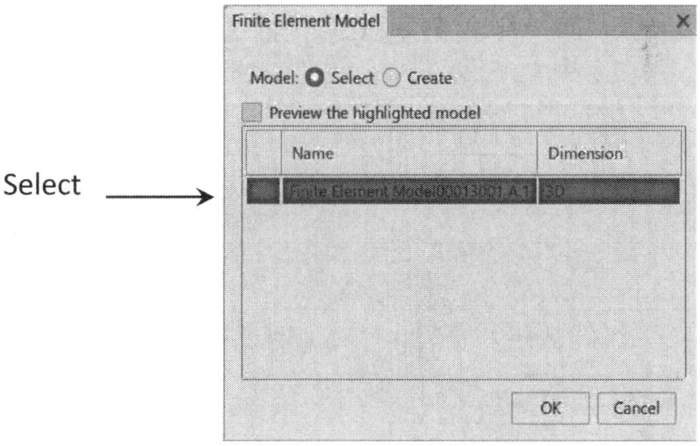

Select ──────→

Select the "Procedures" tab from the action bar (bottom row).

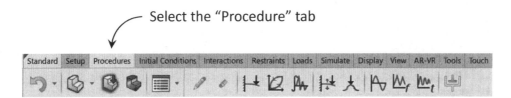

Select the "Procedure" tab

Select the "Buckle Step" icon ⊥ from the
bottom row. Accept the defaults in the ensuing
dialogue box.

Buckle Step ✕

Name: Buckle Step.1

Solver type: Subspace ▾

Number of eigenvalues: 10

Maximum iterations: 30

OK   Cancel

(✓ Structural Analysis Case) (✓ Buckle Step.1) Green check marks

Applying the Restraints:

Select the Restraints tab from the action bar. Choose the "Planar Symmetry" icon
and apply it to the symmetry faces and the ends where there are roller conditions.

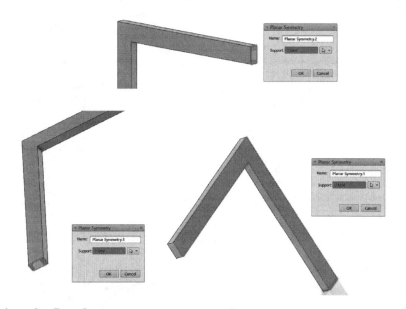

Applying the Load:

Choose the Loads tab from the action bar. Select the "Force" icon and apply 1 lb
to the vertex **which lies in the plane of symmetry** in the two directions shown.

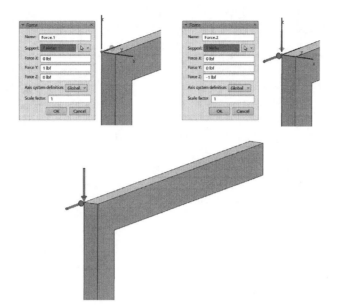

Consistency, Model Check, and Simulation:

Select the "Simulation" tab from the bottom row of icons on your screen (i.e. from the action bar).

"Simulate" tab

It is a good practice to perform the model and consistency check before submitting the work for the final run.
Select the "Model and Scenario Check" icon from the bottom row

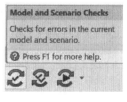

The software goes through a check phase and if there are no issues, a message with a "Green" check mark is returned.

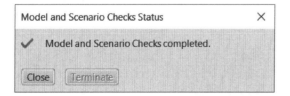

Next select the "Simulation Checks" icon 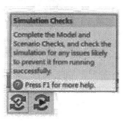 from the bottom row of icons. Accept the number of "cores" in the pop up box below.

Upon the completion of the "Simulation Check", some warning messages are created.

Choose the "Simulation" icon from the bottom row.

Accept the number of "cores" in the pop up box, and wait for the simulation to complete.

The program successfully runs the simulation reporting a single warning.

Simulation Status

✓ Structural Analysis Case.1 completed.

| Messages | Licensing Messages | Plots | Iterations | Diagnostic files |

▶ Errors (0)

▼ Warnings (1)

Buckle option is not supported for element loop parallelization. If you have specified element loop parallelization, it will be turned off for this analysis.

▶ Information (0)

Close   Terminate

Results (Post processing):

Once you close (or move) the obstructing dialogue boxes, you must be in the "Results" section and the bottom row should appear as shown on the right.

Standard | Setup | Plots | Sensors | Calculations | Display | View | AR-VR | Tools | Touch

If not, click on the "Results" icon   .

Results (Alt+R)
Switches to Results. (Alt+R)
Initial Conditions

The first buckling load is reported as 2 x 10214 = 20414 lbf which is in the same ballpark as the estimated theoretical load of 23125 lb. The multiplier "2" comes from the fact that using the plane of symmetry, only half of the thickness is modeled. This mode is shown below. One should be very careful in utilizing such loads which are non-conservative. Another buckling mode is also displayed.

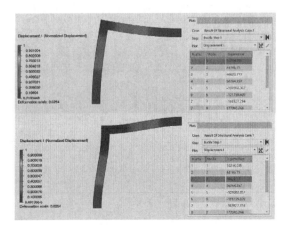

Exercise 1

An aluminum tube has a wall thickness of 0.1 in, nominal radius of 12 in., and length of 48 in. The bottom edge of the tube is clamped (no translation or rotation). Using shell elements, estimate the smallest buckling load applied in the axial direction.

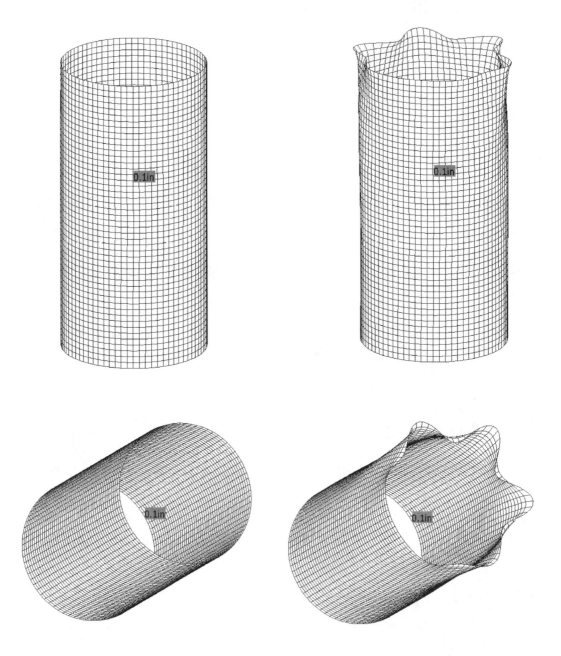

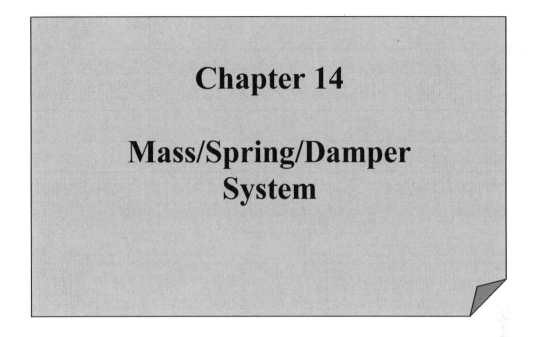

Chapter 14

Mass/Spring/Damper System

Objective:

In this chapter, an assembly of mass, spring, and dampers is modeled and a linear dynamics analysis is performed. Two problems are being considered, a single degree of freedom system (SDOF) and a multi degree of freedom assembly (MDOF).

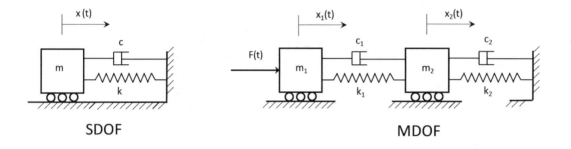

SDOF   MDOF

Problem Statement:

Single Degree of Freedom Case:

Consider the SDOF system shown above where $m = 10000\ kg$, $k = 10^7 N/m$, and $c = 30000\ N.s/m$. The mass is given an initial velocity of $v_0 = 1\ m/s$ at the initial location $d_0 = 0$. The data above leads to the following parameters for the system.

Undamped natural frequency $\omega_n = \sqrt{\dfrac{k}{m}} = 31.623\dfrac{rad}{s} = 5.033\ Hz$

Undamped period of oscillation $T_n = \dfrac{2\pi}{\omega_n} \approx 0.2\ s$

Critical damping $c_{crit} = 2\sqrt{mk} = 6.325 \times 10^5 N.s/m$

Damping ratio $\zeta = \dfrac{c}{c_{crit}} = 0.047 = 4.7\%$

Damped natural frequency $\omega_d = \sqrt{1 - \zeta^2} = 31.587\dfrac{rad}{s}$

Damped period of oscillation $T_d = \dfrac{2\pi}{\omega_d} \approx 0.2\ s$

The exact displacement of the mass as a function of time is given below.

$$x(t) = e^{-\zeta\omega_n t}\left[d_0 \cos(\omega_d t) + \frac{v_0 + \zeta\omega_n d_0}{\omega_d}\sin(\omega_d t)\right]$$

The expression for the reaction force at the wall is described by $RF(t) = -kx(t)$

The plots of the displacement of the mass and the reaction force at the wall are displayed below. The displacement and the reaction force are in meter and Newton respectively.

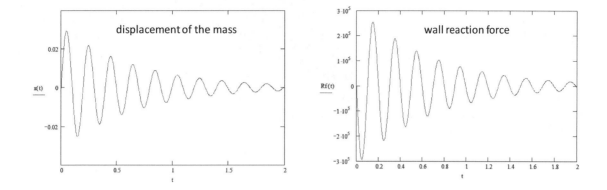

Multi Degree of Freedom Case:

Consider the MDOF system shown in the objective section where $m_1 = 2 \times 10^5 \; kg$, $m_2 = 2.5 \times 10^5 \; kg$, $k_1 = 150 \times 10^6 \; N/m$, and $k_2 = 75 \times 10^6 \; N/m$. Initially, it will be assumed that there is no damping, i.e. $c_1 = c_2 = 0$. But eventually different degrees of damping will be introduced.

The two natural frequencies associated with this system are given approximately by $\omega_1 = 12.2474 \; \frac{rad}{s} = 1.95 \; Hz$ and $\omega_2 = 38.7298 \frac{rad}{s} = 6.16 \; Hz$.

Once these frequencies are calculated by the software, a modal dynamic analysis will be performed where the mass on the left is subjected to an impulsive load as shown in the figure below. The masses are assumed to start the motion from the rest condition.

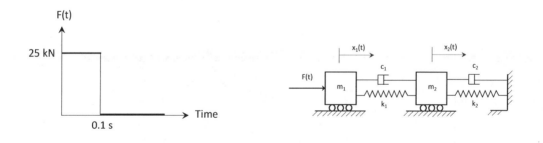

The Model:

First, using the Part Design App

create two points.
Point A with coordinates (0,30 mm, 0) and
point B with coordinates (0, 60mm, 0) as
shown on the right. These points represent
the location of the mass and the wall
respectively.

A: (0,30mm,0)

B: (0,60mm,0)

Creating the Finite Element Model:

Locate the compass on the top left corner of
the screen and click on it. Scroll through the
applications and select the "Structural
Model Creation" App.

Structural Model
Creation

The row of icons on the bottom of your screen (action bar) changes as shown below.

The dialogue box shown on the right "Create Finite
Element Model" appears. For the present problem, keep all
the defaults.

Select the "Abstractions" tab from action bar and from the

menu choose the "Point Inertia" icon 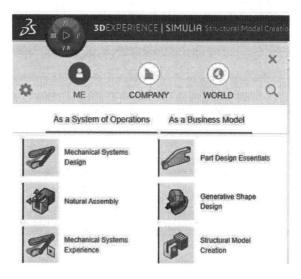.

Abstractions tab

In the resulting dialogue box, for the "Support" choose the point A from the screen. As for the value of the mass, input 10000 kg.

Close the dialogue box by pressing on "OK". The mass icon appears on the screen as displayed.

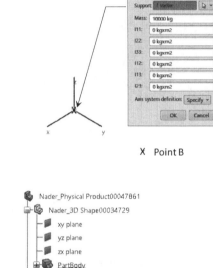

Mass at point A

Point A

X
Point B

X Point B

The tree clearly indicates that the mass has been created. Note that both the mass and the spring are discrete elements and therefore do not appear in the branches that you are used to.

Next, select the "Connections" tab from the action bar.

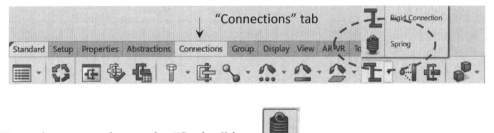

"Connections" tab

Rigid Connection

Spring

From the menu, choose the "Spring" icon [icon].

In the spring dialogue box, follow the steps 1 through 3 to create the spring element. Note that in principle, a spring has no physical length. Therefore, in the present problem, the

30mm is assumed to be the natural (undeformed) length. The length, if necessary, can be specified in the "Ref Length" box. The creation of the spring following the three steps is reflected in the tree as depicted.

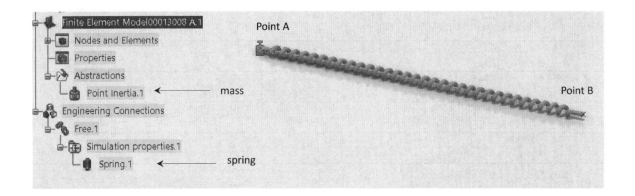

Keep in mind that the point B will be representing the wall. In the present construction the spring is resting along the y -direction. This observation will dictate the nature of the restraints to be imposed on both point A and point B.

Creating a Scenario:

The nature of the analysis, namely, Static, Dynamic, Buckling, etc., is set in the "Structural Scenario Creation" App. Furthermore, the loads, restraints, and interaction are also defined in this application.

It is also important to point out that that one could have created the Scenario before the Finite Element model. In fact, it can be created from within the Structural Scenario App.

Locate the compass on the top left corner of the screen and click it. Scroll through the applications and select the "Structural Scenario

 Structural Scenario Creation

Creation" App

The row of icons on the bottom of your screen changes and will appear as displayed below.

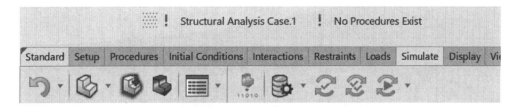

The pop up window "Simulation Initialization" shown below appears on the screen.
Since this is strictly a structural problem, the radio button "Structural" should be selected.

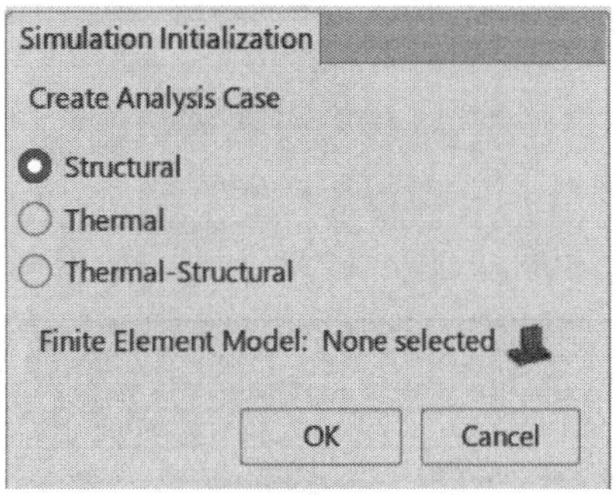

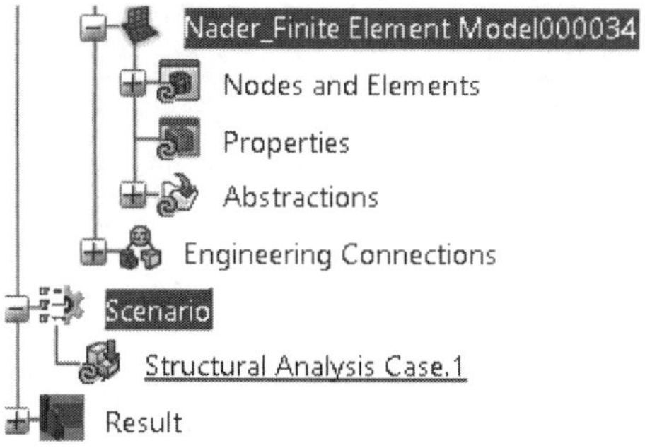

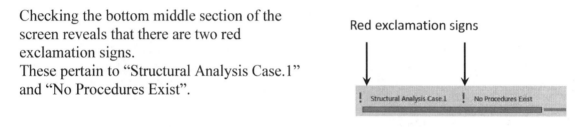

A quick glance at the tree confirms that a "Scenario" has been created.

Checking the bottom middle section of the
screen reveals that there are two red
exclamation signs.
These pertain to "Structural Analysis Case.1"
and "No Procedures Exist".

Red exclamation signs

Structural Analysis Case.1   No Procedures Exist

Next, select the "Setup" tab.

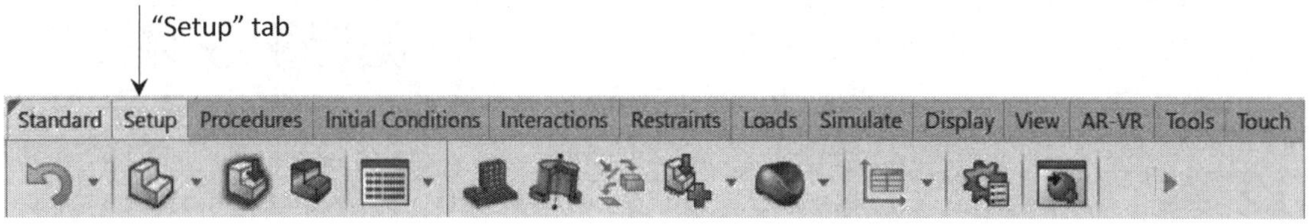

"Setup" tab

Standard | Setup | Procedures | Initial Conditions | Interactions | Restraints | Loads | Simulate | Display | View | AR-VR | Tools | Touch

Click the "Select the Finite

Element Model" icon 
from the bottom row. The
following pop-up window
appears.

Since there is already a finite
element model created, it
appears in the list and make sure
that you select that row.

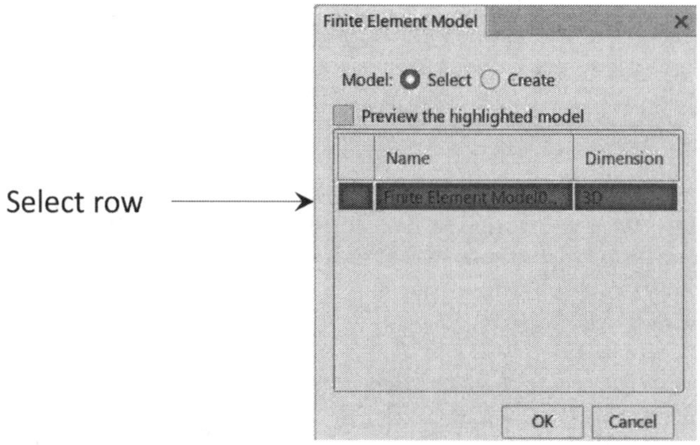

Finite Element Model   ×

Model: ● Select ○ Create
☐ Preview the highlighted model

Name	Dimension
Finite Element Model0...	3D

Select row ⟶

OK   Cancel

Note that the above action creates a "Green" checkmark next to the "Structural Analysis Case.1"

The complete tree is shown below and hopefully allows you to debug your work in case it is needed.

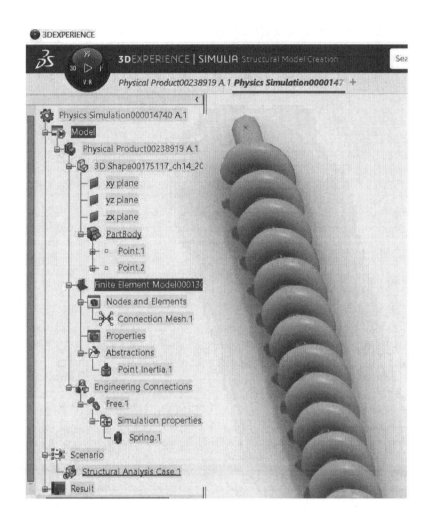

Select the "Procedures" tab from the action bar (bottom row).

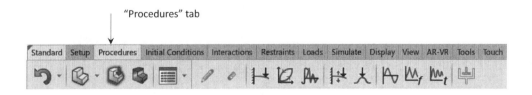

From the menu choose the "Frequency Step" icon ![icon]. Note that this leads to the second "Green" checkmark in the bottom left margin of the screen.

✓ Structural Analysis Case.1   ✓ Frequency Step.1

In the ensuing "Frequency Step" dialogue box, change the number of modes to "1". Needless to say, this is a single degree of freedom system and therefore only one mode can be calculated. Even if this change is not made, a single mode will be calculated.

Frequency Step   ✕

Name: Frequency Step.1

Solver type: Lanczos   ▼

Number of modes: 1   ⟵ ——————————— Change to 1

Minimum frequency: None

Maximum frequency: None

Property evaluation: 0Hz

Shift point: None

OK   Cancel

The next step is to apply the proper restraints which allow translation (and only translation) along the y-axis. Select the "Restraints" tab from the action bar.

"Restraints" tab

| Standard | Setup | Procedures | Initial Conditions | Interactions | Restraints | Loads | Simulate | Display | Vie |

From the available choices, pick the "Fixed Displacement" icon ![icon].

For the "Support", select the Point A where the mass is located and allow only the translation in the y direction as shown. Close the dialogue box by pressing "OK".

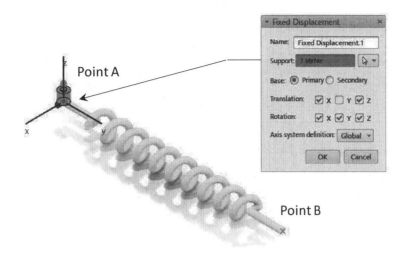

Select the "Fixed Displacement" icon 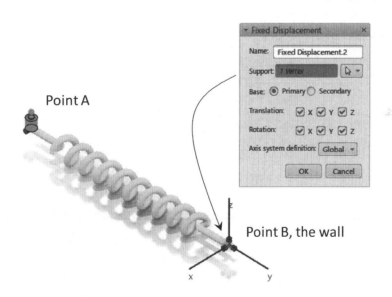 again. Fix all the degrees of freedom at Point B.

Since the present stage deals with the "Frequency Step", the loads are irrelevant and only the restraints (the displacement boundary conditions) are required. In fact, the load icons are all dimmed. Therefore, at this point, one can start the simulation process. Select the "Simulation" tab from the action bar.

"Simulate" tab

| Standard | Setup | Procedures | Initial Conditions | Interactions | Restraints | Loads | Simulate | Displ |

Pick the "Model and Scenario Check" icon.
Assuming that there are no error messages, this will
perform a preliminary scan of the model. In our case, the
model successfully passed.

Model and Scenario Checks Status	✕
✓ Model and Scenario Checks completed.	
Close Abort	

Next select the "Simulation Checks" icon and accept the default number of the
cores.

After the checking completes, our model successfully passes with no warning messages.

Simulation Checks Status

✓ Simulation checks completed.

  ▸ **Errors (0)**

  ▸ **Warnings (0)**

  ▸ **Information (0)**

Finally, use the "Simulate" icon to run the software for producing the simulation.
Our model successfully ran.

Simulation Status

✓ Structural Analysis Case.1 completed.

Messages	Licensing Messages	Plots	Iterations	Diagnostic files
▸ **Errors (0)**				
▸ **Warnings (0)**				
▸ **Information (0)**				

Results (Post processing):

Once you close (or move) the obstructing dialogue boxes, you must be in the "Results" section and the bottom row should appear as shown on the right.

If not, click on the "Results" icon 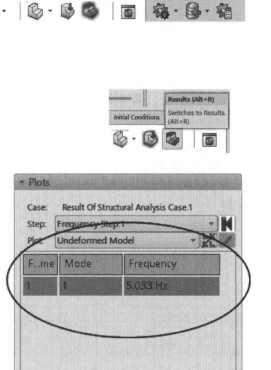 .

In the present problem (and the present step), there is not much to display. Because the discrete "spring" and "mass" elements were used, the deformation modes cannot be displayed. However, the frequency value is prominently shown in the "Plots" window and matches the theoretical value described on page 2 of this chapter.

The Modal Dynamic Step:

In modal dynamics, once the frequencies (modes) are extracted, they can be superimposed to solve the linear dynamic problems. In the present problem, a single frequency of 5.033 Hz was extracted. At this point, we have to return to the "Scenario" tab and create another step.

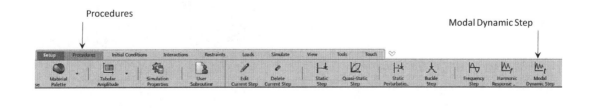

After choosing the "Procedures" tab, select the "Modal Dynamic Step" icon .

In the resulting dialogue box, change the "Total time" to 1s and the "Time increment" to 0.1s.

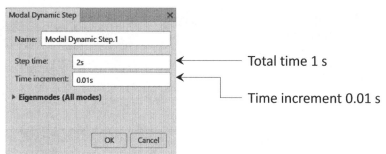

The mass is put in motion by giving it an initial velocity of $v_0 = 1\ m/s$ in the positive y-direction. In order to apply this condition, select the "Initial Conditions" tab in the menu.

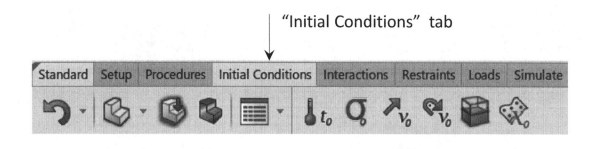

From the resulting menu, choose the "Initial Velocity" icon. The resulting dialogue box is shown below. For the support, pick Point A, where the mass is located. For the direction of the translation, choose y-direction (for our model) and for the "Velocity" use 1 m_s.

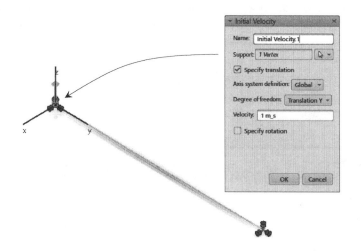

After closing the dialogue box, the proper direction of the imposed initial velocity is displayed.

Before simulating the model, additional output must be requested. This is referred to as the "History" plot. Select the "Simulate" tab from the action bar.

"Simulate" tab

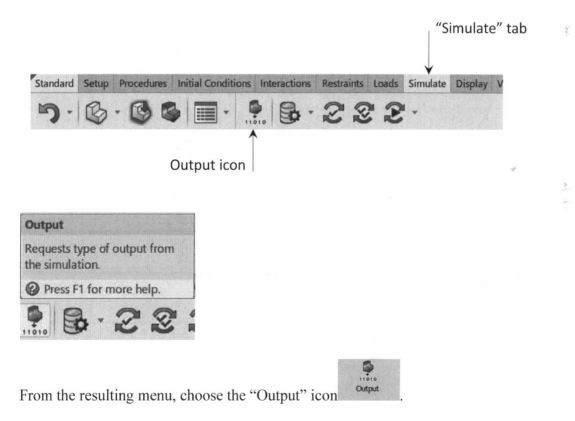

Output icon

Output

Requests type of output from the simulation.

❓ Press F1 for more help.

From the resulting menu, choose the "Output" icon   .

In the ensuing dialogue box, use the pull down menu and select "History".

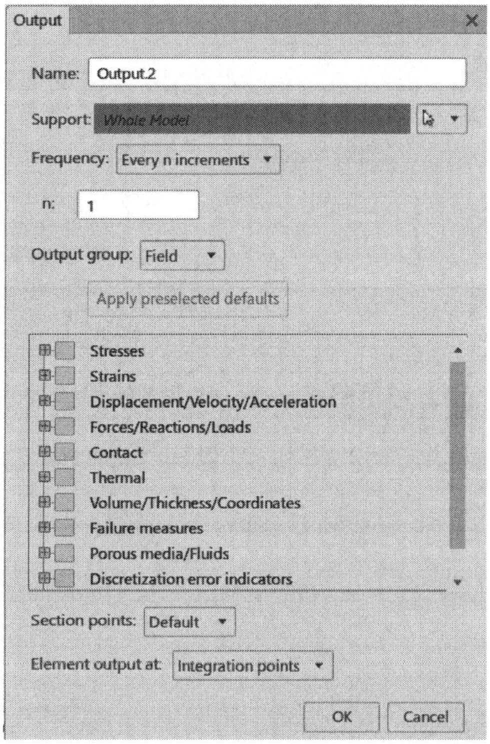

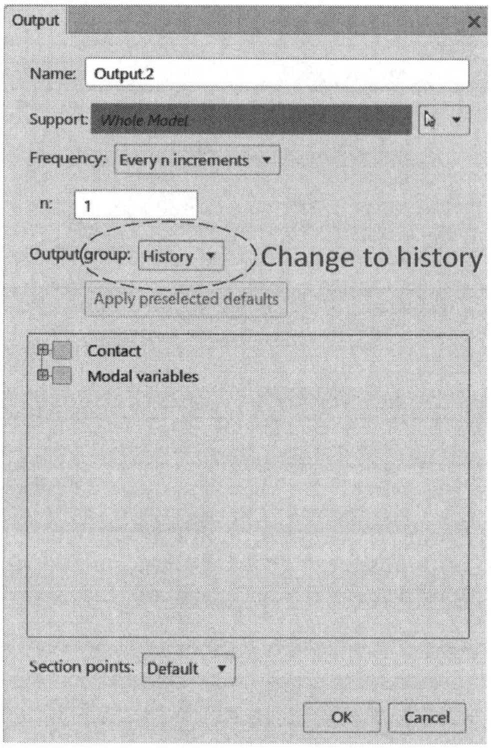

Check the two boxes indicated and for the "Support" pick the mass (i.e. Point A).

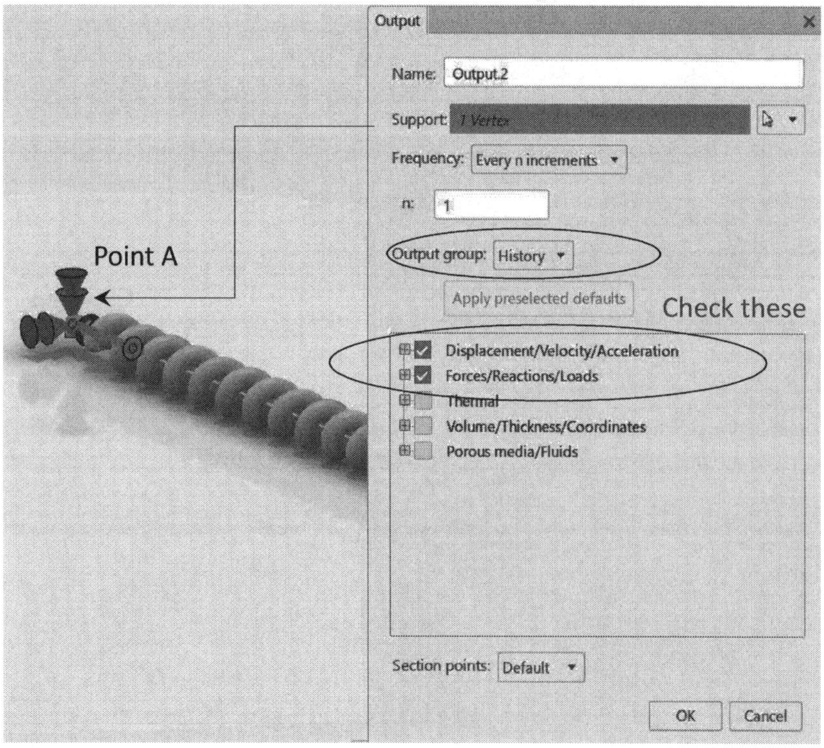

We will next specify the damping value. It is important to point out that at this point, there is no "dashpot" element available in 3DEXPERIENCE. Select the procedures tab once again.

Procedures tab

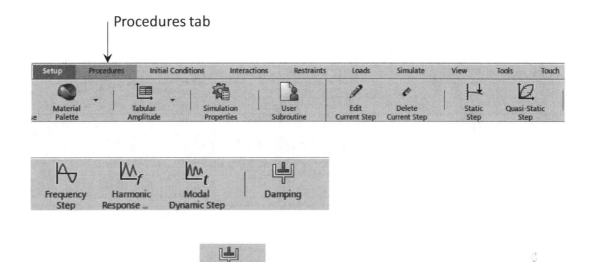

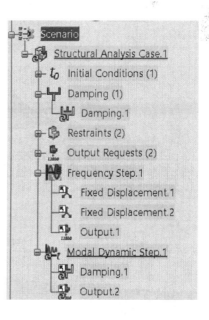

Choose the "Damping" icon from the list. The resulting dialogue box is shown below. We will be using the "Fractional" damping type. In the available table, indicate that the mode with frequency 5Hz is damped by 4.7%. This means $\zeta = 0.047$. The tree, after defining the damping ratio, is also shown for your viewing.

Finally, use the "Simulate" icon 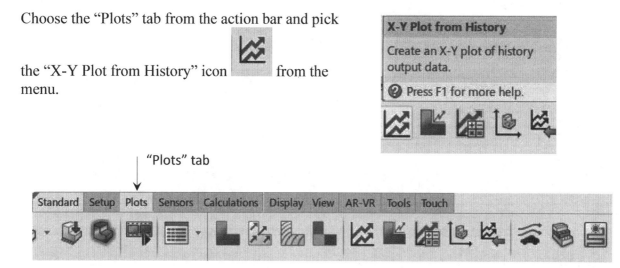 to run the software for producing the simulation. Our model successfully ran but some warning messages were generated.

Choose the "Plots" tab from the action bar and pick

the "X-Y Plot from History" icon from the menu.

"Plots" tab

In the "X-Y Plot from History" dialogue box, use the pull down menu to choose "UT Translations" and the "Vector Component 2". This means plotting the displacement in the y-direction. Clearly the displacements in the other directions are zero. Click on "Apply" to get the plot.

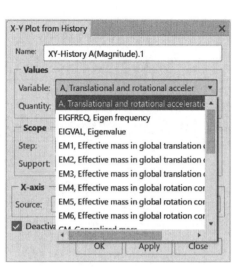

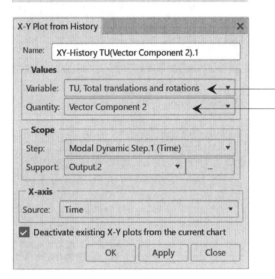

Select UT, Translations

Use the pulldown menu
to select the translation
in the appropriate direction,
not necessarily the magnitude.

The plot of the displacement
of the mass as a function of
time appears on the screen.
The graph is in excellent
agreement with the
theoretical graph presented
on page 3.

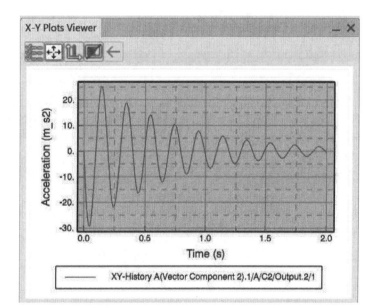

Using the pull down menu, for the variable, select "RF, Reaction Forces" and for the quantity, select "Vector Component 2". Upon clicking on "Apply" the plot shown below appears. This is not surprising. We are requesting the reaction force at Point A where the mass is located. This point is free to move and therefore, the reaction force RF is zero.

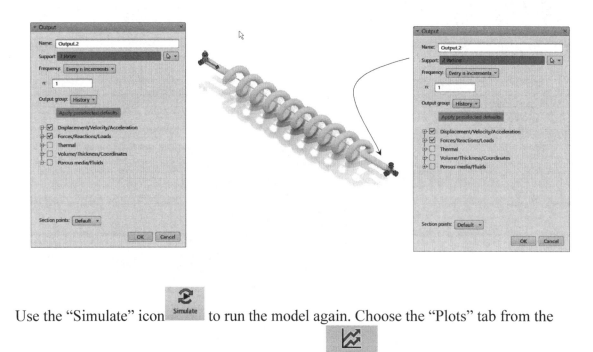

In order to plot the reaction force, we have to request the information at the wall. Double click on the branch of the tree dealing with "Output.2". This is where the additional output was requested in the first place. Use the cursor to pick Point B (i.e. the wall). This stores the information for both points. The process is shown below.

Use the "Simulate" icon ![Simulate] to run the model again. Choose the "Plots" tab from the action bar and pick the "Create History Plot" icon ![Create History Plot] from the menu.

Using the pull down menu for the variable, select "RF, Reaction Forces" and for the quantity, select "Vector Component 2". Upon clicking on "Apply" the plot shown below appears. This is in excellent agreement with the theoretical plot generated on page 3 of this chapter.

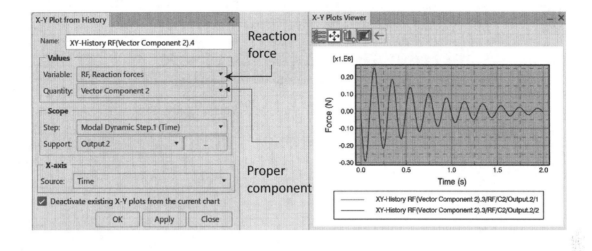

The Two Degree of Freedom System:

Creating the Finite Element Model:

Locate the compass on the top left corner of the screen and click on it. Scroll through the applications and select the "Structural Model

 Structural Model Creation

Creation" App.

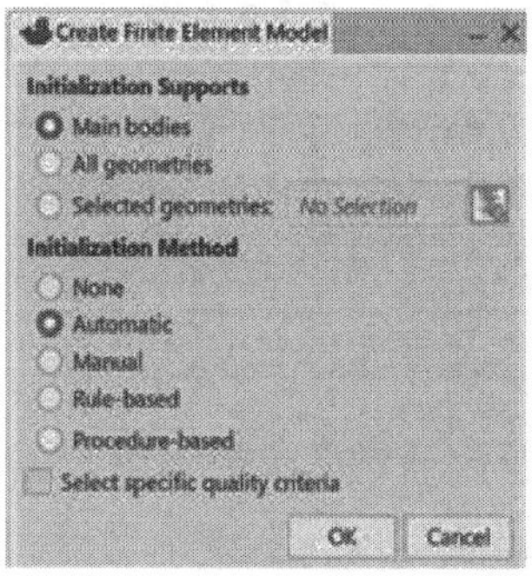

The dialogue box shown below "Create Finite Element Model" appears. For now, use the "Automatic" radio button. Other options are for a user control of the meshing process.

The process of creating the model, namely two masses and two springs, is the same as before. The model is shown below.

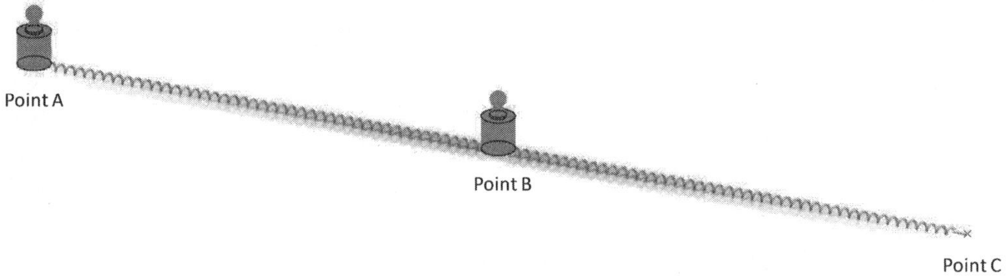

The points from left to right are labled as A, B, and C, 30mm apart.

Creating a Scenario:

The nature of the analysis, namely, Static, Dynamic, Buckling, etc. is set in the "Structural Scenario Creation" App. Furthermore, the loads, restraints, and interaction are also defined in this application.

It is also important to point out that that one could have created the Scenario before the FE model generation. In fact, it can be created from within the "Structural Scenario Creation" App.

Locate the compass on the top left corner of the screen and click. Scroll through the applications and select the Structural Scenario Creation"

 Structural Scenario Creation

App

The row of icons in the bottom of your screen changes and will appear as displayed below.

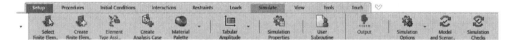

The pop-up window "Simulation Initialization" shown below appears on the screen. Since this is strictly a structural problem, the radio button "Structural" should be selected.

Simulation Initialization
Create Analysis Case
● Structural
○ Thermal
○ Thermal-Structural
Finite Element Model: None selected 🔩
OK   Cancel

A quick glance of the tree confirms that a "Scenario" has been created.

Click the "Select the Finite Element Model"

icon ![icon] from the bottom row. The following
pop-up window appears.

Since there is already a finite element model
created, it appears in the list and make sure that
you select that row.

Select row →

Note that the above action creates a "Green"
checkmark next to the "Structural Analysis
Case.1".

✓ Structural Analysis Case.1   ! No Procedures Exist

Select the "Procedures" tab from the action bar (bottom row).

Procedures tab

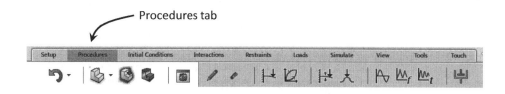

From the menu choose the "Frequency Step" icon 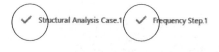. Note that this leads to the
second "Green" checkmark in the bottom left margin of the screen.

✓ Structural Analysis Case.1   ✓ Frequency Step.1

In the ensuing "Frequency Step" dialogue box, change the number of modes to "2".
Needless to say, this is a two degree of freedom system and therefore only two modes can
be calculated. Even if this change is not made, only two modes will be calculated.

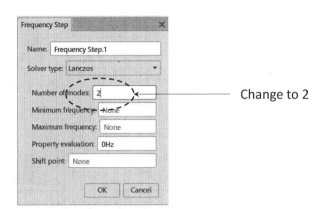

Change to 2

The next step is to apply the proper restraints which allow translation (and only translation) along the y-axis. Select the "Restraints" tab from the action bar.

"Restraints" tab

From the available choices, pick the "Fixed Displacement" icon and apply the restraints. With the exception of Point C (the wall), where all six degrees of freedom are fixed, the points A and B are allowed to translate along the y-direction. Therefore, five of the six degrees of freedom are fixed. The situation is displayed below.

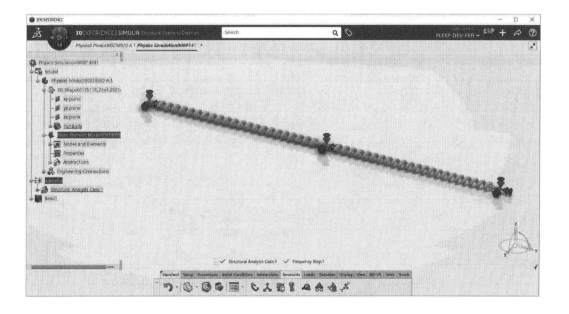

Finally, use the "Simulate" icon  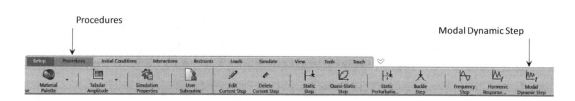 to run the software for producing the simulation. Our model successfully ran.

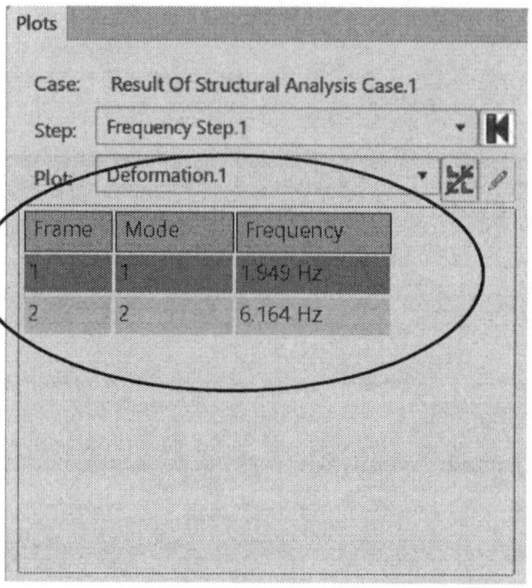

In the present problem (and the present step), there is not much to display. Because the discrete "spring" and "mass" elements were used, the deformation modes cannot be displayed. However, the two frequency values are prominently shown in the "Plots" window and match the theoretical value described on page 2 of this chapter.

Plots

Case:	Result Of Structural Analysis Case.1	
Step:	Frequency Step.1	
Plot	Deformation.1	

Frame	Mode	Frequency
1	1	1.949 Hz
2	2	6.164 Hz

Modal Dynamics Step:

In modal dynamics, once the frequencies (modes) are extracted, they can be superimposed to solve the linear dynamic problems. In the present problem, two frequencies of 1.949 Hz and 6.164 Hz were extracted. At this point, we must return to the "Scenario" tab and create another step.

After choosing the "Procedures" tab, select the "Modal Dynamic Step" icon. In the resulting dialogue box, change the "Total time" to 1s and the "Time increment" to 0.01s.

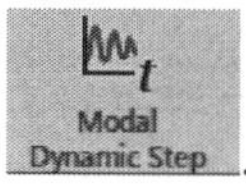

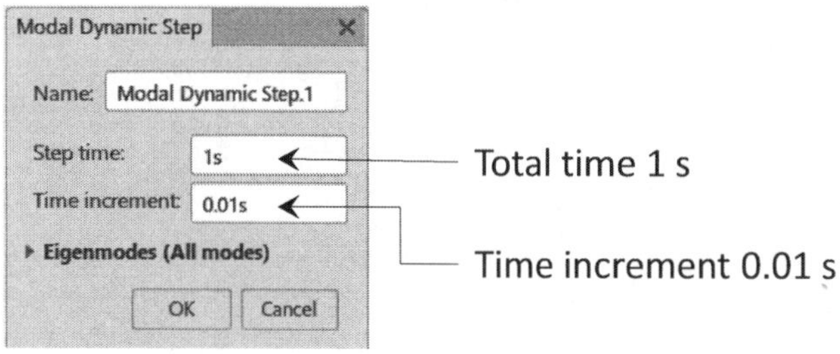

Modal Dynamic Step

Name: Modal Dynamic Step.1

Step time: 1s ⟵ ——— Total time 1 s

Time increment: 0.01s ⟵

▸ **Eigenmodes (All modes)** ——— Time increment 0.01 s

OK   Cancel

Select the "Setup" tab from the action bar. From this action bar, choose "Tabular Amplitude" icon 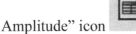.

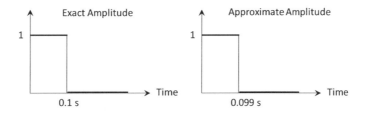

From the menu, choose the "Tabular Amplitude" icon 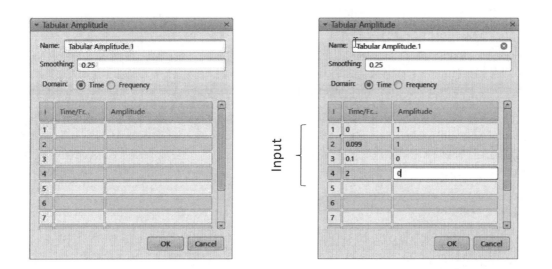. Here, you will be creating an amplitude curve which is almost the step load defined on page 3.

Input the amplitude information as shown below. Note that I have defined the amplitude curve over a 2s interval which is fine because it is larger than the 1s needed.

Close the dialogue box by clicking on "OK". The location where the amplitude curve is displayed in the tree is shown on the next page. The dialogue box for the amplitude curve can easily be accessed by double clicking on the appropriate branches. Note that the

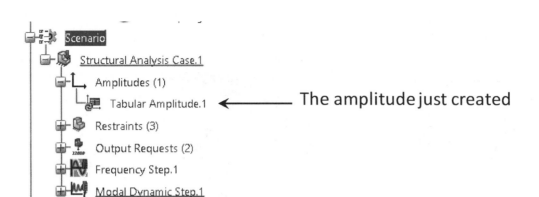

amplitude curve could have had a value of 25000N for the load but we chose to use 1 N.

Applying the Load:

Select the "Force" icon ![Force] from the action bar. For the "Support", choose Point A (the left mass) as shown. Input 25000 N for the "Force Y". Finally, use the pull down menu in the "Amplitude" section, and select "Tabular Amplitude 1".

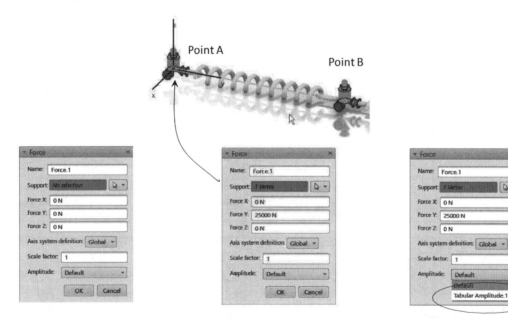

The force is displayed on the screen as expected.

Here is the force

Before simulating the model, additional output must be requested. This is referred to as the "History" plot. Select the "Simulate" tab from the action bar.

"Simulations" tab

From the resulting menu, choose the "Output" icon 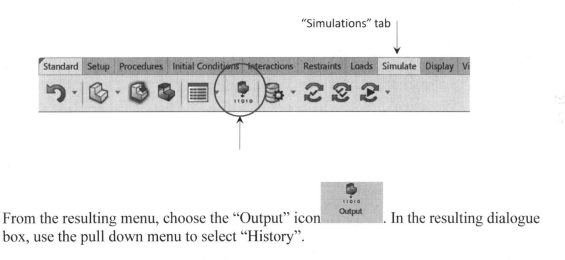. In the resulting dialogue box, use the pull down menu to select "History".

Change to history

Check the proper box and for the "Support" pick the two masses (i.e. Point A and Point B).

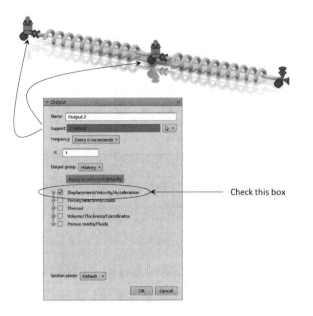

Check this box

Pick the "Simulate" icon ![Simulate] to run the software for producing the simulation. The simulation runs successfully as shown below. Some warning messages have been generated.

Simulation Status

✓ Structural Analysis Case.1 completed.

| Messages | Plots | Iterations |

▼ Warnings (4)

MODAL DYNAMIC OPTION IS NOT SUPPORTED FOR ELEMENT LOOP PARALLELIZATION. IF YOU HAVE SPECIFIED ELEMENT LOOP PARALLELIZATION, IT WILL BE TURNED OFF FOR THIS ANALYSIS.

OUTPUT VARIABLE UR HAS NO COMPONENTS IN THIS ANALYSIS

Boundary conditions are specified on inactive dof of 1 nodes. The nodes have been identified in node set WarnNodeBCInactiveDof.

A STEADY STATE, SUBSPACE PROJECTION BASED, OR MODE-BASED DYNAMIC ANALYSIS IS REQUESTED FOR A MODEL INVOLVING LAGRANGE MULTIPLIERS. INCORRECT STRESSES AND REACTION FORCES MAY BE OBTAINED AT DEGREES OF FREEDOM DIRECTLY DEPENDING ON THESE LAGRANGE MULTIPLIERS (E.G. DISTRIBUTING COUPLING CONSTRAINTS, HYBRID ELEMENTS, OR CONNECTOR ELEMENTS). HOWEVER, ALL OTHER NODAL OUTPUT QUANTITIES SUCH AS DISPLACEMENTS AS WELL AS ELEMENT STRAINS WILL BE CORRECT.

Post Processing of the Results:

Choose the "Plots" tab from the action bar and pick

the "X-Y Plot from History" icon ![icon] from the menu.

> **X-Y Plot from History**
>
> Create an X-Y plot of history output data.
>
> ⑦ Press F1 for more help.

"Plots" tab

| Standard | Setup | Plots | Sensors | Calculations | Display | View | AR-VR | Tools | Touch |

In the "X-Y Plot from History" dialogue box, use the pull down menu to choose "UT Translations" and the "Vector Component 2". This means plotting the displacement in the y-direction. Clearly the displacements in the other directions are zero. Click on "Apply" to get the plot.

Select UT, Translations

Use the pulldown menu
to select the translation
in the appropriate direction,
not necessarily the magnitude.

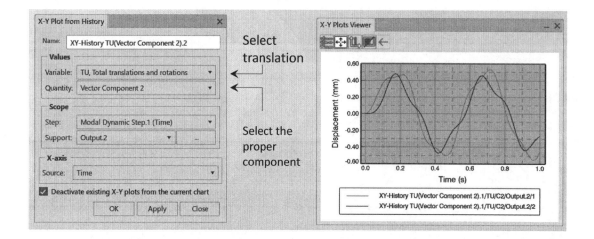

Specifying the Damping:

We will next specify the damping value. It is important to point out that at this point, there is no "dashpot" element available in 3DEXPERIENCE. Select the procedures tab once again.

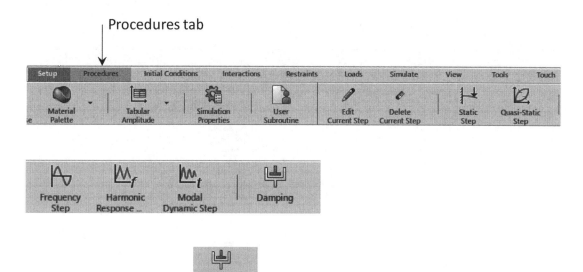

Choose the "Damping" icon from the list. The resulting dialogue box is shown below. We will be using the "Fractional" damping type. To begin with, both modes are assigned 10% damping.

After simulating the model and postprocessing, the displacement curves shown below are generated.

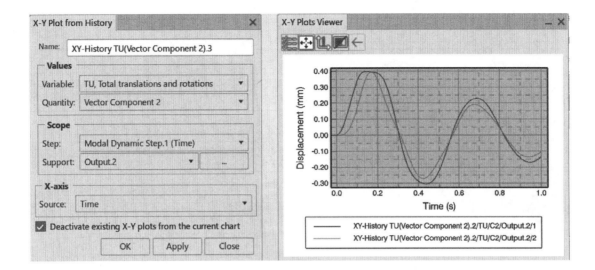

The figure below corresponds to 50% percent damping of each mode.

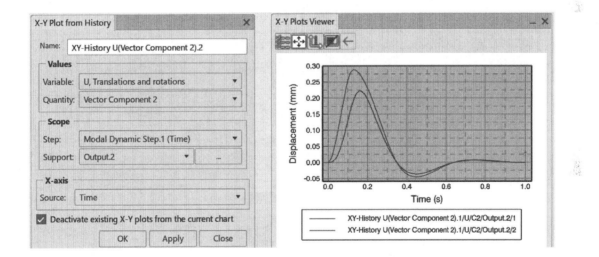

This completes the chapter.

Notes:

Chapter 15

Harmonic Response, Simply Supported Beam

Objective:

In this chapter, the midspan of a simply supported beam is subjected to a sinusoidal (harmonic) load causing it to vibrate in the transverse direction. The objective is to find the amplitude of the vibration of a node as a function of the applied frequency.

Problem Statement:

The simply supported beam shown below is subjected to the harmonic load $F(t) = 4000\sin(\omega t)$ Newton at its midspan. The harmonic force is driven at the circular frequency $\omega = 900\,\frac{rad}{s} = 143\,Hz$

The beam is assumed to be made of steel with $E = 200\,GPa, \rho = 7800\,\frac{kg}{m^3}, \nu = 0.3$.
The length of the beam is L =1000 mm and it has a circular cross section with a radius of R=10 mm.

The theoretical deflection of the beam at the midpoint is described by the expression

$$w(t) = \frac{2*(4000)}{\rho AL}\sum_{n=1}^{\infty}\frac{1}{\omega_{2n-1}^2 - \omega^2}\sin \omega t \text{ where } \omega_n \text{ represents the natural frequencies of a}$$

simply supported beam given by $\omega_n = (n\pi)^2\sqrt{\dfrac{EI}{\rho AL^4}}$ rad/s.

F(t)=4000 sin(ω t)

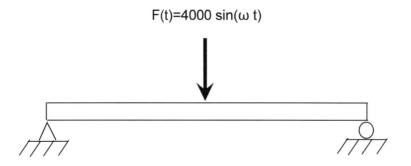

The exact solution based on infinite number of modes, the single mode and two modes approximation are described below and plotted also. One can see that a two-mode approximation produces almost the exact solution at the midspan location.

$$w(t) = \frac{2*4000}{\rho A L} * \left[\sum_{n=1}^{\infty} \frac{1}{\omega_{2n-1}^2 - \omega^2}\right] \sin(\omega t)$$

$$w_1(t) = \frac{2*4000}{\rho A L} * \left[\frac{1}{\omega_1^2 - \omega^2}\right] \sin(\omega t)$$

$$w_2(t) = \frac{2*4000}{\rho A L} * \left[\frac{1}{\omega_1^2 - \omega^2} + \frac{1}{\omega_3^2 - \omega^2}\right] \sin(\omega t)$$

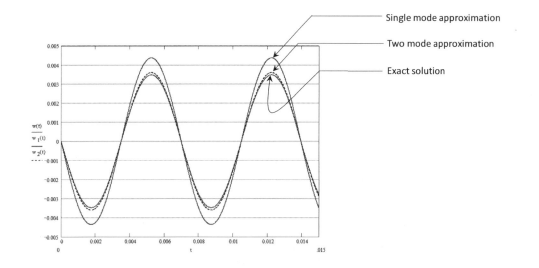

The first two natural frequencies of the transverse vibration of the simply supported beam are also given below which will be used for comparison purposes.

$$\omega_1 = 250 \ \frac{rad}{s} = 39.7 \ Hz$$
$$\omega_2 = 1000 \ \frac{rad}{s} = 159 \ Hz$$

The Model and Material Properties:

Use the Part Design App to create three points as shown followed by creating two lines. The first line is between the points 1 and 2. The second line is between the points 2 and 3.

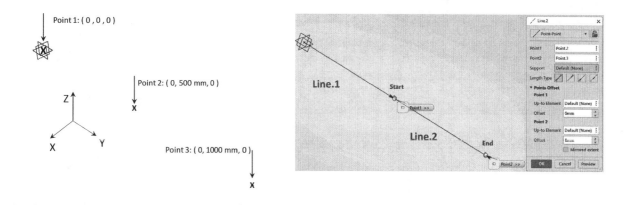

Apply the material properties to this part. The dialogue box with the inputted data is shown below. The part is now completed and needs to be meshed.

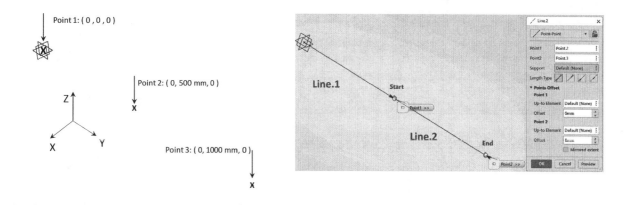

Creating the Finite Element Model:

Locate the compass on the top left corner of the
screen and click on it. Scroll through the
applications and select the "Structural Model

 Structural Model
Creation

Creation" App   .

The appropriate branches are created in the tree
automatically; however, since the lines are to be
meshed with beam elements, the meshing
process must be done manually by the user as
was done in the chapter "Simple Analysis of
Frame".

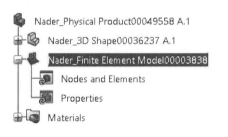

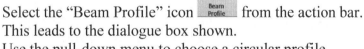

Select the "Beam Profile" icon from the action bar.
This leads to the dialogue box shown.
Use the pull-down menu to choose a circular profile.

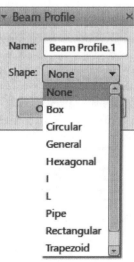

For the radius of the cross-section input 10mm and close the dialogue box. This profile is recorded in the tree.

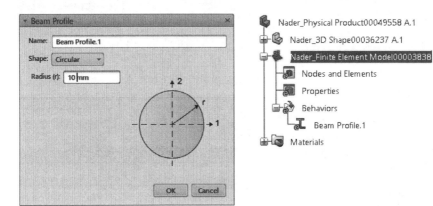

Choose the "Beam Section" icon [Beam Section] from the action bar and upon the appearance of the dialogue box, use the pull down menu to select the "Profile.1" that was just created.

For the "Support" pick the two lines in the model. Note that there is no need to define "Orientation geometry" as the cross section is a circle.

The section is shown on the screen and if necessary you can hide it to avoid distraction.

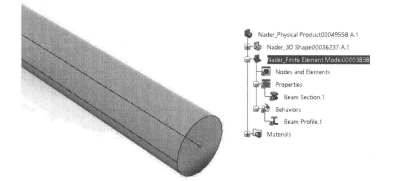

Note that the part is still not meshed. This will be done in the next step.

Switch to the meshing module 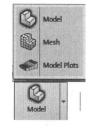.

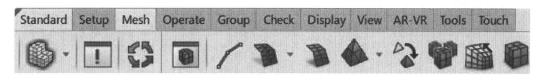

Choose the "Beam Mesh" icon from the action bar. This leads to the dialogue box shown below. For the "Support", you will be selecting the two lines constructed earlier (needs to be done separately). The size is set to 50 mm. This results in 20 beam elements generated on the lines.

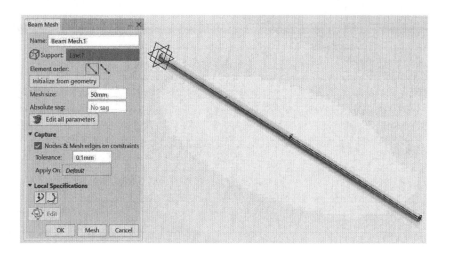

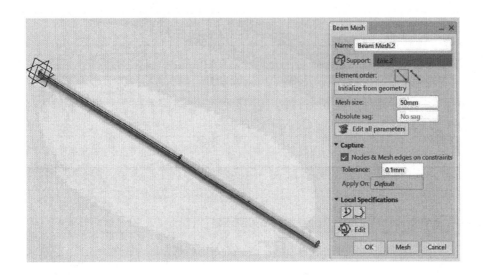

This ensures that there is a point (vertex) where load can be applied. The utility features can be used effectively to display the 1D beam mesh.

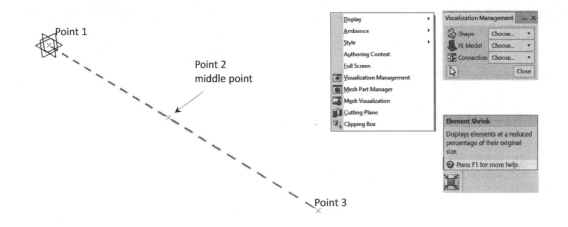

This completes the needed tasks in the "Structural Model Creation" App.

Creating a Scenario:

Locate the compass on the top left corner of the screen and click. Scroll through the applications and select the "Structural Scenario Creation"

 Structural Scenario Creation

App   .

The pop-up window "Simulation Initialization" on the right appears. Since this is strictly a structural problem, the radio button "Structural" should be selected.

Click the "Finite Element Model" icon from the bottom row. The following pop-up window appears.

Since there is already a finite element model created, it appears in the list and make sure that you select that row.

select ⟶

Select the "Procedures" tab from the action bar (bottom row).

Select the "Procedure" tab

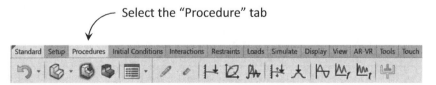

Select the "Frequency Step" icon from the bottom row. For the "Number of modes", type "2".

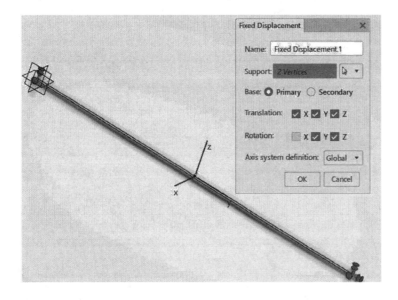

Both with "Green" check marks

Frequency Step	X
Name:	Frequency Step.1
Solver type:	Lanczos ▼
Number of modes:	2
Minimum frequency:	None
Maximum frequency:	None
Property evaluation:	0Hz
Shift point:	None

OK   Cancel

Applying the Restraints:

From the menu, select the Restraints tab. Make sure that the end points are hidden first.

Choose the "Fixed Displacement" icon . Select the two end vertices of the line. Applying the restraints to the actual geometric Point.1 and Point.3 leads to error messages.

Choose the "Fixed Displacement" icon again. For the "Support" select the line in the problem and prevent the motion in the x-direction. This eliminates the out of plane deflection in the x-direction.

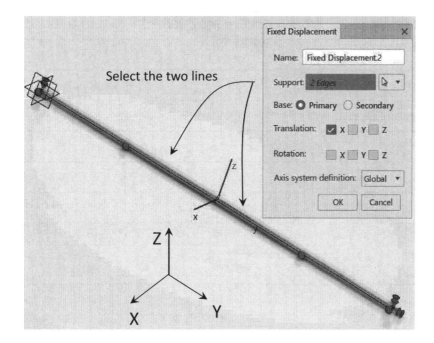

Consistency, Model Check, and Simulation:

Select the "Simulation" tab from the bottom row of icons on your screen (i.e. from the action bar).

"Simulate" tab

It is a good practice to perform the model and consistency check before submitting the work for the final run.

Select the "Model and Scenario Check" icon from the bottom row .

The software goes through a check phase and if there are no issues, a message with a "Green" check mark is returned.

Next select the "Simulation Checks" icon 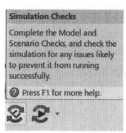 from the bottom row of icons. Accept the number of "cores" in the pop up box below.

The "Simulation Check" runs successfully.

Choose the "Simulation" icon from the bottom row.

Accept the number of "cores" in the pop-up box, and wait for the simulation to complete.

The program successfully runs, and no messages are reported.

Results (Post processing):

Once you close (or move) the obstructing dialogue boxes, you must be in the "Results" section and the bottom row should appear as shown on the right.

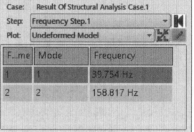

If not, click on the "Results" icon .

The "Plots" dialogue box is shown below. It displays the two modal frequencies requested. The predicted values are in excellent agreement with the numbers reported in page 3 of this chapter. Using the pull-down menu and selecting the "displacement", actual mode shapes can be displayed too.

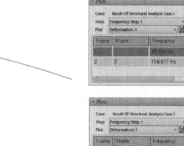

Performing a Harmonic Step:

Select the "Procedures" tab from the action bar. From the menu, pick the "Harmonic Step" icon .

The following dialogue box appears which needs to be filled.

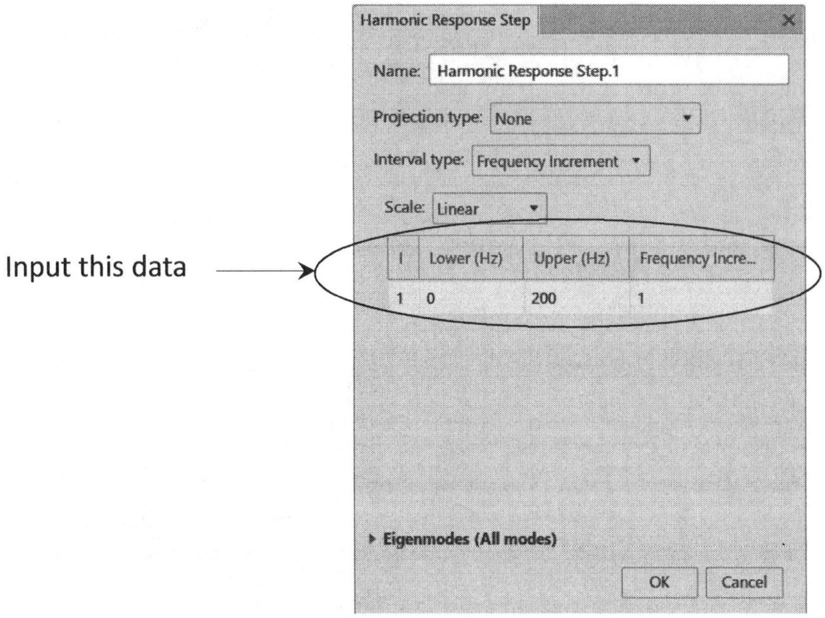

Input this data

The "Lower" frequency being zero leads to a warning message, indicating that it was adjusted to be a small yet not-zero value. The "Upper" frequency indicates the maximum driving frequency range of interest. Finally, the third column indicates the sweeping resolution. The smaller the value, the smoother the frequency response graph will be.

Choose the "Loads" tab, and from the menu, pick the "Force" icon .

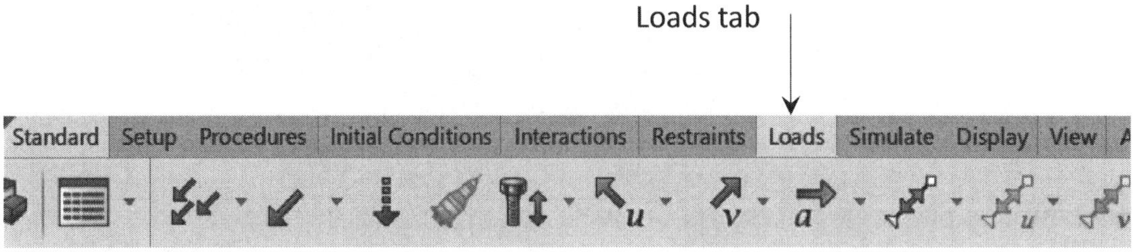

Loads tab

Use the cursor to choose the midpoint (Point.2) and apply a concentrated force of 4000 N to that location. This is the amplitude of the harmonic load being considered.

Requesting Addition Output

From the action bar select the "Output" icon 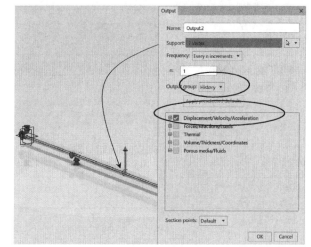.

In the resulting dialogue box, make the selections shown.

For the "Support" choose the midpoint of the beam (Point.2). Use the pull-down menu to pick "History".

Finally, check "Displacement/Velocity/Acceleration" output.

Select the "Simulation" icon ⟳ from the bottom row. The simulation completes with a "warning" message as shown.

Simulation Status

✓ Structural Analysis Case.1 completed.

Messages	Licensing Messages	Plots	Iterations	Diagnostic files

▶ Errors (0)

▼ Warnings (2)

   Output requests in the following steps will override requests from previous steps: harmonic response step.1. Delete the output requests to modify that behavior.

   The minimum frequency is increased to 1.50487e-08 to avoid numerical issues that occur at very small frequencies. If frequencies below this value are of interest, then the workaround is to increase the units of time.

▶ Information (0)

[Close]   [Terminate]

Choose the "Plots" tab from the action bar.

"Plots" tab

| Standard | Setup | Plots | Sensors | Calculations | Display | View | AR-VR | Tools | Touch |

From the menu, pick the "X-Y Create Plot from History" icon, make the following selections and click on "Apply".

X-Y Plot from History

Create an X-Y plot of history output data.

🕐 Press F1 for more help.

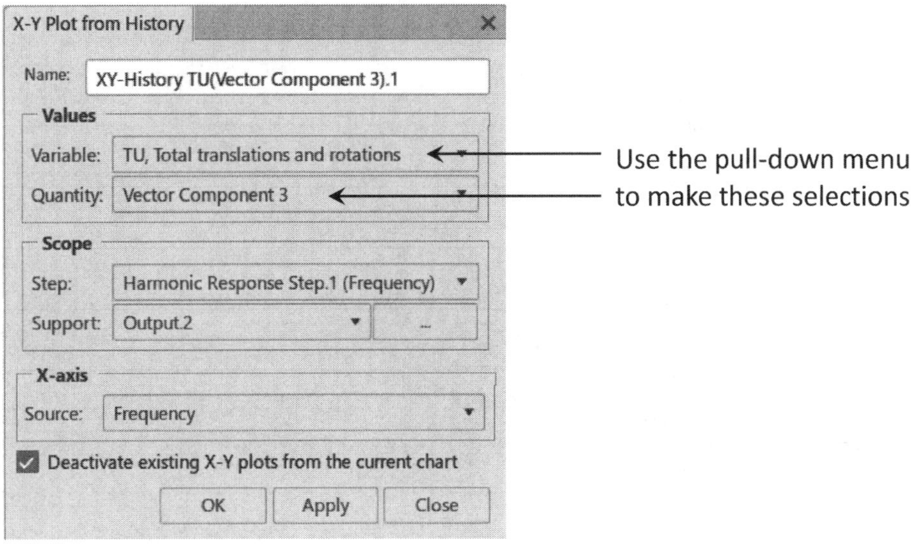

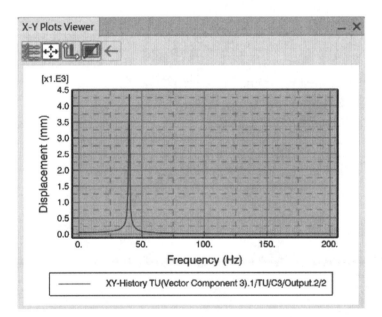

The following frequency response graph is generated.

A reasonable question to ask is how the above curve can be used. Let us recall that the force is applied at the driving frequency of 900 rad/s or 143 Hz. Using the above graph one can find the amplitude of displacement at 143 H which is stated to be 4.38 mm. Therefore, the steady state vibration of the midpoint of the beam is described by $z(t) = 4.38\sin(900t)$. This is in reasonable agreement with the solutions proposed on page 3.

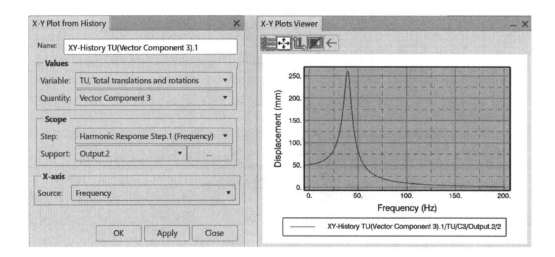

The above frequency response plot is based on zero damping. Let us introduce some modal damping into the model. Select the "Damping" icon from the list of available choices in the menu .

In the resulting dialogue box, indicate 10% damping on modes with frequencies 39 Hz and 158 Hz. Based on these damping values, the frequency response curve is modified as shown below.

Note that the sharp peaks (infinite amplitude) are now reduced to a finite value because of the damping introduced.

Exercise 1: Motor Unbalance

A clamped-clamped beam carries a motor of mass 50 kg and an operational speed of 2000 rpm as shown. If the motor has a rotational unbalance of 0.25 kg.m, use finite elements to find the steady state amplitude of the motor displacement. The beam length is 2 m and the cross section is a 10 cm x 10 cm square.

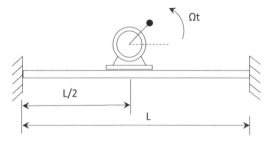

Exercise 2: Harmonic Response of a TDOF System

Consider the TDOF system shown in the objective section where $m_1 = 2 \times 10^5 \ kg$, $m_2 = 2.5 \times 10^5 \ kg$, $k_1 = 150 \times 10^6 \ N/m$, $k_2 = 75 \times 10^6 \ N/m$, and $\zeta_1 = \zeta_2 = 1\%$. Assuming that $F(t) = 100\sin(40t)$, use finite elements to find the frequency response of the masses.

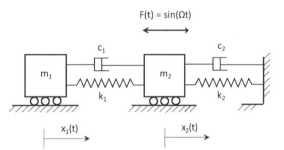

Exercise 3: Harmonic Response of a Clamped-Clamped Beam

Conduct a frequency response analysis of the clamped-clamped beam shown below using the data provided and the transverse distributed load $P = P_0\sin(\omega t)$.

$$EI = 30 \times 10^8, m = 0.1 \ lb.\frac{s^2}{in^2}, P_0 = \frac{lb}{in}, \omega = 300 \frac{rad}{s}, L = 240 \ in.$$

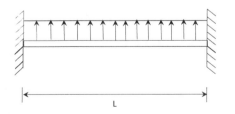

Notes:

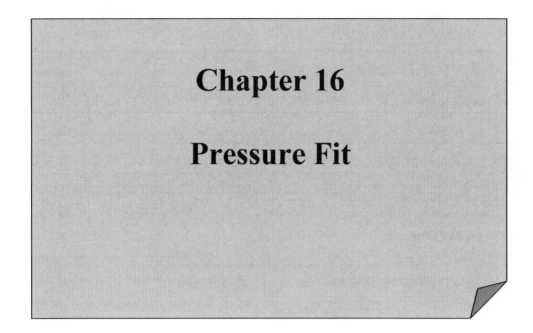

Chapter 16

Pressure Fit

Objective:

In this tutorial, you will analyze the assembly of two disks made of different materials which are shrink fitted (pressure fitted) within each other. The inside disk has a diameter 4.002" which is slightly larger than the outside disk being 4.000".

Problem Statement

The two cylinders, shown below, are shrink fitted. The outside cylinder, made of steel, has inside and outside diameters of 4 in. and 5 in. respectively. The inside cylinder, made of bronze, has inside and outside diameters of 2 in. and 4.002 in. respectively. This implies that diametral interference is 0.002 in.

The material properties of steel are $E_S = 30E6\,psi$ and $v_S = .29$. The corresponding properties for bronze are $E_B = 15E6\,psi$ and $v_B = .32$. Due to symmetry conditions, only a 60-degree sector is being modeled.

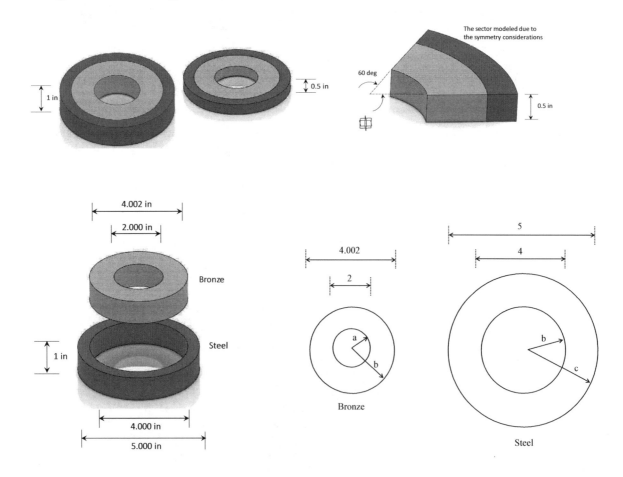

The variables "a", "b" and "c" are called the nominal radii. Here, $a = 1$ in., $b = 2$ in., and $c = 2.5$ in.; furthermore, the radial interference is $\delta = 0.002 / 2 = .001$ in.

The contact pressure can be calculated from the following expression.

$$p = \frac{\delta}{b\left[\dfrac{1}{E_S}\left(\dfrac{c^2 + b^2}{c^2 - b^2} + \nu_S\right) + \dfrac{1}{E_B}\left(\dfrac{b^2 + a^2}{b^2 - a^2} - \nu_B\right)\right]}$$

Based on the supplied parameters, the contact pressure is estimated as $p = 1990$ psi. The stress distribution can then be evaluated from the following formulas.

For Steel:
$$\begin{cases} \sigma_{hoop} = 3537 + \dfrac{22108}{r^2} \\[2mm] \sigma_{radial} = 3537 - \dfrac{22108}{r^2} \end{cases}$$

For Bronze:
$$\begin{cases} \sigma_{hoop} = -2653 - \dfrac{2653}{r^2} \\[2mm] \sigma_{radial} = -2653 + \dfrac{2653}{r^2} \end{cases}$$

The variable "r" represents the distance of the point under consideration to the origin.

The graphical representation of the hoop and radial stress is provided in the figure below. Note that the radial stress is continuous, whereas there is jump discontinuity in the hoop stress at the interface.

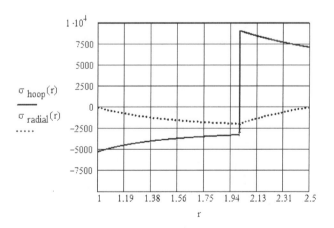

Creation of the Assembly:

Click on the compass on the top left corner of
the screen. This will open the CAD applications
available in 3DEXPERIENCE.

From the list, select the "Assembly Design"

Application  .

It is assumed that you have already created the two parts, the steel and the bronze sectors,
and applied the material properties at the part level prior to the assembly process.
You then insert them into the assembly as "Existing 3D Part" and position them properly.
The positioning can be achieved using the "Engineering Connections" icon, if necessary.
The screen looks as shown below.

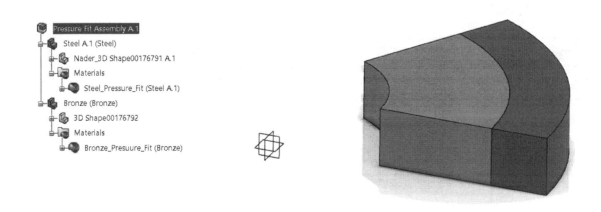

At this point, there are two ways to proceed. One can take the assembly and create the
mesh for the assembly. Alternatively, mesh each of the two parts (at the part level) and
create an assembly of meshes. The first approach was used in chapter 9. To demonstrate
something new, here we will use the latter, namely, and assembly of meshes. For small
assemblies, there is no clear advantage/disadvantage to either strategy. For large
assemblies, however, the assembly of meshes may be preferable.

Double click on the "steel" part to ensure that you are in that location of the model.

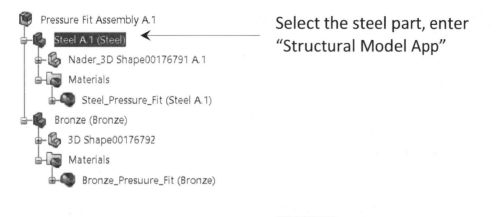

Select the steel part, enter "Structural Model App"

Select the "Structural Model Creation" App from the list of applications and enter that module. Because you are in the steel part, immediately it is meshed.

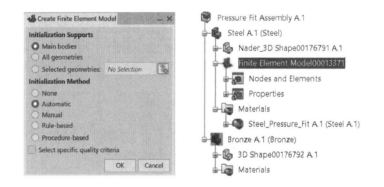

One way to see the mesh is to click on the

"Update" icon .
There are many other ways to display the mesh though.

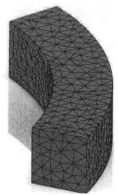

Before you proceed with the other tasks, double click on the "Nodes and Elements" branch in the tree to open the corresponding dialogue box shown below. This is to ensure that the size and type are appropriate and can be changed if necessary.

Once again, double click on the "Nodes and Elements" branch in the tree to open the corresponding dialogue box shown on the right. Make sure that the "Element order" 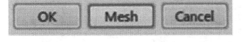 is parabolic and the element size is "0.105in" as shown.

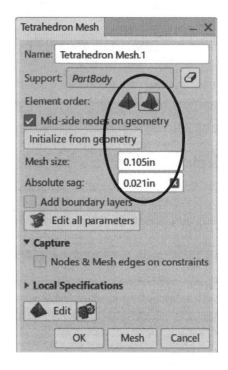

If necessary, click on the "Mesh" button at the bottom of the dialogue box to update the information chosen.

OK	Mesh	Cancel

Next "Hide" the mesh just discussed; double click on the "Bronze" part in the tree. This will land you in that part.

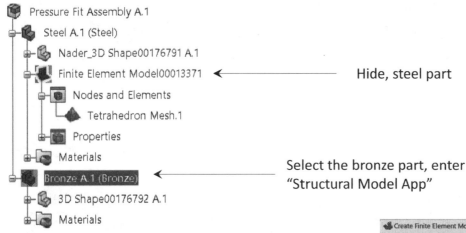

Hide, steel part

Select the bronze part, enter "Structural Model App"

Once again, select the "Structural Model Creation" App

 Structural Model Creation   from the list of applications and enter that module.

Because you are in the "Bronze" part, immediately it is meshed.

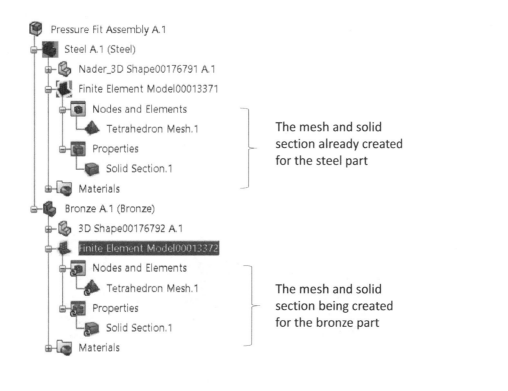

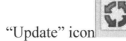 Pressure Fit Assembly A.1
    Steel A.1 (Steel)
        Nader_3D Shape00176791 A.1
        Finite Element Model00013371
            Nodes and Elements
                Tetrahedron Mesh.1
            Properties
                Solid Section.1
        Materials
    Bronze A.1 (Bronze)
        3D Shape00176792 A.1
        Finite Element Model00013372
            Nodes and Elements
                Tetrahedron Mesh.1
            Properties
                Solid Section.1
        Materials

The mesh and solid section already created for the steel part

The mesh and solid section being created for the bronze part

Once again to see the mesh, click on the

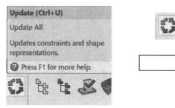

"Update" icon   .

Before you proceed with the other tasks, double click on the "Nodes and Elements" branch in the tree to open the corresponding dialogue box shown on the right. This is to ensure that the size and type are appropriate and can be changed if necessary.

Once again, double click on the "Nodes and Elements" branch in the tree to open the corresponding dialogue box shown on the right. Make

sure that the "Element order" 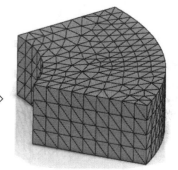 is parabolic and the element size is "0.115in" as shown.

If necessary, click on the "Mesh" button at the bottom of the dialogue box to update the information chosen.

To see both meshes simultaneously you can select the "Visualization Management" icon

Visualization Management and then manipulating the corresponding dialogue box.

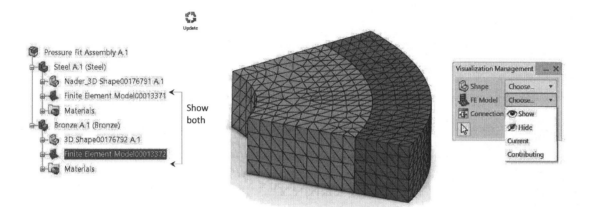

*The next step is to **move back to the "Assembly Design App"**. Double click on the top level branch of the tree. This will move you to the "Assembly Design" App.*

Select the "Structural Model Creation" App   Structural Model Creation   from the list of applications and enter that module. Immediately the familiar "Create Finite Element Model" dialogue box shown below appears.

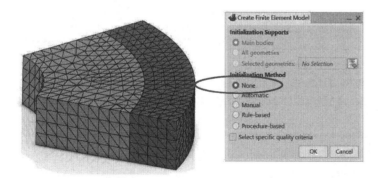

Make sure the radio button "None" is selected.

Note that on the top section of the tree, two branches have been created. This is where the mesh information is submitted. ***By the way, if the radio button "Automatic" is chosen***, the entire assembly is meshed once again which was not the plan. We want to use the meshes that are already created at the part level.

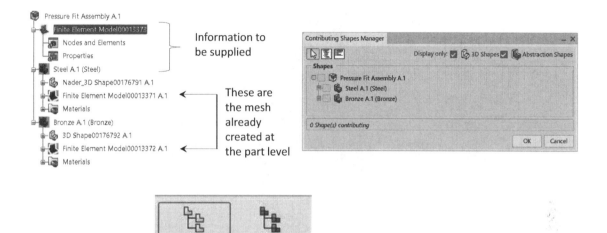

There are two icons 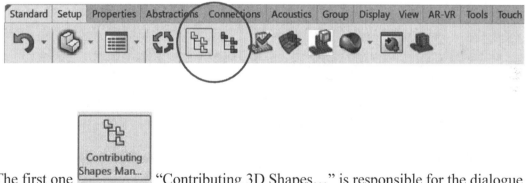 in the action bar which are instrumental to what is about to be done.

The first one "Contributing 3D Shapes…" is responsible for the dialogue box shown above. Through this dialogue box, the software is told which 3D Shapes are participating in the analysis of the assembly. Place a check mark in the boxes shown below and close the dialogue box.

The second icon, named "Contributing Finite Elemen…" instructs which meshes are used to participate in the analysis of the assembly. Select this icon which leads to the next dialogue box.

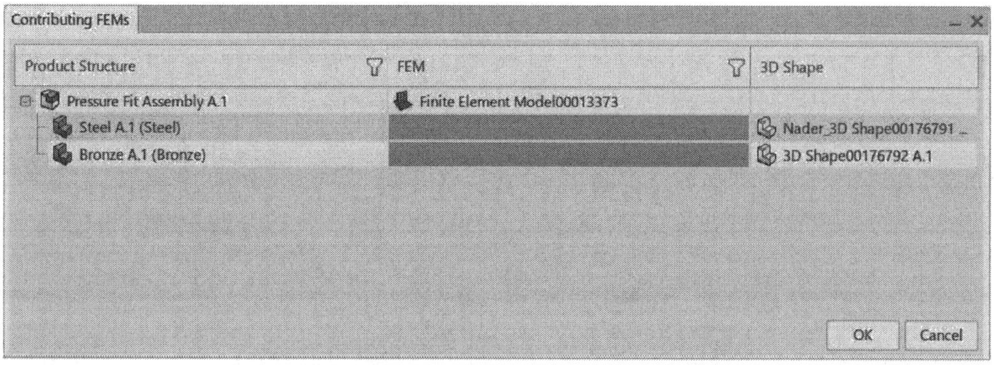

Place the cursor in the position shown, right click, and make the indicated selection.

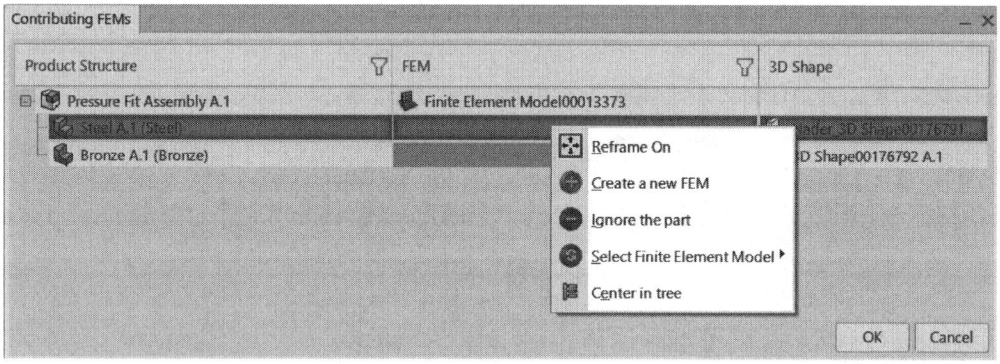

The result of this selection is shown below.

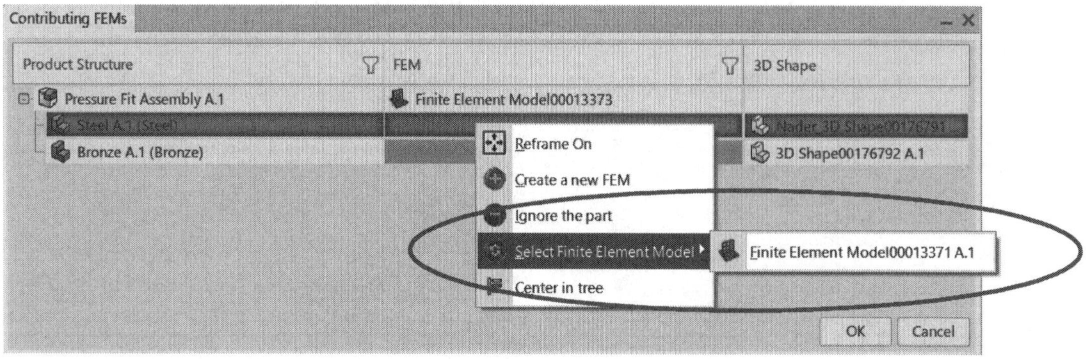

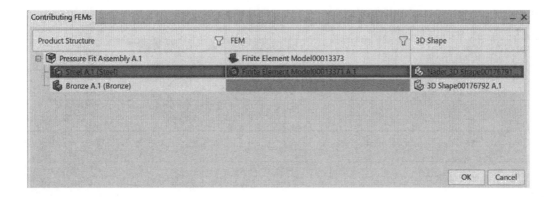

The above process must be repeated for the lower line in the dialogue box. These are also shown below for completeness.

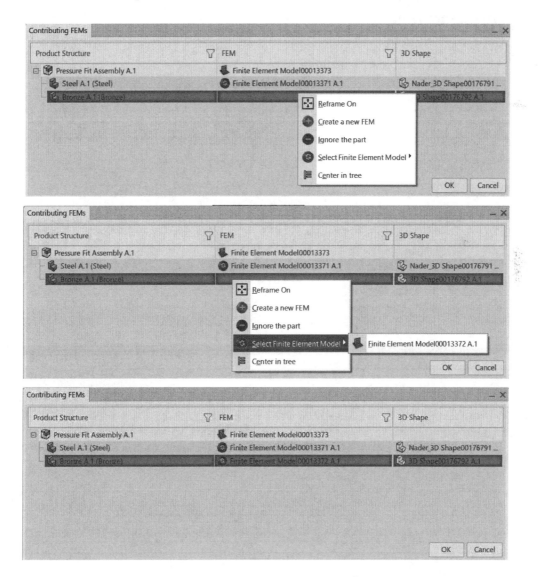

Although the steps mentioned above include the part meshes in the analysis of the assembly, there is no indication of this in the tree "visually". The tree still looks as before.

There is a way to confirm that the above steps have in fact taken place. Select the "Feature Manager" icon

Feature
Manager   from the action bar. The ensuing dialogue box (below)

confirms the adaptation of the part meshes for the analysis of the assembly.

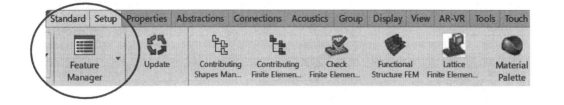

The following tree diagram is taken from the documentation of an earlier release of 3DEXPERIENCE but may still be useful in reference to what was done above.

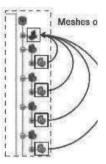

FEM Rep Management Strategies

i) Meshes of an assembly (**MOA**)
    Meshes and associated properties
    for all parts are created at the
    global (i.e. assembly) level.

ii) Assembly of Meshes (**AOM**)
    Part-level FEM Reps containing
    mesh parts and associated properties
    are linked to a global FEM Rep.

Note: One can also create a FEM Rep using
      a combination of the above strategies

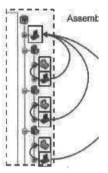

Creating a Scenario:

Locate the compass on the top left corner of the
screen, and click on it as shown on the right.
Scroll through the applications and select the
"Structural Scenario Creation" App

  Structural Scenario
Creation

The pop-up window "Simulation Initialization"
shown appears on the screen. Since this is strictly a
structural problem, the radio button "Structural"
should be selected.

Click the "Finite Element Model" icon from the bottom row. This is referring to the Finite Element which is already created. The following pop-up window appears.

Since there is already a finite element model created, it appears in the list, and make sure that you select that row.

Select this row

Finite Element Model

Model: ● Select ○ Create

☐ Preview the highlighted model

Name	Dimension
Finite Element Model0...	3D

OK   Cancel

Select the "Procedures" tab from the action bar (bottom row).

Select the "Procedures" tab from the action bar (bottom row).

"Procedures" tab

Standard Setup Procedures Initial Conditions Interactions Restraints Loads Simulate Display AR-VR Tools Touch

Select the "Static Step" icon from the bottom row.

At this point, there should be two "Green" checkmarks in the bottom left corner.

✓ Structural Analysis Case.1   ✓ Static Step.1

Static Step

Name: Static Step.1

Step time: 1s

▼ **Incrementation**

Maximum increments: 1000

Time incrementation selection: Automatic ▼

Initial time increment: 1s

Minimum time increment: 1e-005s

Maximum time increment: 1s

▶ **Stabilization**
▶ **Advanced**

OK   Cancel

Applying the Restraints:

Choose the "Restraints" tab in the action bar and pick the "Planar Symmetry" icon 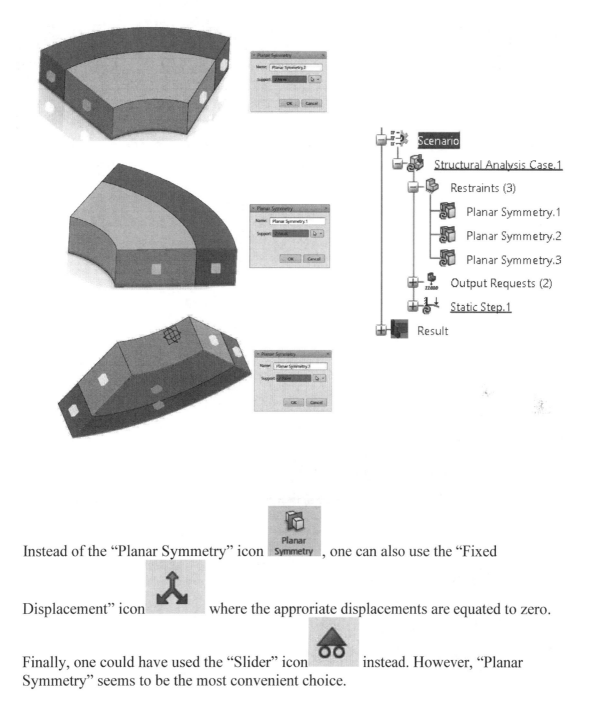 from the menu. Using the cursor, select the six symmetry surfaces; these need to be done in groups of two.

Instead of the "Planar Symmetry" icon , one can also use the "Fixed

Displacement" icon where the approriate displacements are equated to zero.

Finally, one could have used the "Slider" icon instead. However, "Planar Symmetry" seems to be the most convenient choice.

Defining the Interaction:

Select the "Interactions" tab from the action bar.

"Interactions" tab

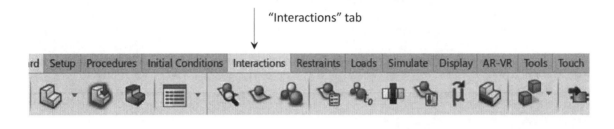

From the menu list, choose the "Surface-based Contact" icon and in the resulting dialogue box shown, make the indicated choices.

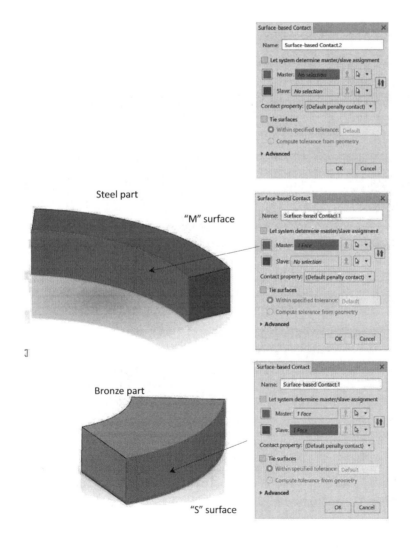

Steel part

"M" surface

Bronze part

"S" surface

The tree at this point has the appearance below.

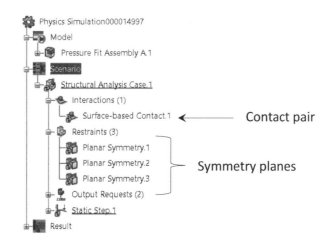

Choose the "Contact Interference" icon 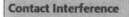 from the menu. The only selection that needs to be made is the "Surface-based Contact.1" created in the earlier step as the "Contact Surface".

Contact Interference

Controls handling of overclosed surfaces used in surface contact interactions.

Press F1 for more help.

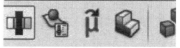

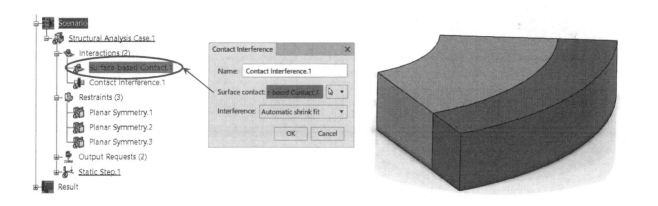

Consistency, Model Check, and Simulation:

Select the "Simulation" tab from the bottom row of icons on your screen (i.e. from the action bar).

"Simulate" tab

It is a good practice to perform the model and consistency check before submitting the work for the final run.
Select the "Model and Scenario Check" icon from the bottom row.

The software goes through a check phase and if there are no issues, a message with a "Green" check mark is returned.

Model and Scenario Checks Status	✕
✓ Model and Scenario Checks completed.	
Close Terminate	

Next select the "Simulation Checks" icon from the bottom row of icons. Accept the number of "cores" in the pop up box below.

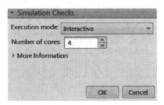

The "Simulation Check" runs successfully.

Simulation Checks Status

✓ Simulation checks completed.

▼ Warnings (2)

C3D10HS AND HYBRID TETRAHEDRAL ELEMENTS WILL ENFORCE PRESSURE CONTINUITY ACROSS MATERIAL BOUNDARIES. IN ORDER TO ALLOW DISCONTINUITIES IN THE VOLUMETRIC FIELD USE *TIE.

OUTPUT REQUEST PE IS NOT AVAILABLE FOR THE MATERIAL FOR ELEMENT TYPE C3D10HS

Choose the "Simulation" icon 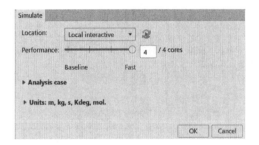 from the bottom row.

Accept the number of "cores" in the pop up box, and wait for the simulation to complete.

Simulate

Location: Local interactive   ▼

Performance: ————————○   [4] / 4 cores

       Baseline   Fast

▶ Analysis case

▶ Units: m, kg, s, Kdeg, mol.

OK   Cancel

The program successfully runs, and no messages are reported.

Simulation Status

✓ Structural Analysis Case.1 completed.

| Messages | Plots | Iterations | Diagnostic files |

▶ Errors (0)

▼ Warnings (1)

    Output request cf has been removed as there are no applicable loads in this step

▶ Information (0)

Close   Terminate

Results (Post processing):

Once you close (or move) the obstructing dialogue boxes, you must be in the "Results" section and the bottom row should appear as shown on the right.

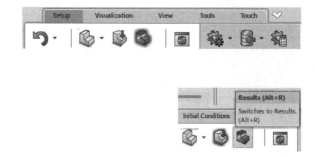

If not, click on the "Results" icon 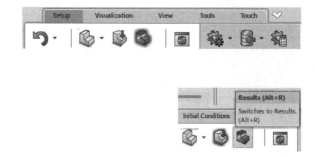 .

In the background, you can see the "Plot" window; select the Frame.2 and use the pulldown menu to choose the "displacement", "von Mises stress", and the "Contact Pressure". These are all shown on the next page.

We can compare the maximum value of the contact pressure contour with the theoretical value of 1990 psi obtained by the formula below. The agreement is quite good.

$$p = \frac{\delta}{b\left[\dfrac{1}{E_S}\left(\dfrac{c^2+b^2}{c^2-b^2}+\nu_S\right)+\dfrac{1}{E_B}\left(\dfrac{b^2+a^2}{b^2-a^2}-\nu_B\right)\right]}$$

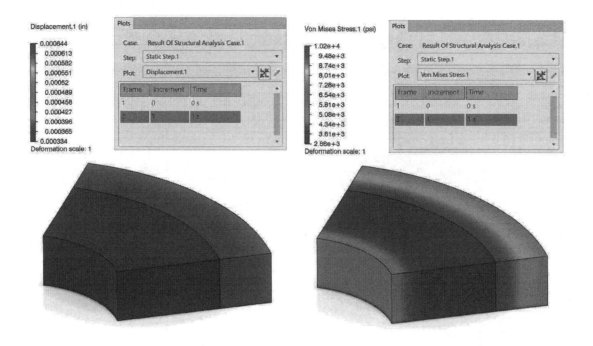

Note that the contact pressure contour legend agrees quite well with the theoretical calculation of 1990 psi.

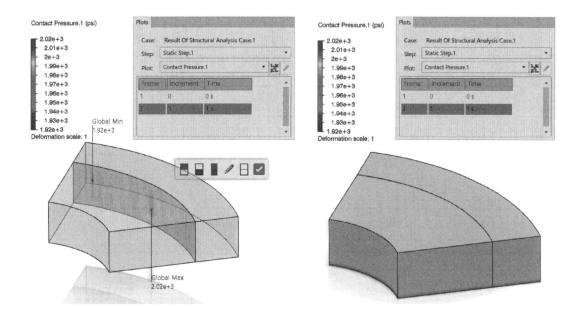

Notes:

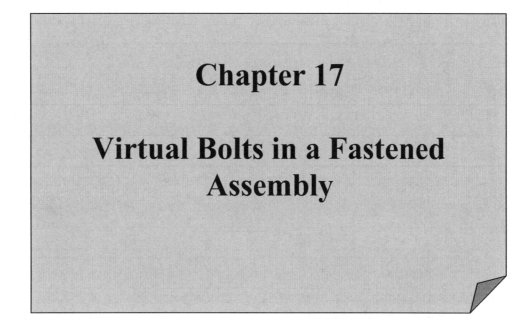

Chapter 17

Virtual Bolts in a Fastened Assembly

Objective:

In this chapter, a simple assembly consisting of two parts which are fastened together is considered where the virtual bolt is employed for modeling purposes. The parts are assumed to be made of steel and the entire assembly behaves elastically.

NOTE: It is assumed that you have basic familiarity with CAD modeling in 3DEXPERIENCE allowing you to create two blocks with two holes in each that can be lined up for bolt insertion. If that is not the case, please consult the following tutorial book.

CAD Modeling Essentials in 3DEXPERIENCE, by Nader Zamani, SDC Publications, ISBN 978-1-63057-095-8.

Problem Statement:

The assembly shown below is fastened together with two bolts. The left end of the bottom part is clamped, and the end of the top part is subjected to a downward force of 1000N causing the entire assembly to bend downward. The entire structure is assumed to be made of structural steel with a Young's modulus of 200GPa and Poisson's ratio of 0.3. Furthermore, it is assumed that the entire assembly remains in the linear elastic range. The bolts are not modeled but instead represented by "Virtual Bolt". The axial stiffness of these bolts is assumed to be 1.0E+6 N/m (kg_s2) and a preload of 1000 N is present upon tightening.

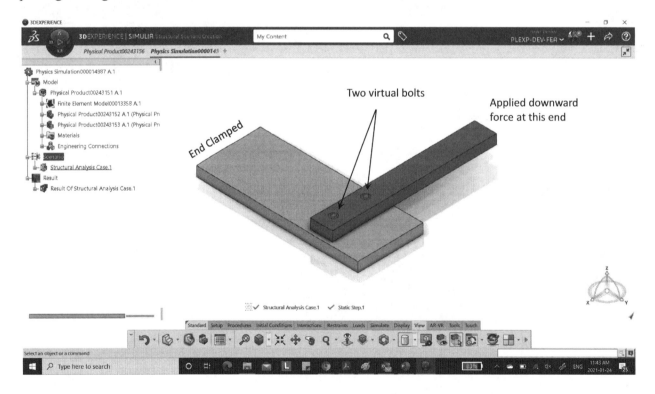

The dimensions of the parts are provided below and are all in millimeters.

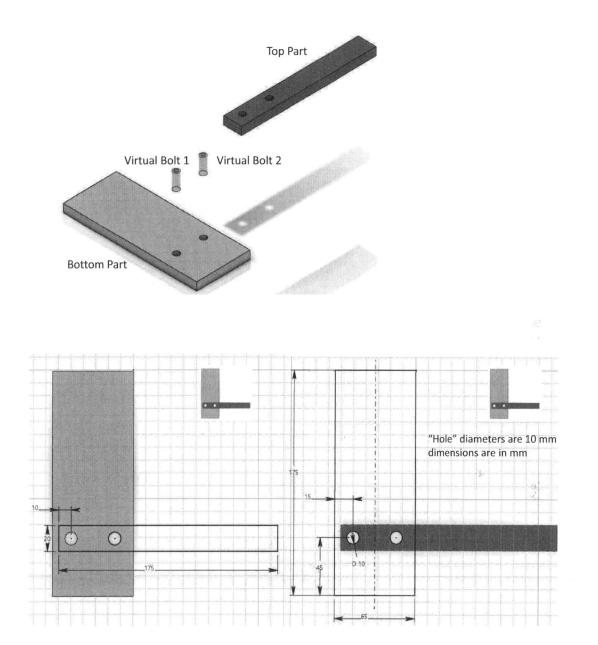

The reason behind using the virtual bolt instead of the three-dimensional model of a bolt is simply efficiency. Needless to say, such a crude model does not provide any information of the stress distribution within the bolt. Its primary role is to transfer the loads from one part to another. In case the stress analysis of the fasteners and/or threads is needed, there is no option but to perform a three-dimensional discretization of the bolts. It is also worth mentioning that within 3DEXPERIENCE, there are three models for a virtual bolt. They are "Deformable", "Rigid", and the "Beam". In this chapter, we utilize the "Deformable" virtual bolt due to its popularity and ease of use.

Creation of the Assembly

Click on the compass on the top left corner of
the screen. This will open the applications
available in 3DEXPERIENCE.

From the list, select the "Assembly Design"

 Assembly Design
App   .

It is assumed that you have already created the
two parts, the "Top" and the "Bottom". You
then insert them into the assembly as "Existing
3D Part" and position them properly. The
positioning can be achieved using the
"Engineering Connections" icon, if necessary.

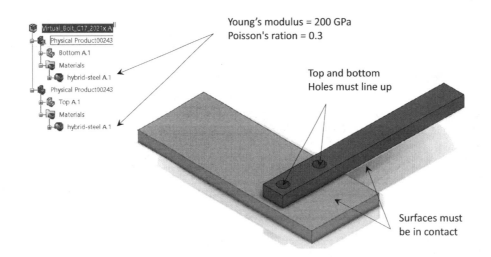

Young's modulus = 200 GPa
Poisson's ration = 0.3

Top and bottom
Holes must line up

Surfaces must
be in contact

The next step is to create and apply the elastic material data. This process was explained
in detail on several occasions in the earlier chapters. Due to the space limitations, we skip
the step; however, specifically refer to chapters 9 where an assembly involving two parts

was present. As a reminder to the reader, create the material using ![Create materials] and then apply
to each of the two parts individually. The case of chapter 9 was even more involved as
both the elastic and elastic-plastic data had to be supplied. In the present assembly, only
elastic material data, namely Young's modulus and Poisson's ratio, is inputted.

Warning:

Before you proceed to the next step, make sure that you are in the top branch of the tree, i.e., the "Assembly Design" workbench. This can be achieved by double clicking on the top branch.

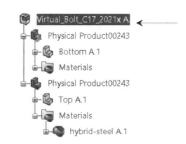

Double click on the top branch to make sure that you are in "Assembly Design"

Creating the Finite Element Model:

Locate the compass on the top left corner of the screen and click on it. Scroll through the applications and select the "Structural Model

 Structural Model Creation

Creation" App   .

The dialogue box shown on the right appears. For now, use the "Automatic" radio button. Other options are for user control of the meshing process. In the case of "Automatic", tetrahedral parabolic elements are created.

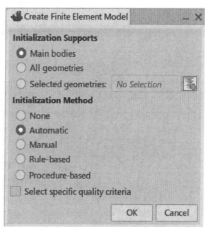

The entire assembly consisting of two parts has been meshed. These two elements and two solid sections are displayed in the tree.

The main reason behind the "Warning" statement earlier is to make sure that both parts (Top and Bottom) are meshed simultaneously.

From the bottom row of icons, select the "Mesh" icon   .

The bottom row's appearance now looks as shown below.

Select the "Update" icon   . Upon updating, the mesh appears on the screen.

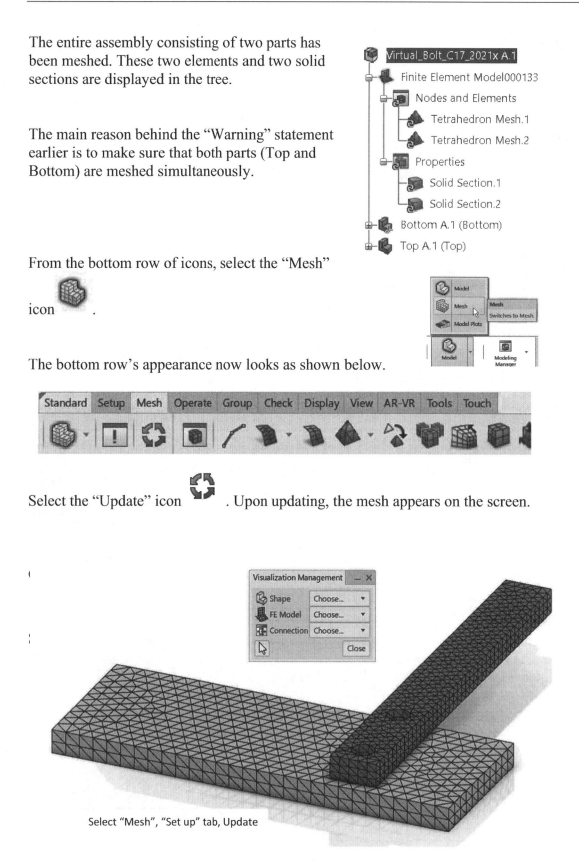

Select "Mesh", "Set up" tab, Update

From the available options, choose the icon 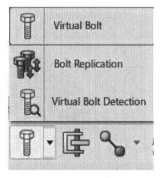 .

Note that the idea behind a "Virtual Bolt" is that the actual physical bolt is not created and therefore not meshed. Meshing a bolt is impractical when many of such components are present.

The steps needed to create the "Virtual Bolt.1" are shown graphically on the next page and also repeated in the paragraph below.

Step 1:
For "Support 1" pick the inner cylindrical surface of the top hole. Note that after you do this, the "Support 2" still indicates "Ground".

Step 2:
For "Support 2" pick the inner cylindrical surface of the corresponding bottom hole. You will need to rotate the assembly to be able to reach that hole.

Step 3:
For the "Mechanical Behavior", use "Deformable" and input an Axial Stiffness of 1E+6 kg_s2. For the "Nominal diameter" input 10mm.

Step 4:

Press the "Update Mesh" button

This closes the "Virtual Bolt" dialogue box.

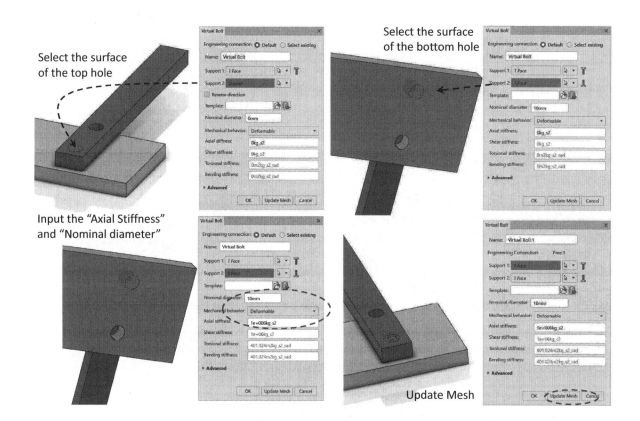

Select the surface of the top hole

Input the "Axial Stiffness" and "Nominal diameter"

Select the surface of the bottom hole

Update Mesh

Repeat the same steps for the other hole, creating "Virtual Bolt 2".

Note that both bolts are in fact created as they appear in the tree.

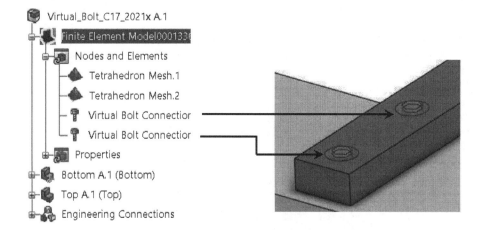

If a rigid virtual bolt is selected, there is no axial stiffness associated with it and therefore a bolt tightening force is meaningless. We will be applying a preload (bolt tightening load) to our "Deformable" choice later.

Connection
Manager

Selection of the "Connection Manager" icon from the action bar provides a table summarizing the status of the virtual bolts created. Note that from within this table, one can hide the bolts if needed.

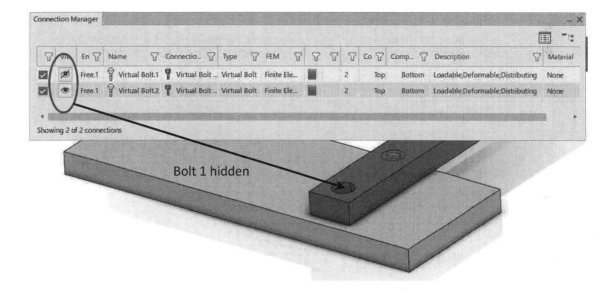

It is also worth mentioning that the "Deformable" and "Rigid" virtual bolts do not require a material. That, however, is not the case with the "Beam" type of virtual bolt.

Creating a Scenario:

Locate the compass on the top left corner of the screen and click on it. Scroll through the applications and select the "Structural Scenario Creation" App

Structural Model
Creation

.

The row of icons on the bottom of your screen changes as shown here.

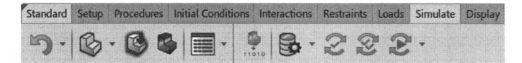

The pop-up window "Simulation Initialization" shown on the right appears on the screen. Since this is strictly a structural problem, the radio button "Structural" should be selected.

A quick glance at the tree confirms that a "Scenario" has been created.

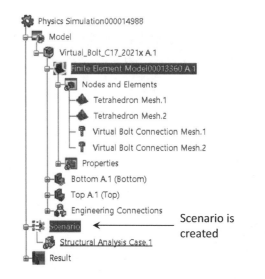

Checking the bottom middle section of the screen reveals that there are two red exclamation signs.

These pertain to "Structural Analysis Case.1" and "No Procedures Exist".

Red exclamation signs

| Structural Analysis Case.1 | No Procedures Exist |

Click the "Select the Finite Element Model" icon from the bottom row. The following pop-up window appears.

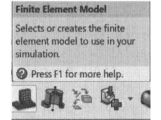

Since there is already a finite element model created, it appears in the list, and make sure that you select that row.

Select this line

Select the "Procedures" tab from the action bar (bottom row).

Select the "Procedure" tab

Standard | Setup | Procedures | Initial Conditions | Interactions | Restraints | Loads | Simulate | Display | View | AR-VR | Tools | Touch

Select the "Static Step" icon from the bottom row.

The "Static Step" dialogue box pops up. Make the appropriate changes as shown. Note that if the "Advanced" pulldown list is selected, it becomes clear that this is the point in the software where "Geometric Nonlinearities" are included, or excluded.

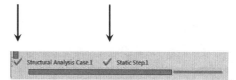

NLGEOM is "on" ⟶

Choose these values

A quick glance at the bottom middle section of the screen reveals "Green" checkmarks instead of "Red" exclamation marks.

Note the "Green" checkmarks instead of "Red" exclamations

Applying the Restraints:

Select the "Restraints" tab from the action bar. Choose the "Clamp" icon [Clamp] and use it for the face of the assembly as shown.

Restraints tab

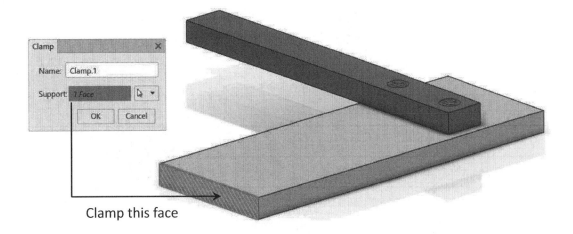

Clamp this face

Applying the Load:

The free end face of the top member is given a downward force of 1000 N. Choose the "Loads" tab of the action bar.

Loads tab

Select the "Force" icon and apply 1000 N downward as shown.

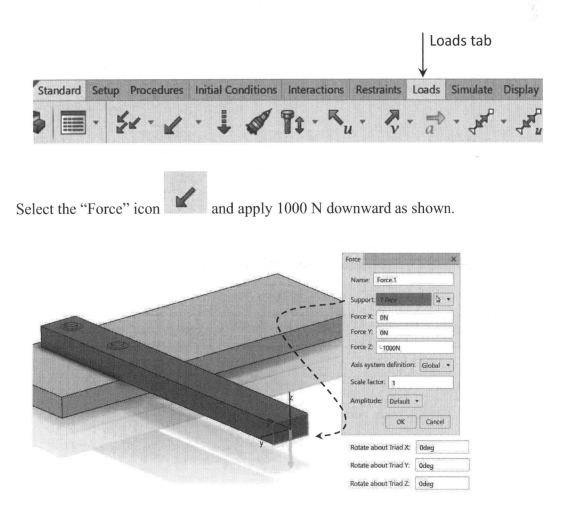

Next select the "Bolt Force" icon 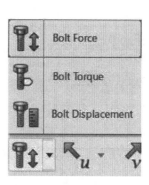 from the menu available.

In the resulting dialogue box for the "Support", select Virtual Bolt.1 on the screen and for the input type 1000N. Repeat the same process for Virtual Bolt.2

The tree displays the types of forces applied in each case.

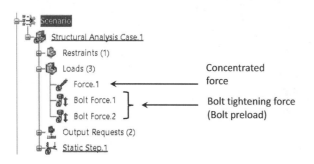

Defining the Contact Interaction:

Choose the "Interactions" tab from the Scenario action bar. This tab was not used in the previous chapters because they all consisted of a single part. The role of this tab is only meaningful for assemblies (or self-contact) where there are several parts interacting with each other.
Clearly, in this context, interaction means parts contacting each other.

Interactions tab

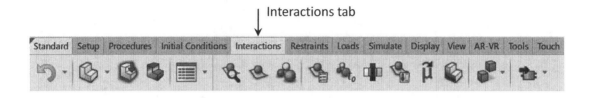

Note that the name of all icons pertaining to this tab has the word "contact" associated

with them. From the list, select the "Surface-based Contact" icon . In the present problem, the bottom face of the narrower part is in direct contact with the surface of the wider part. These two surfaces are traditionally referred to as the ""Contact Pair". In these situations, one of the surfaces can be viewed as the "M" whereas the other one as the "S".

There are some guidelines for this selection. For example, the surface which has a finer mesh and/or the surface with substantial curvature is ordinarily taken as the "S". In our situation, make the selection as shown below.

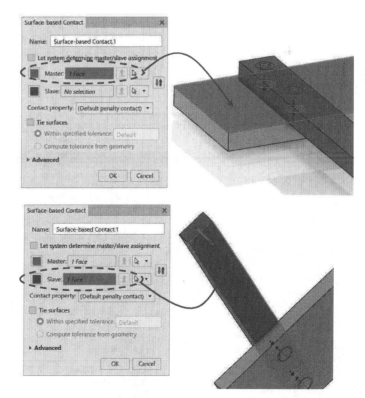

Simulation Stage:

At this point, all the preliminary work is completed, and one can simulate the problem. Select the "Simulation" tab from the action bar.

"Simulate" tab

It was pointed out earlier in the other chapters that it is a good idea to perform consistency check and scenario check before submitting the job for a full-blown simulation. These can be done by the first two icons on the left of this list below.

We will ignore this recommendation and by selecting the "Simulate" icon submit the job.

Accept the defaults in the resulting dialogue box.

A large number of warning messages are generated which is not surprising. The mesh used is very coarse and no attempt for getting a good mesh was made. Despite this, the job successfully completes as shown in the bottom figure.

In the present run, although successful, we get a warning message displayed on the right. This may be due to the lack of coincident constraints at the assembly stage. However, it did not lead to any errors.

Simulation Status ✕

⚠ The revolution axis of the feature Virtual Bolt.2 is not coincident.

Close   Terminate

The other tabs associated with the "Simulate" command are also displayed below.

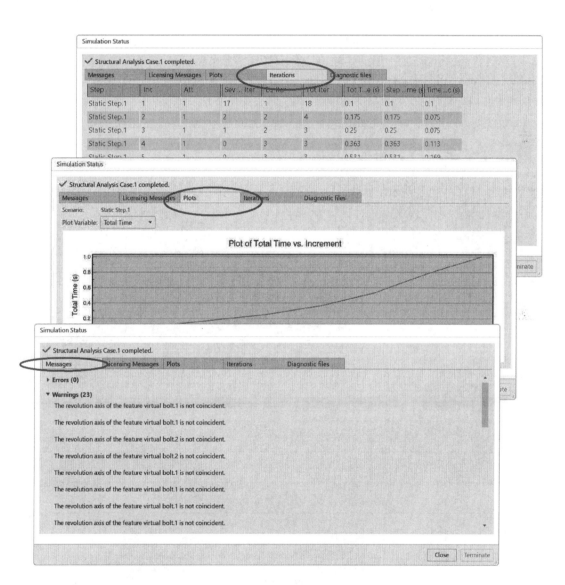

Results (Post processing):

Once you close (or move) the obstructing dialogue boxes, you must be in the "Results" section and the bottom row should appear as shown on the right.

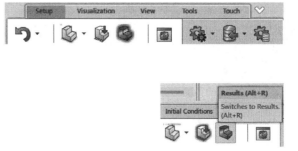

If not, click on the "Results" icon   .

In the background, you should see the "Plots" dialogue box which shows the results of Frame1, and the results after the first iteration. If the first of the "Plots" dialogue box is highlighted, the value of the von Mises stress is zero as shown below. The two generated plots correspond to frame 2 and frame 8 (the final frame)

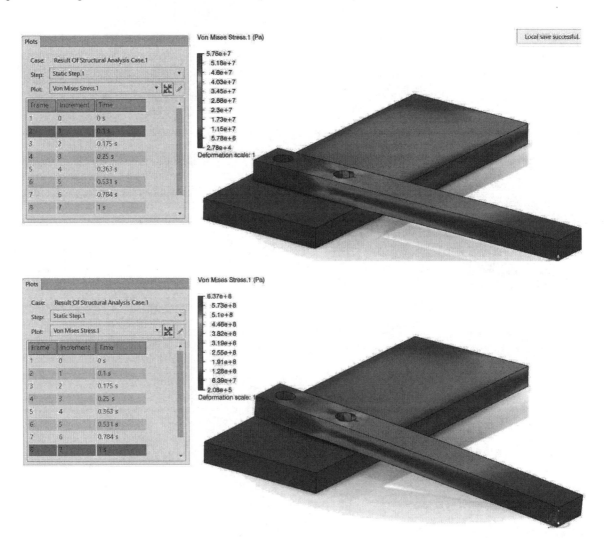

The two plots below represent the displacements corresponding to the same frames.

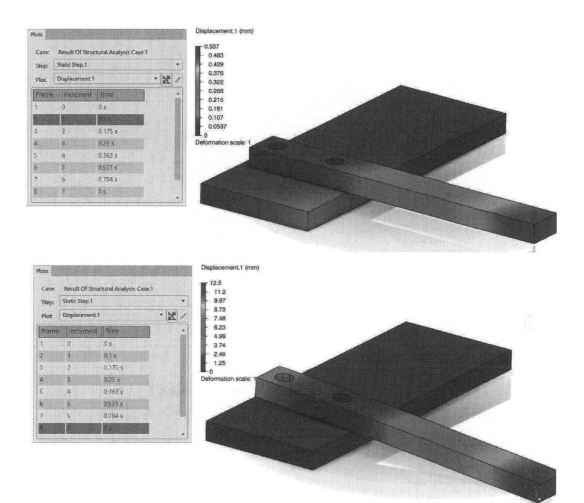

The view from the side indicates a significant "lift off" from the lower surface. This is due to the low tightening force value for the Virtual Bolt.1.

To explore this further, the tightening load for Virtual Bolt.1 is doubled, namely 2000 N. The result is presented below and clearly indicates the better outcome.

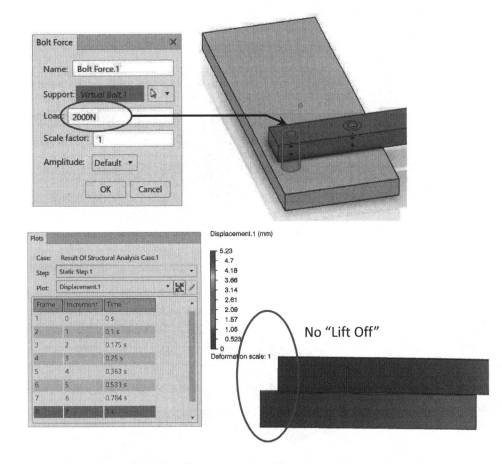

No "Lift Off"

To demonstrates the significance of the "Bolt Force", we deleted the concentrated downward force acting at the end of the top member. As for the bolt forces, we kept the 2000 N and 1000 N respectively.

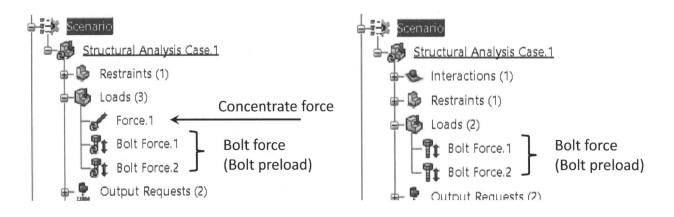

The resulting von Mises stress distribution and the displacements are shown below. Note the stress concentration around the bolts. Furthermore, the bolt force in one of the bolts is double the other one, and therefore the stress is higher in that vicinity.

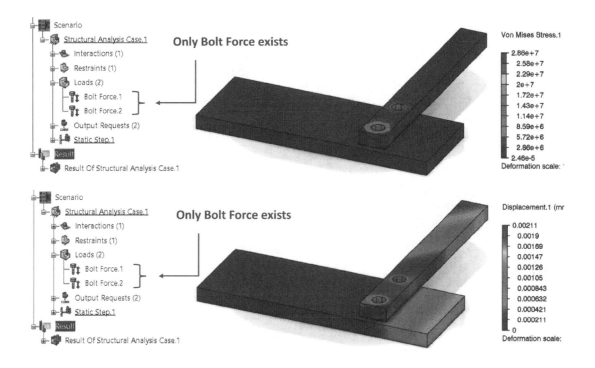

Notes:

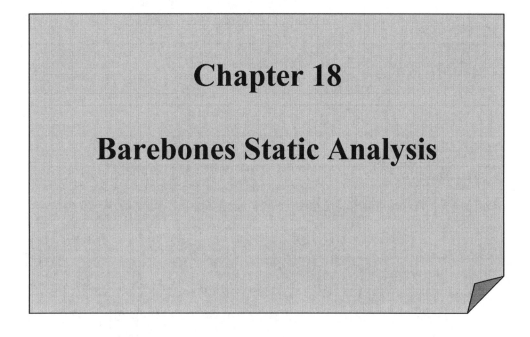

Chapter 18

Barebones Static Analysis

Objective:

A cantilever structure is loaded on a portion of the top face and the deformation is restricted to be in the linear elastic range. The problem is to be modeled with the barebones "Static Analysis" App available in 3DEXPERIENCE.

Problem Statement:

The simple part shown below is made of steel with Young's modulus 200GPa and Poisson's ratio of 0.3. It is subjected to a concentrated load F in an oblique orientation and a pressure load P applied in a circular region as shown below. This is a very simple problem, much simpler than some other problems presented in the book.

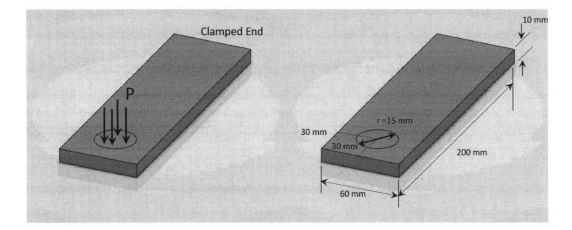

There are two reasons for discussing this problem. The first one (which is a peripheral topic) is to show the reader how to apply a pressure load on the circular region. This will be achieved by the "Sew" operation in the Part Design workbench. The second reason is to demonstrate the use of the "Static Analysis" App for barebones finite element analysis of a problem. I would prefer calling it the "quick and dirty way" of performing linear static analysis for "solid" models with solid elements.

Creating the Geometric Model:

Using the "Part Design" App ![Part Design], create the box of dimensions 200x60x10 mm as shown above. Note that since the top face of the box has no circular feature, once the geometry is meshed, the pressure load P cannot be applied as intended. It may be tempting to create a circle on the face and pad it (or pocket it) by a small amount. One can then apply the pressure on the raised (or sunk) circular feature. Although this may be legitimate in many problems, we have modified the part which can lead to manufacturing inconsistencies. We will present an alternative approach to maintain the same geometry.

On the top face of the block made, create a sketch representing the circle; dimension and position it accordingly.

In the tree shown, this is represented by the name "Sketch.2". In our case, "Sketch.1" was used to create the block.

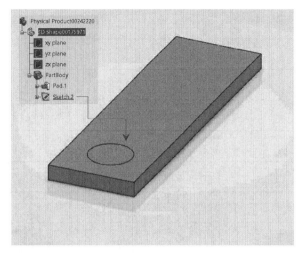

Select the compass in the top left corner of the screen and from the resulting list, choose the "Generative Shape Design"

 Generative Shape Design

This is the application that is devoted to surface operations. Obviously, one needs a surface if shell elements are expected to be used but that is not the plan here.

The action bar for the selected App is shown below. The "Essentials" tab is where the desired icon resides.

"Essentials" tab

Choose the "Fill" icon . In the resulting dialogue box, select the Sketch.2 which was already created on the top face of the block. This will act as the "Curve" in the "Fill Surface Definition" dialogue box as depicted.

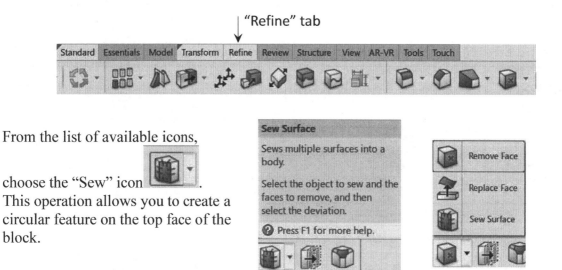

Upon performing the operation, return to the "Part Design" workbench . From the action bar on the bottom of the screen, select the "Refine" tab.

"Refine" tab

From the list of available icons,

choose the "Sew" icon .
This operation allows you to create a
circular feature on the top face of the
block.

Sew Surface

Sews multiple surfaces into a
body.

Select the object to sew and the
faces to remove, and then
select the deviation.

❓ Press F1 for more help.

Remove Face

Replace Face

Sew Surface

In the resulting dialogue box, for "Object to sew", choose fill.1 created in the earlier step.

Make sure that the check box "Simplify Geometry" is deactivated Simplify geometry .
Failure to do this will not create the circular patch needed.
Note that the arrow associated with the sewing operation is pointing "Up"; you can use
the mouse cursor to flip the arrow. For a successful operation, the arrow must point in the
direction of the target surface that the patch is expected to be sewn to.

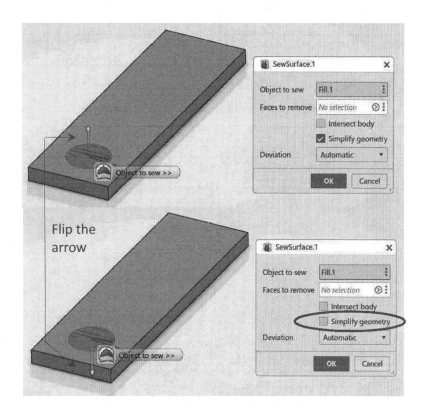

The created circular feature now reveals itself as shown below.

The pressure P will then be applied to this patch avoiding the exterior portion. It is important to point out that there is also a "Sew" icon in the Generative Shape Design workbench that cannot sew a surface to a solid.

Entering the "Static Analysis":

Select the compass in the top left corner of the screen and in the "Search" section type "Static

 Static Study

Analysis" App.

As indicated earlier, this is a barebones finite element analysis of a problem. It uses only solid elements and deals with linear elastic material.

Upon entering the workbench, the "Tree" immediately disappears and the action bar at the bottom of the screen takes the following form. Note that it is sparsely populated and has a limited number of options. It is important to realize that you have access to the part generated by the tabs on top of the screen. In fact, if you select that tab, you will see that the "Tree" is present, and a Finite Element Model has been created. Return to the most recent tab to proceed with your work in "Static Analysis".

Note that we could have applied the material properties earlier while being in the Part Design workbench; however, we neglected to do so. It can also be done here as the

material icon is also available in the action bar.

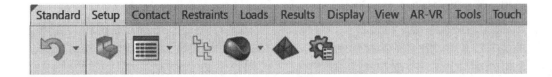

Select the icon which will land you in the "Material Palette" database.

In this problem, the material properties "Steel_in_FEA_Ch2" which was created in a different chapter fits the description needed and can be used. Therefore, right click on the name and apply it to the part as shown on the next page. The other option is to go back to the part, create, and apply the desired material.

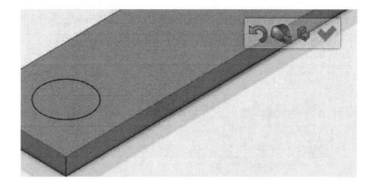

Select the "Global Mesh Density" icon  from the action bar and use the default sliding bar position. This results in a mesh that is neither very coarse, nor very fine.

Select the "Restraints" tab and "Clamp" icon and apply the clamp.

"Restraints" tab

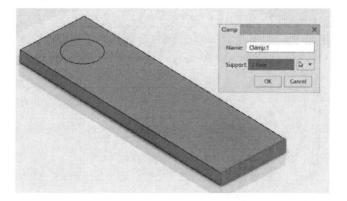

Select the "Tools" tab and "Pressure" 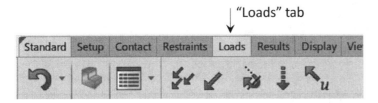 icon.

"Loads" tab

For the pressure value use 4MPa. Note that the circular patch can be selected because it is a feature associated with the top face.

It remains to apply the concentrated force at the desired vertex. This requires the actual magnitude of the force and the correct direction.

Select the "Force" icon from the action bar, and for the point of application of the force, pick the indicated vertex. Note that as soon as the vertex is selected, a local xyz coordinate system is created and the magnitude of the force 1000N is applied to the +z direction of this coordinate system.

In the bottom right corner, one can rotate the xyz coordinate system to ensure that the +z direction represents the direction of the applied load.

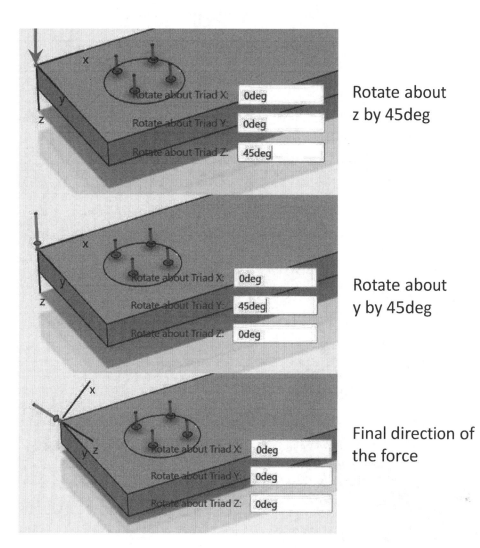

Rotate about
z by 45deg

Rotate about
y by 45deg

Final direction of
the force

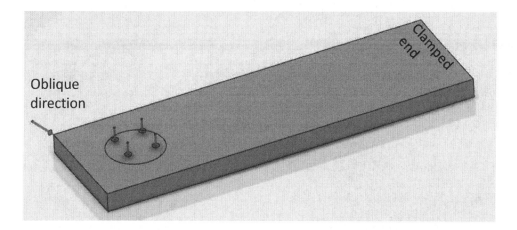

The "Static Analysis" App now has all the necessary information to run the analysis.

Select the "Results" tab from the action bar and choose the "Simulate" icon .

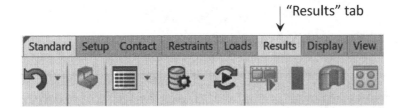

"Results" tab

The simulation runs successfully, and the post processing results will appear on the screen. One can select different entities to be plotted.

Simulation Status   ×

✓   Simulation completed.

Close   Terminate

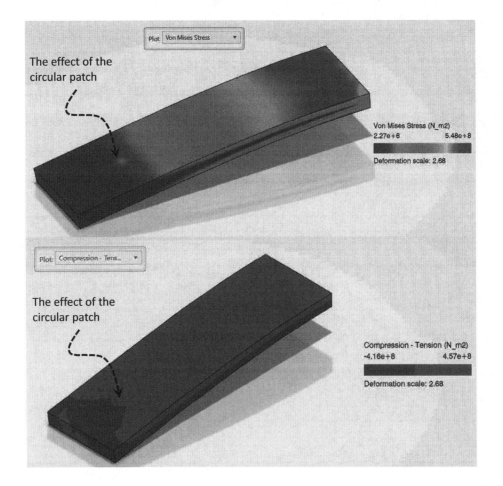

In the event that you intend to change the magnitude of the concentrated force, a specific set of steps have to be followed. Select the "Feature Manager" icon 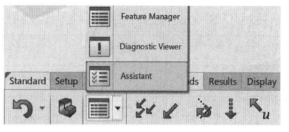 from the action bar.

Upon selecting this icon, the dialogue box below pops up.

In	Vi	Name	Type	Category	Definition
☑	👁	Clamp.1	Clamp	Restraints	
☑	👁	Force.1	Force	Loads	Magnitude: 1000 N
☑	👁	Pressure.1	Pressure	Loads	4e+006 N_m2

Double click on the third row i.e., Force.1; the value can be changed easily. Obviously upon changing the force value, the problem must be simulated again.

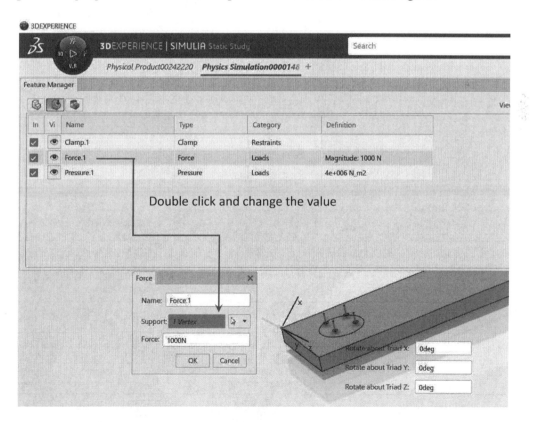

Seeing the mesh is also not as straightforward as one expects. Choose the physical product tab where the original part is residing.

Choose the tab where the physical product is residing.

Note that the tree indicates that the mesh is hidden.

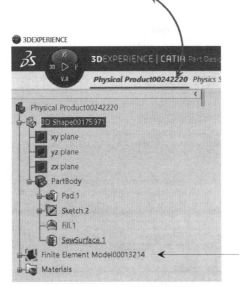

Mesh is Hidden

In the bottom right corner of the screen, select the arrow which takes you to the hidden space.

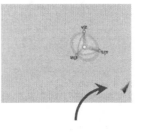

Access the Hidden Space by selecting the "Arrow" "bottom right" corner of the screen.

One can easily see the coarse mesh generated earlier. The circular patch is clearly visible.

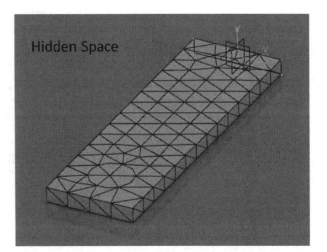

This completes chapter 18.